Learning from Entrepreneurial Failure

Learning from Entrepreneurial Failure provides an important counter-weight to the multitude of books that focus on entrepreneurial success. Failure is by far the most common scenario for new businesses and a critical part of the entrepreneurial process is learning from failure and having the motivation to try again. This book examines the various obstacles to learning from failure and explores how they can be overcome. A range of topics are discussed that include why some people have a more negative emotional reaction to failure than others and how these negative emotions can be managed; why some people delay the decision to terminate a poorly performing entrepreneurial venture; the prevalence of anti-failure biases and stigmatization in organizations and society; and the role that the emotional content of narratives plays in the sensemaking process. This thought-provoking book will appeal to academic researchers, graduate students, and professionals in the fields of entrepreneurship and industrial psychology.

DEAN A. SHEPHERD is the David H. Jacobs Chair in Strategic Entrepreneurship at the Kelley School of Business, Indiana University. His research investigates both the decision making involved in leveraging cognitive and other resources to act on opportunities, and the processes of learning from experimentation (including failure), in ways that ultimately lead to high levels of individual and organizational performance.

TRENTON WILLIAMS is an Assistant Professor in the Entrepreneurship and Emerging Enterprises Department at Syracuse University's Whitman School of Management. His research interests generally focus on resilience, organizational emergence and new venture formation under resource constraints.

MARCUS WOLFE is an Assistant Professor of Management in the Miller College of Business at Ball State University. Prior to a career in academia, Marcus was involved with founding and serving in senior leadership positions for a number of entrepreneurial firms. His research focuses on entrepreneurial failure, emotions, and decision making.

HOLGER PATZELT is the Chair of Entrepreneurship at the Technische Universität München (TUM), Germany. His research focuses on entrepreneurial decision making and the economic, emotional, and psychological consequences of failure. He currently also serves as the Vice Dean of Academic Affairs at TUM School of Management.

Learning from Entrepreneurial Failure

Emotions, Cognitions, and Actions

DEAN A. SHEPHERD
Kelley School of Business, Indiana University

TRENTON WILLIAMS
Whitman School of Management, Syracuse University

MARCUS WOLFE
Miller College of Business, Ball State University

HOLGER PATZELT
Technische Universität München

CAMBRIDGE
UNIVERSITY PRESS

CAMBRIDGE
UNIVERSITY PRESS

University Printing House, Cambridge CB2 8BS, United Kingdom

Cambridge University Press is part of the University of Cambridge.

It furthers the University's mission by disseminating knowledge in the pursuit of education, learning and research at the highest international levels of excellence.

www.cambridge.org
Information on this title: www.cambridge.org/9781107129276

© Dean A. Shepherd, Trenton Williams, Marcus Wolfe and Holger Patzelt 2016

First published 2016

A catalogue record for this publication is available from the British Library

Library of Congress Cataloging-in-Publication Data
Names: Shepherd, Dean A.
Title: Learning from entrepreneurial failure : emotions, cognitions, and actions /
Dean A. Shepherd, Trenton Williams, Marcus Wolfe, Holger Patzelt.
Description: 1 Edition. | New York : Cambridge University Press, 2016. |
Includes bibliographical references and index.
Identifiers: LCCN 2015034759| ISBN 9781107129276 (Hardback) |
ISBN 9781107569836 (Paper back)
Subjects: LCSH: Entrepreneurship. | Business failures.
Classification: LCC HB615 .S49638 2016 | DDC 658.4/21–dc23 LC record available
at http://lccn.loc.gov/2015034759

ISBN 978-1-107-12927-6 Hardback

Dean would like to dedicate this book to the newest members of the Shepherd clan: Henry and Olivia Seager.

Trent would like to dedicate this book to his family, namely Natalee, Millie, Tristan, Hallie, and Kate Williams.

Marcus would like to dedicate this book to his parents for their constant support and his brother who first sparked his interest in entrepreneurship.

Holger would like to dedicate this book to Silvia and Helen, who always help him moving forward from his own failures.

Contents

Figures

Acknowledgments

We gratefully acknowledge Paula Parish and Claire Wood
(from Cambridge University Press) for their support; Ali Ferguson
and Alisa Boguslavskaya for their help in preparing the manuscript;
and Judith Behrens, Nicki Breugst, Orla Byrne, Melissa Cardon, Julio
DeCastro, Dawn DeTienne, Dan Holland, Kathie Sutcliffe, Dennis
Warnecke, and Johan Wiklund for their help in developing some of the
concepts covered in the book.

1 Introduction

We start with a real-life story. A young lecturer has just returned to his office after teaching one of his favorite classes. In this class, he discussed the high risks associated with entrepreneurial action – that failure was a very real possibility. But importantly, and to quote from the textbook, "Businesses fail, but entrepreneurs do not. Failure is the fire that tempers the entrepreneur's steel and street savvy" (Timmons 1999). The point is that the entrepreneur and the business are separate entities such that when a business fails, the entrepreneur can go on to create a subsequent business. The failure experience informs and motivates entrepreneurial action.

The lecturer's contemplation of the discussions in class was interrupted by a phone call from his father who revealed that the family business was performing poorly. After hearing more details about the financial state of the business, the lecturer advised his father to close the business. The business was subsequently closed, and his father experienced a range of negative emotions. He was angry with others who let him down. He was disappointed that his dreams for the business could not be realized. He believed that he had not only failed as a business person, but because he could no longer hand the business on to his other son, he felt like he was a failure as a father. He became depressed. This caused his family great anxiety.

The next time the lecturer taught the class on entrepreneurial failure, he was highly sceptical of the optimistic story told by textbooks that entrepreneurs automatically and instantaneously learn from failure. This no longer rang true given his experience with his father.

The young lecturer described here was the first author of this book (Dean Shepherd) as a doctoral student almost twenty years ago.

The disconnect between the explanations of failure in the entrepreneurial textbook and his experience with his father's failed entrepreneurial endeavor motivated him to explore the academic literature. Surprisingly, the entrepreneurship and management literature largely ignored the personal implications for those who experience failure. There was little understanding of how and why failure impacts individuals, and as a result, there were few prescriptions for helping individuals cope with this situation. This raised a few fundamental questions that the authorship team has worked on over the last decade, the outcome of which culminates in the current book.

First, although Dean had personal experience with his father's severe negative emotional reaction to business failure, a fundamental question in this context is why a person has such a considerable negative emotional reaction to failure. Do people have similar negative emotional reactions to the failure of entrepreneurial projects within established organizations? Why might some people experience negative emotions from the failure of an entrepreneurial endeavor while others do not (or why do they experience a less negative emotional reaction)? Perhaps it is not just an attribute of individuals but also an attribute of what is lost and the context in which it occurs. In other words, when might an individual experience a more severe (or less severe) negative emotional reaction to a failure experience? In Chapter 2, we address these questions by building on self-determination theory to explain variance in people's negative emotional reactions to failure in terms of how entrepreneurial failure thwarts the satisfaction of individuals' basic psychological needs.

Second, although Dean's father experienced a failure, it did not seem that he was in a state to be able to learn from the experience. How do negative emotional reactions to failure impact individuals' ability to learn from the experience? Given the same negative emotional reaction to failure, why are some individuals able to more quickly reduce their negative emotions and learn from the experience? Do all people who experience failure feel that their self-worth is threatened and therefore activate ego-protective strategies, or are some people able to detach feelings of self-worth from these failure events? Why are people often compassionate to others who experience failure but overly harsh on themselves? What happens when people are compassionate to themselves after experiencing a failure event? In Chapter 3, we address these questions by building on the notion of self-compassion, which can help reduce threats to self-esteem, reduce the generation of negative emotions, and also keep negative emotions in balance to enhance learning from the experience.

Third, it was only after Dean's discussion with his father that the decision was made to terminate the business. However, had his father realized quite some time before that the business was going to fail, or was he in denial about the inevitable outcome? Indeed, Dean's father continued to invest resources into the firm despite its poor performance, and as a result, when the business eventually failed, the family lost all its financial wealth. When people realize that their endeavor is failing, why do some choose to persist and others choose to terminate? That is, why do some choose to "throw good money after bad" such that when failure eventually occurs, the financial cost is larger than it needed to be? Is such a delay caused by procrastination, sunk costs, or some other form of biased decision making, or is there some benefit in delaying despite the financial costs? That is, are some people able to benefit from a delayed termination? If yes, then why are some people able to benefit from delayed termination while others are not? In Chapter 4, we address these questions by exploring the role of procrastination in delaying termination and making failure more costly than it needs to be. However, we also build on the notion of anticipatory grief to gain a deeper understanding of how some delay in termination can facilitate recovery from failure when it eventually occurs.

Fourth, Dean's father was not in an emotional state to learn from his experiences after the failure event nor was he able to learn during the period immediately preceding the failure event. However, perhaps, if he had quickly started a new business (which was difficult to do given the financial costs of failure), his negative emotional reactions to the business failure may not have been so great. Does quickly re-engaging in a new entrepreneurial endeavor reduce the negative emotions from a failure event? If so, is such a reduction in negative emotions associated with increased learning from the failure experience, or are there some circumstances in which higher negative emotions are associated with superior learning outcomes? Does a failure event always cause negative emotions, or are there situations in which a delay in failure (i.e., the termination) generates negative emotional reactions? Does learning from a failure experience only occur after the failure event, or can some people learn from their experiences before the failure event occurs? In Chapter 5, we address these questions by building on the notion of "creeping death" and the rapid redeployment of human resources to explain how delaying termination can lead to both the generation of negative emotions and enhanced learning from the failing experience.

Fifth, although it was Dean's father who directly experienced the business failure, he was embedded in a family and a broader social context. Dean's family tried to help the patriarch emotionally recover from the failure but with only limited success in the short run. How do "others" help reduce an individual's negative emotions generated by failure? Are some people more effective at managing their emotions to more quickly reduce negative emotions and/or more effectively use others' to more quickly reduce negative emotions? Are some others more helpful to the person suffering, and if so, under what circumstances? Can effective help along with reducing the negative emotions generated from failure and/or learning from the experience be organized at the systems level? For example, are some families more capable of helping a member recover from a business failure to learn from the experience, and are some organizations more capable of helping employees recover from project failure to learn from the experience? In Chapter 6, we address these questions by building on the role of emotional intelligence (at the individual level) and emotional capability (at the organizational level) to gain a deeper understanding of the factors that facilitate an individual's recovery from failure so that the individual and the organization can enhance their learning from the experience.

Sixth, Dean's father felt further anxiety because outsiders harshly blamed him for the failure of the business. As a result, he withdrew from social interactions with those who knew the business had failed and concealed the failure from all others. Indeed, audiences can stigmatize individuals involved with failure. How does stigmatization influence the level of negative emotions an individual feels over an entrepreneurial failure? Why are some who fail stigmatized more than others? Are some audiences less likely to stigmatize individuals for their entrepreneurial failures than other audiences? Are some regions less "entrepreneurial" (i.e., stigmatize failure more) than other regions? In Chapter 7, we address these questions by combining our understanding of the psychological foundations of grief from failure (Chapter 2) with the notion of stigmatization to explore biases in evaluating individuals whose entrepreneurial endeavors fail, impression management to explore actions to enhance the individual's psychological well-being, and perspective taking to understand how audiences differ in harshness of their blame for an entrepreneurial failure.

Seventh, although Dean's father never talked about the business failure (to others and avoided thinking about it himself), by telling more and more plausible stories in his research, Dean has developed a narrative of the failure. What role do narratives play in enabling people involved with a failure to make sense of their experience with it? How much emotional content is used in failure narratives? Given that failure is a frequent occurrence for entrepreneurs and entrepreneurial firms, to what extent do narratives reflect an entrepreneurial orientation? What impact does the narrative content have on subsequent performance? In Chapter 8, we address these questions by building on the sensemaking and entrepreneurial orientation literatures to explore how and why cognitive approaches reflected in narratives are impacted by failure and, in turn, how these impact performance.

Finally, one of the main motivations for undertaking this research journey toward an increased understanding of learning from failure was to offer practical implications for those who experience entrepreneurial failure. In the final chapter (Chapter 9), we offer a summary of the book with a focus on its practical implications.

Overall, the book builds on and extends our research over the last decade or so on the topic of learning from failure. Our research on this topic began with Shepherd (2003) and continues to this day (i.e., papers published in 2014 and 2015 and in press). The book covers (1) the failures of projects, businesses, family businesses, and even college football matches with (2) rich data from a variety of industries – from knowledge-intensive research and development to drug development to founding teams to college football teams – (3) across a variety of countries, such as the United States, Germany, the United Kingdom, Ireland, and Australia, (4) and across multiple levels of analysis, including the individual entrepreneur, his or her team, his or her business, and his or her regional location. By recombining knowledge from our existing studies with new material and rich examples (including from original qualitative data), we are able to offer a cohesive story of learning from failure that generates many new insights over and above the accumulation of our published research on the topic.

REFERENCE

Timmons, J. A. 1999. *New Venture Creation: Entrepreneurship for the 21st Century*. Boston, MA: Irwin McGraw-Hill.

2 Grief over entrepreneurial failures

Although we started this journey with the failure of a business in Chapter 1, entrepreneurial endeavors also exist as projects within organizations, and these entrepreneurial projects can fail. Project failure occurs when "a project's activities cease due to unsatisfactory or insufficient progress" (Shepherd, Covin, and Kuratko, 2009: 589). For example, "seventy percent of Nokia's new ventures were either discontinued or entirely divested [between 1998 and 2002]. Another 21 percent were absorbed into existing business units and ceased to exist as independent ventures" (McGrath, Keil, and Tukiainen, 2012: 51). Further, 35 to 45 percent of all new products are estimated to be failures (Boulding, Morgan, and Staelin, 1997); half of all information system projects are reported as failures (Keil and Robey, 1999); and in an extensive study of venturing units, there were no instances of success (Campbell, Birkinshaw, Morrison, and van Basten Batenburg, 2003). But are people likely to experience the same level of grief over project failure as they would over business failure? Do all people experience the same level of grief over project failure? Given that the answer to these questions is likely to be no, what explains these differences? In this chapter, we explore differences in both entrepreneurial projects and entrepreneurial business settings to explain the emotional and motivational consequences of failure.

NEGATIVE EMOTIONAL REACTIONS TO PROJECT FAILURES

We turn to the psychology literature for theorizing on possible answers to these questions. Specifically, by building on self-determination theory (Deci and Ryan, 2000; Shepherd and Cardon, 2009), we gain new insights into the generation of grief over project failure.

Self-determination theory is concerned with explaining an individual's psychological well-being. Individuals have three fundamental psychological needs (i.e., nutrients), and these provide a basis for understanding why some projects are more important than others and why some people find one project more important than another. Given that grief is the negative emotional reaction to something lost, by understanding the importance of a project, we gain some insights into the level of grief generated by its loss through failure. The three fundamental psychological needs are for competence, relatedness, and autonomy. As illustrated in Figure 2.1, the more an entrepreneurial venture satisfies an individual's needs for competence, relatedness, and autonomy, the more it contributes to that individual's psychological well-being, but it also generates more grief when these needs are thwarted by failure.

PROJECT FAILURE THWARTING THE NEED FOR COMPETENCE

The more a project satisfies an individual's need for competence, the more grief he or she will feel when the project fails. The need for competence is satisfied when feedback provides information that the individual is performing well at a particular task (Deci and Ryan, 2000). Some projects satisfy the need for competence by providing the opportunity to learn new skills (Dweck, 1986), demonstrate mastery of the project's tasks (Butler, 1992), successfully compete against

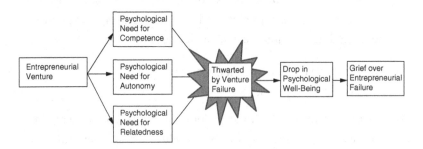

FIGURE 2.1: A self-determination model of grief over entrepreneurial failure

other groups (Tjosvold, Johnson, Johnson, and Sun, 2003), and thus be a member of a competent team (Lindsley, Brass, and Thomas, 1995). Various managers and employees who we interviewed in our studies and were involved in innovation and new product development projects emphasized that project work can contribute to fulfilling their need for competence. For example, we conducted a study with 257 research scientists working on highly uncertain projects in different academic disciplines (Shepherd and Patzelt, 2011). Before we used a questionnaire to explore the emotional and learning consequences of project failure, we interviewed seven scientists in the areas of chemistry, biochemistry, mechanical engineering, behavioral economics, theoretical physics, aerospace engineering, and biology. These scientists had considerable project experience, including past project failures. The aim of the interviews was to gain a deeper understanding of how scientists and engineers perceive their projects and how they emotionally react to project failure. On various occasions during the interviews, these scientists emphasized the importance of their projects for their self-image as a competent scientist and how failure can threaten this self-image. For instance, an aerospace engineer reported, "The view (of others on us) is they do clean work, it is well documented, it keeps costs and time. . . . So you must deliver. I personally experience it as substantial pressure, which I generated myself but which is important and for me part of defining myself."

Similarly, a biologist reported that being successful at work for her is "very important, without any question . . . without work, well, it defines me. I am happy [when I can prove myself]. This is very important for me."

However, if a project fails and the subsequent project does not satisfy the need for competence to the same degree, the deficit between the two likely contributes to the grief generated by the project's failure. The greater the deficit, the greater the generation of negative emotions. In our interviews with engineers and scientists (Shepherd, Patzelt, and Wolfe, 2011), the leader of the aerospace engineering project continued by describing his reaction to a failure as follows:

There is one case, which frustrated me personally. We had a
super-exciting and super-interesting project ... where [we] wanted
to finish a benchmark example [by] last October, but now we hope
to be done by this October. We have [a] one-year delay, which
frustrates me a lot. On the one hand, you can of course argue that
we do something that does not yet exist and is very new, which
suggests that time cannot be determined in advance, but on the
other hand, one must clearly say that for us engineers, it is clearly
the goal to determine timelines for projects that have not been
done yet. So this is indeed very frustrating.

Obviously, the fact that this project leader could not deliver the desired
outcome in time thwarted his self-image as a competent engineer.
Similarly, in the same study, the leader of a mechanical engineering
project reported that the project's failure "hurt me as an engineer ...
because, it was simply the case that we failed with a technological
challenge." This engineer's project employed about 200 people and was
highly visible within his organization and beyond.

We found similar results in another study on project terminations in a large German technology company (Shepherd, Patzelt,
Williams, and Warnecke, 2014). In this company, we explored eight
engineering projects from four subsidiaries in the fields of energy and
electricity. These projects differed substantially in scope, their
budgets ranged $750,000 to $140 million, and they had been between
3 and 200 employees working on the projects. All together, we conducted 28 interviews with top managers, project leaders, and project
team members about the failed projects. Specifically, these interviews
covered topics like the project termination process, emotional reactions to these terminations, and learning from the experience. The
interviews provided evidence for how project failure can thwart the
need for competence for those involved. For example, a project team
member described the reaction of the project's chief technology devel-
oper as follows, "He was very frustrated because he thought that what
he had designed aerodynamically was the best. He was going to have

serious discussions [with other team members] about the engine because he thought that they must have built it wrong. He continuously asked, 'Have you checked this, have you checked that?'"

Another manager of a failed project explained his emotional reaction to project failure as follows:

> I had a sudden feeling of being embarrassed about it [the project failure] because the rest of the business was a relatively small company... I felt embarrassed because, you know, other people know that you failed. So, you know other people. People on the department floor, people in the testing department, etc., they know that the group failed to do what they should have done. That was quite hard I think.... I felt embarrassed because I knew other people knew that we failed. As a collective team, irrespective of what was wrong with it, we failed to successfully complete the task ... But, probably the worst time was when you were basically talking to people within manufacturing or production because they obviously would not have heard about it [the project failure]. And then you had to explain to them [about the failure] and you just felt ... you know, the way that they reacted: "You got it wrong, didn't you?" That felt uncomfortable. Your group being probably one of the most educated groups in the company, etc., doctors, PhDs, and things, and most people have got a degree and everything. You just felt ... you know ... people of your group, they do not know what they are doing, etc. That felt quite uncomfortable.

Obviously, this manager perceived that others would no longer view him and his team members as competent managers and engineers, leading to feelings of embarrassment and shame.

The need for competence is important as it contributes to an individual's psychological well-being. Project failure can thwart this psychological need by providing negative feedback about competence, sending a signal to important others about one's competence and perhaps also resulting in deployment to a subsequent project that does not provide positive feedback on competence and/or does not provide the same opportunity to develop skills and knowledge. To the extent that project failure thwarts the psychological need for competence, the individual will have a negative emotional reaction to the loss of that project.

PROJECT FAILURE THWARTING THE NEED FOR AUTONOMY

A similar effect likely occurs for individuals' psychological need for autonomy (Shepherd and Cardon, 2009). Autonomy in a work-related context refers to "volition, to having the experience of choice, to endorsing one's actions at the highest level of reflection" (Deci and Ryan, 2008). A project can satisfy the need for autonomy through structures and processes (Bennis and Nanus, 1985) that empower (Logan and Ganster, 2007), facilitate participative decision making (Liden and Tewksbury, 1995), and delegate decision-making authority to the team (Blanchard, Carlos, and Randolph, 1995).

In our interviews, several participants indicated the need for autonomy as an important motivating factor. For example, in one study, Behrens and colleagues (2014) explored how large firms organize when developing radical innovations and then bringing them to market quickly. In this study, we conducted 55 interviews with leaders and team members of 16 innovation departments in mid-sized and large German firms in innovation-driven industries. These industries included, for example, automotive, telecommunications, consumer goods, industrial goods, and medical technology, and size of the companies ranged from 600 to 400,000 employees. While the research project's primary goal was to explore how firms organize their innovation departments in terms of incentives, resource provisions, and organizational structures, the interviews also provided insights into what the project leaders and team members perceive as important drivers of their motivation. For example, we interviewed the top manager who was responsible for the strategy of a large firm. This manager told us about a successful project in his firm, and in his view, autonomy was one of the key motivational factors for team leaders and members:

> It was important [for the success of the project] that the leader of this project had, I would say, enough freedom in allocating his resources. This is really important, that he had a certain freedom.... At the beginning, the project had just three people; today it has 60 or 70 team members.... [At the beginning of the project] there was little need for the leader to convince others or overcome resistance.

In another firm captured by the same study, an employee in the R&D department described the importance of autonomously developing new ideas:

> Particularly in pre-development, but also in development [of new products], every single employee can initiate something based on his or her own ideas. It would be very disappointing for an employee who wants to start something new if the ideas just evaporate or there is no possibility to put them into action. At our firm, I feel that it is indeed the case [that one can initiate new ideas and put them into action]. With your own initiative, you can start new projects.... For me, it is crucial that one [employees] works on projects that they like. It must be fun.... For me, this includes having the freedom to make up my mind about particular projects. I think, it is also important not to have the feeling that one's own ideas have somehow "dried up" or do not have consequences. It is important for me to personally come up with projects.

Again, to the extent that termination of a project creates a deficit in perceived autonomy, the individual will experience grief from the project failure. For example, in our study on eight failed projects of a large German technology corporation (Shepherd et al., 2014), a manager experienced top management's decision to abandon his engineering project prematurely as a personal lack of freedom to make decisions autonomously:

> I personally then thought, well, no matter how much effort and time you invest, you are only a minor cog in the overall process.

The actual decision and strategy is made at a different level. My impact that this is going to be successful is indeed minimal. This was my first reaction. Because then I thought, no matter what you do, whether you perform like crazy or whether you take it easy, it would not have been different. This was my first emotional reaction. . . . It was totally disappointing because I tried to exert influence internal to the organization to make the project better, but because the way it [the organizational process] was set up, it [the project] could not work.

The need for autonomy is important as it contributes to an individual's psychological well-being. Project failure can thwart this psychological need by revealing a lack of autonomy over the decisions necessary to make the project successful and/or a lack of autonomy over the decision of whether to terminate and persist with the project. After project failure, the individual may be reassigned to a project in which he or she has less autonomy over how the project tasks are to be completed. To the extent that project failure thwarts the psychological need for autonomy, the individual will have a negative emotional reaction to the loss of that project.

PROJECT FAILURE THWARTING THE NEED FOR RELATEDNESS

The final psychological nutrient is relatedness. Relatedness refers to "feeling connected to others, to caring for by those others, to having a sense of belongingness both with other individuals and with one's community" (Deci and Ryan, 2002: 7). A project can satisfy this need for relatedness by providing access to supportive supervision and/or coworkers (Thompson and Prottas, 2006), a group with which to identify (Richter, West, Van Dick, and Dawson, 2006), and a basis for interactions and friendships. For example, in our interviews with engineers at a large German company (Shepherd et al., 2014), one interviewee reported about a past project team experience:

In the team, I worked together with the colleagues very well and we built personal relationships and one suddenly realized, "Wow, we are indeed a great team. You have a great team, and this is important for a project." ... It was a pity that we had to be separated [after project termination] although we thought we are a great team, we could make it.

Similarly, another project team member in our study on 55 members of 16 innovation departments of large German firms reported, "The everyday interaction within the team is really important.... We have ties of friendship in the team; trust each other; and once in a while, enjoy a drink together after work."

If a project that satisfies managers' and employees' need for relatedness fails, this can lead to the experience of grief. For example, in one study (Shepherd et al., 2014), we found that after project failure, a team member reported that he feared the loss of important relationships with both his colleagues and external stakeholders:

> You start to get angry and you shake your head because a lot of effort and money would have been wasted. You then have to wonder why you did this stressful work over the last three years.... It is extremely bad if you have the feeling that motivation is not only getting lost but is switching completely because you cannot provide any perspective to the people [including external suppliers] because you cannot provide a clear explanation.... It is painful that the efforts up to this phase suddenly are not important for the project anymore.

Similarly, his colleague on the same project feared that he might lose standing in and connection with the scientific community and reported, "I mean, let's be clear about it: a year ago, we were the pioneers, and everyone in the community around the world knew it.... The fact is we have not gotten that far.... That hurt me personally."

An engineer leading another failed project in the same company described the eroding social structures of the team when the failure became obvious:

There have been many conflicts that we faced during this period [leading up to the failure of the project] because people were convinced that if we did it differently this way or that way, then we could keep the deadline nevertheless. . . . You start making compromises, some more easily, some more difficult. There were many fights. . . . Partly this was constructive, but even then it costs a lot of energy to cope with such issues. I think this [project failure] has led to a real disappointment in the whole team.

Further, one of our interviewees (Shepherd et al., 2011) was a leader of a mechanical engineering project that had been running for years, cost millions of euros, and had a high level of public visibility. He reported that immediately after his project had failed, there were "considerable tensions" among team members. One year later, almost all the team members had left the firm "just due to frustration," and "from the team, which we used to have, one is retired, and I am the only one left." When a project fails and team members are relocated within or leave the organization, the replacement project might not provide the same level of (perceived) relatedness than the failed project. In this case, the individual is likely to experience grief over the losses caused by project failure (Shepherd and Cardon, 2009).

In sum, our interviews with leaders and members of entrepreneurial projects provided multiple examples of how these projects can help satisfy individuals' needs for competence, autonomy, and relatedness and how project failure can thwart the fulfillment of these needs and lead to the generation of negative emotions – namely, grief over the loss of the valued project.

MOTIVATIONAL CONSEQUENCES OF NEGATIVE EMOTIONAL REACTION TO PROJECT FAILURES

The generation of grief over failed projects creates a problem for organizations. The organization often needs to be entrepreneurial to succeed (for a review see Rauch, Wiklund, Lumpkin, and Frese, 2009; Wiklund and Shepherd, 2005), and this means using projects as experiments to reveal opportunity (Brown and Eisenhardt, 1997; McGrath, 1999). Many of these projects will fail (Boulding et al., 1997; Campbell et al., 2003). As illustrated in the previous section, when project failure thwarts an individual's psychological needs, it generates grief, and these negative emotions diminish the individual's motivation to move on and invest energy and effort into subsequent projects (Shepherd and Cardon, 2009), that is, unless the organization can consistently provide replacement projects of equal or greater psychological value to the project lost. Therefore, the organization is faced with the challenge of somehow overcoming this emotional downside to maintain employees' motivation after project failure.

Indeed, there is evidence that negative emotional reactions to project failure impact project team members' motivation. For example, in his article "When IT Projects Flounder, Emotions Run High," Fitzgerald (2010) described the case of Dana B. Harris, who had worked on sonar acoustics software for Arleigh Burke guided missile destroyers in the 1980s. When developing this highly sophisticated software, Harris "was really into it, really excited about it." However, after the end of the Cold War in 1990, the project was abandoned due to budgetary cuts, and Harris and his team experienced substantial emotional troubles, as he recalled 20 years later: "Not having the excitement of developing that kind of software, it was like I'd lost something. I remember that feeling very, very clearly." Obviously, Harris and his team lost something they found very important to them, which generated grief. As a consequence, Harris found it difficult to motivate himself for subsequent projects and decided to leave the defense industry.

Similarly, in interviewing research scientists in Germany, we (Shepherd et al., 2011) found strong evidence of how grief over project failure impacts motivation. For example, one behavioral economist reported on a project in which she had invested more than one-and-a-half years together with two co-authors. The team had developed a theory about economic decision making and had enrolled participants in an experimental task to collect data for testing the hypotheses. Based on the results obtained, the team had even drafted a working paper for later publication; however, disagreements within the team about the future development of the manuscript dampened the motivation of each team member to invest further resources into the project, which was ultimately terminated before the results had been published. The scientist reported the following, "[The project failure] was a really unpleasant situation. In a sense, of course, you start a project and would like to have results that warrant publication, but you are not able to lead it to a good outcome. To see that you and the team were not able to lead it to successful completion was altogether disappointing."

In another example, as project leader, an aerospace engineer had been awarded a project from a famous airplane manufacturer by winning a competition against several other research groups. The project's aim was to develop an airplane with autonomous navigation that would pass a defined number of defined spots in the landscape within a certain timeframe. However, the project was interrupted and delayed several times because the team failed to deliver the necessary technical solution at the proposed milestones. The project leader noted that the project failure was "frustrating.... You state you can do everything and others cannot.... [And] if we do not deliver, I experience it as personal disappointment and personal failure, which depresses my soul." The project leader was also in fear of losing his reputation as a reliable partner for industry and was thus uncertain about future funding opportunities for his group and the entire research institute.

Similarly, a research scientist in theoretical physics reported on a project for which he and others tried to perform some theoretical calculations on crystalline elastomers. However, the project faced problems because the experimental data did not fit with the team's theoretical calculations, which hindered any project progress. Reflecting on the failure, the scientist noted that he "worked as much as before, but the motivation was not as high.... You do not really have the full drive anymore. In terms of working hours, it was certainly not different, but it was really frustrating. I was quite furious." He went on and emphasized that "You indeed think twice whether it all makes sense what you are doing.... It is indeed that you start doubting more." This emotional reaction is particularly remarkable because describing his work environment, the scientist also found it "pretty normal that some things do not work out." However, the perceptions of normality of project failure did not eliminate his negative emotional reaction to the failure nor the demotivate effect of those negative emotions.

Similarly, a research scientist in biology found it "not surprising" that some projects he had worked on did not work out but also mentioned considerable negative emotional reactions when they occurred. In describing a project on insect–plant interactions for which he "tried to find out how a particular gene influences this interaction, how cankers eating the plant are affected, and how the defense mechanisms of the plant can be regulated anew," he experienced a series of failures and setbacks:

> We had a hypothesis that did not work out.... We had to go back not only weeks or months but almost two years. We completely rejected the hypothesis and started anew. This was not easy....
> Imagine, you work for one-and-a-half years, do all the experiments, and all the graphs look the same.... Motivation is difficult then. If the results are frustrating because the hypothesis was not right, you find yourself without energy. [He went on to describe his work in a more general way.] It is always like this: If something works well and you find something interesting, then immediately everything is on fire and you have to do many things and start rotating. But, if the results are frustrating, just because the hypothesis was wrong once again, then you are out of energy in a certain sense. Yes, one can say it this way.

We found similar demotivational aspects of project failure in our study on failed projects in a large technology firm. For example, one project manager reported the following, "I personally really fell into a hole. This project, these two-and-a-half years,... I had never worked so intensely for the company as during this time. Regarding work effort, regarding responsibility, but also cost responsibility, responsibility for resources. For me, it was the biggest [project] I had done so far... I really fell into a true hole."

Indeed, for this manager, the emotional reaction was extreme as he went on to report about physical consequences toward the end of the project:

> Usually I like doing sports, running and riding the bicycle. But then,
> when the project's end came near, I got personal health problems.
> I had a slipped disk.... I would not make anyone particularly
> responsible; in the end, the responsibility is always my own. But
> I can indeed imagine that it was due to all this tension. For weeks,
> I felt that I had hardening in my back and in my shoulder muscles,
> which did not disappear anymore. I know that this [muscle tension]
> usually goes away when I do sports, go running, swimming, or
> biking. I was not able to do it anymore. When I went to the doctor,
> it went on for another couple of weeks, and then I had the disk slip
> in the back of my neck.... I personally then realized that I had
> crossed a border and that I was not OK.

In sum, our interviews together with existing studies provided considerable evidence of team leaders' and members' negative emotional reactions to project failures. In line with self-determination theory, these individuals perceive projects as important when they fulfill their basic psychological needs, specifically their needs for competence, autonomy, and relatedness. In the case of project failure, these needs are thwarted, leading to negative emotional experiences. One important consequence of these negative emotions is that leaders and members of failed project teams lose their work motivation to a considerable extent, thus depleting organizations of one of their most important resources – a motivated work force.

NEGATIVE EMOTIONAL REACTION TO BUSINESS FAILURES

While the examples provided so far show that social judgment theory is a useful framework to understand how the failure of entrepreneurial projects can thwart team leaders' and members' basic psychological needs for competence, autonomy, and relatedness and thereby generate negative emotions, there is considerable evidence that firm failure can lead to similar outcomes for independent entrepreneurs.

ENTREPRENEURIAL FIRM FAILURE THWARTING THE NEED FOR COMPETENCE

Several studies have emphasized the important role of learning for entrepreneurs (Cope, 2003; Politis, 2005), both in the classroom (Honig, 2004; Kuratko, 2005) and in practice (e.g., Corbett, 2007; Harrison and Leitch, 2005). These learning experiences can lead to feelings of mastery (Butler, 1992), which in turn signal to the entrepreneur that he or she has developed competence (Rawsthorne and Elliot, 1999). Indeed, the desire to learn can be an important motivation for founding and growing a new business. For example, a learning goal orientation refers to individuals' focus on the development of skill, knowledge, and competence, which are associated with more task-focused, adaptive, and mastery-oriented behaviors (Bunderson and Sutcliffe, 2003), and a study with 158 college students found that a learning goal orientation is related to entrepreneurial career motivations (Culbertson, Smith, and Leiva, 2010). Further, in a large study, we interviewed 154 founders from 64 ventures about their motivations to start and run their businesses (among other topics) (Breugst, Patzelt, and Rathgeber, 2015). For this study, we sampled entrepreneurs of incubator ventures in the Munich area, and we followed the ventures and the founders for about eight months. The accumulated interview material amounted to more than 3,000 single-spaced pages of transcripts from 278 interviews and more than 224 of audio material. In this material, there was considerable evidence of a strong learning motivation among the founders. For example, one founder reported, "The variety ... of course we have topics that we focus on, but they are so broad that I have a great bandwidth.... There are always different fields, and one deals with so many interesting people." Another founder stated the following, "About my job, I especially like ... that it covers various topics. I am not only doing development, but I am also some kind of a trainer for employees, which is certainly an interesting role. I do also have contact with customers, and I have the possibility to immediately get customer feedback on what we are doing."

Finally, a third entrepreneur described his learning motivation as follows: "I like to face challenges and to master these challenges.... It is very important to me that the task ... the challenge is motivating."

If their firm fails, entrepreneurs may not be able to sufficiently fulfill their need for competence; the failure might actually signal to them that they are incompetent when it comes to founding and running a business. For example, one of the founders we interviewed was the CEO of a medical technology venture, but due to bad performance, he was forced to leave the firm by his cofounder and the investor. Reflecting on the time when his exit came near, he noted the following:

> [Our investor] said, "We need a new CEO; I do not work this way!" Of course I opposed at the beginning because I thought what role remains for me then if the investor does the marketing and there is a new CEO. Who do you need then? They will not need me anymore then!... He considered me as being incompetent.... I felt quite depressed.... I would not have thought that he considered me replaceable. [But he says that he can] exchange me and things will be better.... You must see it this way. Without me, the firm would not exist, the idea would not exist, and we [would] not have convinced the investor in the first place!

Interestingly, the cofounder's description of his former partner strongly connected to his reactions to the need for competence:

"I believe that he [the partner] is convinced that what he says makes sense and that he can help the firm. It hurts his ego if someone now says it would be best if he does not say anything."

To entrepreneurs, their business is a way to satisfy their need for competence – they can demonstrate their skills and knowledge, and the challenging task gives them the opportunity to further develop their competences. However, business failure (or failure as an entrepreneur resulting from being kicked out of the business) represents negative feedback about one's competence, and the replacement role (including unemployment) may not satisfy the need for competence as much as running a business. To the extent that the entrepreneurial failure thwarts entrepreneurs' psychological need for competence, it will generate negative emotional reactions when the business is lost to them.

ENTREPRENEURIAL FIRM FAILURE THWARTING THE NEED FOR AUTONOMY

The need for autonomy is a major source of motivation to start a business. For example, in a study of 300 alumni of an Australian university, Douglas and Shepherd (2002) analyzed 4,800 assessments of hypothetical career scenarios and found that individuals vary in their desire for independence and that those who value independence more will have stronger intentions to pursue entrepreneurial careers. Our interviews with 154 firm founders confirmed that running their venture can significantly contribute to fulfilling the psychological need for autonomy. For example, when asked about what she likes most about being an entrepreneur, one founder answered, "I can make many decisions – basically make all decisions – myself." Another entrepreneur reported, "In any case, I want to work in a [team] constellation where I have the say! I want to have a clear superiority in terms of influence."

Despite these studies and interview quotes supporting the importance of autonomy for the motivation to start a business, there is less evidence on how (and to what effect) firm failure has on thwarting individuals' needs for autonomy. For example, in our interviews with entrepreneurs of failed businesses, we found little support for an experience of a loss of autonomy. Similarly, although a recent study by Jenkins, Wiklund, and Brundin (2014) hypothesized that the loss of independence would cause grief for failed entrepreneurs, their empirical results did not provide evidence for the hypothesis. Specifically, these authors surveyed 120 entrepreneurs in Sweden who had filed for bankruptcy with a venture they had actively been running and in which they held an ownership stake. Contrary to the hypothesis, regression models showed no statistically significant association between loss of independence and grief, and there was also no statistical difference between entrepreneurs who had experienced failures previous to the focal failure and those who had not. It appears that while the need for autonomy is a driver for starting a venture, once the venture has failed, either (1) the fulfillment of this need becomes less important or (2) failed entrepreneurs fulfill this need by other means, such as starting another business. Indeed, Jenkins et al., (2014) found that portfolio entrepreneurs (i.e., those who run several businesses at a time) and to a certain extent also hybrid entrepreneurs (i.e., those who are in salaried employment in addition to running their own business) experience less loss of independence from business failure (but similar levels of grief) than others.

Therefore, perhaps either running ventures other than the failed business (for portfolio entrepreneurs) or enjoying autonomy in a salaried job (for hybrid entrepreneurs) might be sufficient for fulfilling entrepreneurs' psychological need for autonomy. Future research can make important contributions by further exploring how and when business failure impacts entrepreneurs' need for autonomy.

ENTREPRENEURIAL FIRM FAILURE THWARTING THE NEED FOR BELONGINGNESS

Entrepreneurship is a social endeavor, and founders must entertain multiple relationships with team members, employees, investors, customers, and other stakeholders (Aldrich and Zimmer, 1986;

Birley, 1986). Internal to the venture, perhaps the most important and intense social relationships built are those with other members of the entrepreneurial team. For example, one founder we interviewed reported, "We spent together 12 to 13 hours every day over three years. One does indeed get to know each other." When asked about the most important factors for running a successful venture, another founder emphasized the following: "From my point of view, the most important issue is the trust in the team and the belief in the team and that these are maintained over time. The moment these get broken, I am convinced that it is a very dangerous moment for the venture." Finally, reflecting on her experiences in the past, one founder of an e-commerce startup reported, "2011 was our best year. And we had confidence. We had 10 employees altogether.... It was a great team, and it was really fun."

While these quotes provide evidence for the notion that being part of an entrepreneurial team can contribute to fulfilling one's need for relatedness, our interviews also demonstrated that either the failure of the firm or the disbanding of the entrepreneurial team (i.e., the exit of one team member) can thwart the fulfillment of this need. For example, the remaining team member of a medical technology venture described his feelings after the cofounder had left the firm as follows:

> Of course I felt lonely after Sam left the firm.... He was really the only one in exactly the same situation as me; he was in the same boat. I missed him as a person, a person who has the same interests, who can represent me in certain issues or take some of my work load and also can communicate with me. I was more or less left alone.

When asked about how the relationship with this cofounder had developed after the firm had failed, an entrepreneur of an Internet firm explained, "Before [the failure], we had a deep and daily relationship which was very intense. After that [the failure], we had difficulties talking even about the most marginal issues."

Of course, not all entrepreneurs must satisfy their need for belongingness through work. The founder of a medical technology venture reported that after exiting the firm, he was able to satisfy his psychological need for relatedness by turning to individuals from outside the venture:

> I must say that was a difficult time in any case. If you face such a difficult time, you are happy for anyone supporting you. My girlfriend has helped me quite a bit here. It was really important to have somebody to talk this issue over [with] and who also has an external view. I also talked with a lot of friends about it, and I openly asked: "Am I mad now, or what's the issue?"

Although some entrepreneurs are able to satisfy their need to belong by looking to non-work-related relationships, others lose a sense of belonging when a business fails (or they are forced to exit). To the extent that their psychological need for belongingness is thwarted by failure, they will have a negative emotional reaction. We now turn to the impact of such a negative emotional reaction on motivation.

MOTIVATIONAL CONSEQUENCES OF A NEGATIVE EMOTIONAL REACTION TO FIRM FAILURE

Similar to the motivational effect of grief in the context of entrepreneurial projects, the experience of negative emotions from firm failure can have a profound impact on the motivation of independent entrepreneurs (Shepherd, 2003). For example, one of our interviewees of a failed venture reported the following:

> In this moment, it was a deep moment of defeat which I had never before experienced in a similar way. A moment where I said, yes, now I am giving up, although I am not the person who usually does so. [Interviewer: Why did you experience it as a defeat?] Because I had stopped something I had very, very strongly believed in for two years. To stop something like this had been a defeat from my point of view.

When we interviewed that person several months after the venture had failed, he had still not moved on to another job. Similarly, when we heard of the failure of another entrepreneurial venture in our sample, we tried to contact one of the founders for a follow-up interview. We were, however, not able to make contact with that person – he had cut all his social ties, including removing his mobile and home phone number and deleting all his e-mail addresses and profiles on Facebook and other social networks. As we heard from his cofounder, this individual had left the city and shut down all contacts. Six months later, we found him back in town and willing to give us an interview. He conceded that the grief from failure was so strong that he could not stay in the same place and in the same social environment anymore but had to travel to another part of the world to recover and sort himself out. He only returned when he felt that he had the motivation to move on with his life and look for work again.

These examples are only a few cases providing evidence of the strong motivational effects that negative emotions from venture failure can have on entrepreneurs – effects that are similar to those of members and leaders of project teams. Importantly, however, there is obviously variance in individuals' intensity of negative emotions generated after failure, and how these negative emotions impact motivation.

DISCUSSION

In this chapter, we explored the emotional and motivational consequences of project team members and independent entrepreneurs who experience failure. Using self-determination theory as a theoretical framework and interview data from both independent entrepreneurs whose businesses failed and members of project teams whose projects failed, we provided evidence that the consequences of failure are substantial because the loss of a project or firm thwarts individuals' needs for competence, relatedness, and autonomy. These findings have a number of implications for scholars and open up interesting avenues for future research.

First, our interview data illustrate that self-determination theory is a useful theoretical angle to study the emotional and motivational consequences of failure for entrepreneurs and members of entrepreneurial project teams. Typically, self-determination theory has been used to study the sources of intrinsic motivation in work environments and how such environments should be designed to trigger employees' motivation (Deci and Ryan, 2000). Further, self-determination theory has been used to explain individuals' psychological well-being, arguing that thwarting basic needs diminishes well-being and generates negative emotions (La Guardia, Ryan, Couchman, and Deci, 2000). However, self-determination theory has rarely been applied in project settings (an exception is Shepherd and Cardon, 2009), and few studies have used it to explain entrepreneurial emotions and motivation (Schröder and Schmitt-Rodermund, 2013; Shepherd and Cardon, 2009). Based on our earlier discussion and the fact that the self-determination theory is consistent with our interview data, we encourage scholars to draw on this theoretical foundation to further advance our understanding of failure's emotional and motivational (and perhaps other) consequences for those involved (and others in their environment).

Second, a noteworthy finding relates to differences between the failures of entrepreneurial projects and entrepreneurial firms with respect to thwarting the three basic needs. Specifically, our interview data demonstrate that both types of failures can thwart individuals' needs for competence and relatedness. Interestingly, however, while we provide evidence that project failure also thwarts individuals' need for autonomy, we did not find similarly strong evidence for business failure thwarting this need. This is somewhat surprising given that becoming an independent entrepreneur seems to be ideal to fulfill individuals' autonomy needs (Shane, Locke, and Collins, 2003). A possible explanation for this finding might be that in a corporate environment, project failure usually leads to individuals' involvement in other activities within the organization, activities for which management might grant those who failed less autonomy than before (perhaps as a consequence of/punishment for the failure). Independent entrepreneurs who fail, in contrast, often do not enter into salaried employment but rather try to start anew (after overcoming some period of recovery) or face a period of unemployment. That is, even in the case of failure, there is no corporate environment that imposes rules and structures upon independent entrepreneurs. Future research can test these propositions and explore in more detail when failure (project or business) leads to thwarting individuals' need for autonomy.

Third, although our interview data suggest that the three basic needs do indeed play a role in explaining emotional reactions to entrepreneurial failures, it is also noteworthy that not all individuals experience the loss of a project or a firm in the same manner. That is, while some interviewees indicated that their needs for competence, relatedness, and/or autonomy were thwarted, there was also considerable variance between individuals. Indeed, while self-determination theory posits that all individuals have the three basic needs, it also states that there is variance in "the consequences of the extent to which individuals are able to *satisfy* the needs within social environments" (Gagné and Deci, 2005: 337). That is, some social environments (within or outside corporations) are more likely to buffer against the negative consequences of failure when individuals' experience of negative emotions and grief. In the chapters that follow, we introduce studies showing how differences between individuals and their environments impact negative emotions from failure. However, as we outline later, we also believe that future research can still make important contributions by continuing to explore the characteristics of individuals' social environments that determine to what extent thwarting the needs for competence, relatedness, and autonomy from project and business failure translates into negative emotions for subsequent entrepreneurial endeavors.

Finally, in addition to the negative implications for individuals' emotional well-being, our discussion and interview data illustrate the detrimental effects of project and business failure on the motivations of those involved. One of the central arguments of self-determination theory is that in environments where individuals perceive that their three basic needs have been thwarted, intrinsic motivation diminishes. Again, however, our interview data indicate that the manifestation of how failure impacts entrepreneurs' motivation varies across individuals and situations. Indeed, Deci and Ryan (2000) argued that there are situational differences that impact how central each of the three basic needs is in triggering motivation. It appears that there is variance between situations in corporate environments and those typically experienced by independent entrepreneurs with respect to the centrality of individual needs and that there is variance within corporate and independent entrepreneurial environments with respect to this centrality. It is an open yet important research question as to how these variances can be explained. Answers to this question might have substantial influence on how entrepreneurial environments (e.g., entrepreneurial project settings, the networks independent entrepreneurs operate in) should be designed to accommodate the possibility of project and business failure with respect to minimizing their negative effects on the motivation of those who failed and to maximize the learning opportunities arising from that experience.

Implications for entrepreneurs and managers

Our illustration of the negative emotional and motivational consequences of entrepreneurial project and business failure entail a number of implications for practicing managers and entrepreneurs.

First, it seems important that managers are aware of the emotional consequences of project failures. In a corporate setting, higher-level managers might not have been actively involved in the project that failed, or they might have been supervising multiple projects at a time when only one failed. These low levels of involvement might cause only minor emotional reactions from senior managers, but the situation is quite different for many of the project team members. Due to team members' negative emotional reactions to project failure, team members might not be able to fully and immediately engage in the next project. Instead, some active help in managing negative emotions from failure before and/or during the start of a new project could be necessary for team members to recover effectively and quickly. We will highlight possibilities of managing negative emotions from project failure in subsequent chapters. However, recognizing that such emotions exist and that they can be substantial for project team members is an important first step for managers leading entrepreneurial firms.

Second, independent entrepreneurs can make an important first step of recovering from business failure when they acknowledge the existence of their own negative emotions. These emotions are not exceptional; rather, it seems that they are quite normal when entrepreneurs perceive the failed business as having been something important to them. When independent entrepreneurs acknowledge negative emotions after failure, they can actively and systematically start the recovery process (as we outline in subsequent chapters). Indeed, knowing that these emotions are normal and that the failure experience is shared among many other entrepreneurs in similar situations represents an important first step toward recovery. For example, knowing that they share their current emotional situation with other (perhaps prominent) entrepreneurs who were successful with subsequent businesses might mitigate the extent to which business failure thwarts failed entrepreneurs' needs for competence. That is, knowing that others have failed, emotionally recovered, and subsequently succeeded illustrates that failure is just a normal part of the learning process necessary to build up the competence to become a successful entrepreneur.

Third, similar to knowing about team members' negative emotions from entrepreneurial project failures, managers should be aware about the motivational consequences of such failures. This awareness might help managers develop realistic expectations of team members' performance immediately following a failure. It seems that some team members who are highly demotivated from project failure may not be able to take on particularly challenging tasks. For these team members, managers might assign tasks that are less challenging for a certain amount of time, and they might consider providing them vacations or flexible and reduced working hours to cope with the failure and to regain their motivations. Then again, others might cope better with the grief over project failure by being re-assigned to an equally (or even more) challenging assignment so they feel that their career has not plateaued or worse. Since motivational consequences differ between those involved in the failure, it seems best for supervisors to acknowledge each team member's specific reaction and provide individualized treatment to restore the motivation of the entire project team after failure.

Finally, following business failure, it seems normal for entrepreneurs to experience a decline in motivation and become wary of making emotional investments to start anew. Again, knowing that they share this experience with others and that many of those others have found the motivation to re-enter entrepreneurship and be successful in the end might help entrepreneurs of failed businesses escape the "motivational dip." Indeed, this knowledge might help them escape vicious cycles of ruminations – namely, when a lack of motivation leads to increased negative emotions (e.g., feelings of guilt and shame for not being motivated), which in turn decrease motivation, and so on. Additionally, acknowledging that a lack of motivation for starting a new business after failure is rather normal might help those who failed to channel their motivations to different activities, which could help distract from the failure and thus speed up recovery, enabling the entrepreneur to regain motivation for entrepreneurship (Shepherd, 2003).

REFERENCES

Aldrich, H. E. and Zimmer, C. 1986. Entrepreneurship through social networks. In H. E. Aldrich (ed.), *Population Perspectives on Organizations*: 13–28. Uppsala: Acta Universitatis Upsaliensis.
Behrens, J., Ernst, H., and Shepherd, D. A. 2014. The decision to exploit an RandD project: Divergent thinking across middle and senior managers. *Journal of Product Innovation Management*, 31(1): 144–158.

Bennis, W. and Nanus, B. 1985. *Leadership: The strategies for taking charge*. New York: Harper and Row.

Birley, S. 1986. The role of networks in the entrepreneurial process. *Journal of Business Venturing*, 1(1): 107–117.

Blanchard, K., Carlos, J., and Randolph, W. 1995. *The empowerment barometer and action plan*. Escondido, CA: Blanchard Training and Development.

Boulding, W., Morgan, R., and Staelin, R. 1997. Pulling the plug to stop the new product drain. *Journal of Marketing Research (JMR)*, 34(1): 164–176.

Breugst, N., Patzelt, H., and Rathgeber, P. 2015. How should we divide the pie? Equity distribution and its impact on entrepreneurial teams. *Journal of Business Venturing*, 30(1): 66–94.

Brown, S. L. and Eisenhardt, K. M. 1997. The art of continuous change: Linking complexity theory and time-paced evolution in relentlessly shifting organizations. *Administrative Science Quarterly*, 42(1): 1–34.

Bunderson, J. S. and Sutcliffe, K. M. 2003. Management team learning orientation and business unit performance. *Journal of Applied Psychology*, 88(3): 552.

Butler, R. 1992. What young people want to know when: Effects of mastery and ability goals on interest in different kinds of social comparisons. *Journal of Personality and Social Psychology*, 62(6): 934–943.

Campbell, A., Birkinshaw, J., Morrison, A., and van Basten Batenburg, R. 2003. The future of corporate venturing. *MIT Sloan Management Review*, 45(1): 30–37.

Cope, J. 2003. Entrepreneurial learning and critical reflection discontinuous events as triggers for 'higher-level' learning. *Management Learning*, 34(4): 429–450.

Corbett, A. C. 2007. Learning asymmetries and the discovery of entrepreneurial opportunities. *Journal of Business Venturing*, 22(1): 97–118.

Culbertson, S. S., Smith, M. R., and Leiva, P. I. 2010. Enhancing entrepreneurship: The role of goal orientation and self-efficacy. *Journal of Career Assessment*: 115–129.

Deci, E. L. and Ryan, R. M. 2000. The "what" and "why" of goal pursuits: Human needs and the self-determination of behavior. *Psychological Inquiry*, 11(4): 227–268.

Deci, E. L. and Ryan, R. M. 2002. *Handbook of Self-Determination Research*. New York: University Rochester Press.

Deci, E. L. and Ryan, R. M. 2008. Hedonia, eudaimonia, and well-being: An introduction. *Journal of Happiness Studies*, 9(1): 1–11.

Douglas, E. J. and Shepherd, D. A. 2002. Self-employment as a career choice: Attitudes, entrepreneurial intentions, and utility maximization. *Entrepreneurship Theory and Practice*, 26(3): 81–90.

Dweck, C. S. 1986. Motivational processes affecting learning. *American Psychologist*, 41(10): 1040–1048.

Fitzgerald, M. 2010. When good projects go bad. Computerworld. www.computerworld .com/article/2550660/it-management/when-good-projects-go-bad.html.

Gagné, M. and Deci, E. L. 2005. Self-determination theory and work motivation. *Journal of Organizational Behavior*, 26(4): 331–362.

Harrison, R. T. and Leitch, C. M. 2005. Entrepreneurial learning: Researching the interface between learning and the entrepreneurial context. *Entrepreneurship Theory and Practice*, 29(4): 351–371.

Honig, B. 2004. Entrepreneurship education: Toward a model of contingency-based business planning. *Academy of Management Learning and Education*, 3(3): 258–273.

Jenkins, A. S., Wiklund, J., and Brundin, E. 2014. Individual responses to firm failure: Appraisals, grief, and the influence of prior failure experience. *Journal of Business Venturing*, 29(1): 17–33.

Keil, M. and Robey, D. 1999. Turning around troubled software projects: An exploratory study of the deescalation of commitment to failing courses of action. *Journal of Management Information Systems*, 15(4): 63–87.

Kuratko, D. F. 2005. The emergence of entrepreneurship education: Development, trends, and challenges. *Entrepreneurship Theory and Practice*, 29(5): 577–598.

La Guardia, J. G., Ryan, R. M., Couchman, C. E., and Deci, E. L. 2000. Within-person variation in security of attachment: A self-determination theory perspective on attachment, need fulfillment, and well-being. *Journal of Personality and Social Psychology*, 79(3): 367.

Liden, R. C. and Tewksbury, T. W. 1995. Empowerment and work teams. In G. R. Ferris and S. D. Rosen and D. T. Barnum (eds.), *Handbook of Human Resources Management*: 386–403. Oxford, England: Blackwell.

Lindsley, D. H., Brass, D. J., and Thomas, J. B. 1995. Efficacy-performance spirals: A multilevel perspective. *Academy of Management Review*, 20(3): 645–678.

Logan, M. S. and Ganster, D. C. 2007. The effects of empowerment on attitudes and performance: The role of social support and empowerment beliefs. *Journal of Management Studies*, 44(8): 1523–1550.

McGrath, R. 1999. Falling forward: Real options reasoning and entrepreneurial failure. *Academy of Management Review*, 24: 13–30.

McGrath, R. G., Keil, T., and Tukiainen, T. 2012. Extracting value from corporate venturing. *MIT Sloan Management Review*, 48(1): 50–56.

Politis, D. 2005. The process of entrepreneurial learning: A conceptual framework. *Entrepreneurship Theory and Practice*, 29(4): 399–424.

Rauch, A., Wiklund, J., Lumpkin, G. T., and Frese, M. 2009. Entrepreneurial orientation and business performance: An assessment of past research and suggestions for the future. *Entrepreneurship Theory and Practice*, 33(3): 761–787.

Rawsthorne, L. J. and Elliot, A. J. 1999. Achievement goals and intrinsic motivation: A meta-analytic review. *Personality and Social Psychology Review*, 3(4): 326–344.

Richter, A. W., West, M. A., Van Dick, R., and Dawson, J. F. 2006. Boundary spanners' identification, intergroup contact, and effective intergroup relations. *Academy of Management Journal*, 49(6): 1252–1269.

Schröder, E. and Schmitt-Rodermund, E. 2013. Antecedents and consequences of adolescents' motivations to join the family business. *Journal of Vocational Behavior*, 83(3): 476–485.

Shane, S., Locke, E. A., and Collins, C. J. 2003. Entrepreneurial motivation. *Human Resource Management Review*, 13(2): 257–279.

Shepherd, D. A. 2003. Learning from business failure: Propositions of grief recovery for the self-employed. *Academy of Management Review*, 28(2): 318–328.

Shepherd, D. A. and Cardon, M. S. 2009. Negative emotional reactions to project failure and the self-compassion to learn from the experience. *Journal of Management Studies*, 46(6): 923–949.

Shepherd, D. A., Covin, J. G., and Kuratko, D. F. 2009. Project failure from corporate entrepreneurship: Managing the grief process. *Journal of Business Venturing*, 24(6): 588–600.

Shepherd, D. A. and Patzelt, H. 2011. The new field of sustainable entrepreneurship: Studying entrepreneurial action linking "what is to be sustained" with "what is to be developed." *Entrepreneurship Theory and Practice*, 35(1): 137–163.

Shepherd, D. A., Patzelt, H., and Wolfe, M. 2011. Moving forward from project failure: Negative emotions, affective commitment, and learning from the experience. *Academy of Management Journal*, 54(6): 1229–1259.

Shepherd, D. A., Patzelt, H., Williams, T. A., and Warnecke, D. 2014. How does project termination impact project team members? Rapid termination, 'creeping death', and learning from failure. *Journal of Management Studies*, 51(4): 513–546.

Thompson, C. A. and Prottas, D. J. 2006. Relationships among organizational family support, job autonomy, perceived control, and employee well-being. *Journal of Occupational Health Psychology*, 11(1): 100–118.

Tjosvold, D., Johnson, D. W., Johnson, R. T., and Sun, H. 2003. Can interpersonal competition be constructive within organizations? *The Journal of Psychology*, 137(1): 63–84.

Wiklund, J. and Shepherd, D. A. 2005. Entrepreneurial orientation and small business performance: a configurational approach. *Journal of Business Venturing*, 20(1): 71–91.

3 Self-compassion and learning from failure*

In Chapter 2, we highlighted how entrepreneurial projects can boost individuals' psychological well-being. That is, the more a project satisfies an individual's psychological needs for competence, autonomy, and belongingness, the more important the project is to him or her. Although the importance of a project enhances the motivation for success, it also means that if the project fails, the individual will have a more negative emotional reaction (i.e., grief over the loss of an entrepreneurial project [see Chapter 2]). From the hedonic perspective of psychology (Kahneman, Diener, and Schwarz 1999), an individual's subjective well-being is enhanced by the absence of negative affect (Diener and Lucas 1999). Therefore, people often engage in attempts to avoid and/or quickly eliminate negative emotions in order to return to a high level of subjective well-being.

However, a different perspective of well-being leads to an emphasis on a different outcome for responses to project failure. Rather than focusing on happiness (including the absence of negative affect and the maintenance of self-worth), the eudaimonic approach focuses on "meaning and self-realization" (Ryan and Deci 2001: 141). This approach suggests that not all actions and reactions that reduce negative emotions also promote personal growth (McGregor and Little 1998; Ryan and Deci 2001). For example, protection from threats to perceived self-worth (e.g., those arising from project failure) can reduce or eliminate negative emotions but can simultaneously be maladaptive (for reviews see Blaine and Crocker 1993; Crocker and Park 2004). Such is the case, for instance, when "people wanting to maintain high self-esteem . . . dismiss negative feedback as unreliable

---

* We thank Kathie Sutcliffe for helping develop these ideas.

or biased, trivializing failures or attributing them to external causes. As a consequence, they may take less personal responsibility for harmful actions and develop an inaccurate self-concept, hindering growth and change" (Neff and Vonk 2009: 24).

Thus, cognitions and actions to protect feelings of self-worth in the face of failure can enhance subjective well-being, but can also lead to a rigid and closed mindset that diminishes and rejects alternative explanations (Jost, Glaser, Kruglanski, and Sulloway 2003; Taris 2000) for why a project failed. In doing so, the pursuit of subjective well-being can create obstacles, including blind spots (Sutcliffe and Weick 2003) that obstruct learning. In this chapter, we explore how to overcome some of these blind spots. Specifically, we discuss what self-compassion is; how it fits into the eudaimonic conceptualization of well-being; and how it is achieved across levels, including individual, group, and organizational levels. First, we discuss an overarching model for this chapter. Second, we discuss the individual aspects of the model, including the relationship between self-compassion and learning from failure. Finally, we discuss general implications and offer suggestions for future research.

A SELF-COMPASSION MODEL OF LEARNING FROM FAILURE

Model overview

In the sections that follow, we develop a multilevel model of self-compassion as an approach to learning from failure, which is illustrated in Figure 3.1. Our model differentiates the influence of self-compassion and learning outcomes within and across levels. At the individual level, a person's self-compassion positively influences his or her learning from failure, which is mediated by positive emotions. At the organizational level, self-compassion influences organizational learning from failure, which is mediated by collective positive emotions. Three constructs link the individual and organizational levels: (1) self-compassion (i.e., self-kindness, common humanity, and

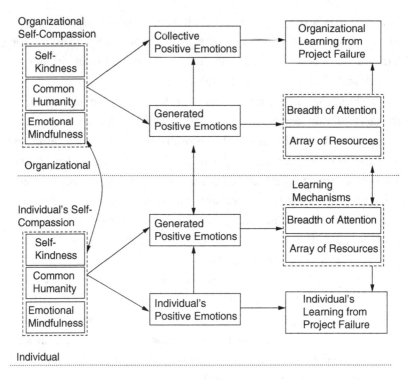

FIGURE 3.1: A self-compassionate model of learning from failure

mindfulness], (2) positive emotions, and (3) learning (i.e., breadth of attention and array of resources). These constructs are applicable at both the individual and the organizational levels and are, therefore, referred to as isomorphic (House, Rousseau, and Thomashunt 1995; Huy 1999).

In developing our model, we make a number of assumptions that establish important boundary conditions for the model. Consistent with other organizational theory, including research on compassion, we acknowledge the organization as an entity. As argued by Kanov et al. (2004: 816), "we are not suggesting that organizations are entities that like individuals, literally notice, feel, and respond to pain; nor are we suggesting that organizational compassion is a mere aggregation of compassion among individuals. Rather organizational compassion involves a set of social processes in which noticing, feeling and responding to pain are shared among a set of organizational members." We make a similar assumption for organizational self-compassion.[1] Further, we assume that entities (i.e., individuals and organizations) are heterogeneous in self-compassion, and we explore the consequences of that heterogeneity but not its antecedents. As such, the processes by which self-compassion becomes legitimated, propagated, and coordinated are outside the bounds of the current chapter but are worthy of future research.

Self-compassion

The concept of self-compassion (at the individual level) comes from Buddhist philosophy (Bennett-Goleman 2002; Rosenberg 1999; Salzberg 2004) and represents part of a larger effort to build on Buddhist notions to inform the Western understanding of suffering and psychological well-being (for a review, see Wallace and Shapiro 2006). Self-compassion in the context of failure events refers to *an individual's emotional response to his or her negative emotional reaction to failure that involves feeling care and kindness toward oneself, recognizing that one's experience is part of the common human experience, and understanding one's inadequacies and flaws in a nonjudgmental way* (adapted from Neff 2003a). Self-compassion at the individual level involves the dimensions of self-kindness, common humanity, and mindfulness (Neff 2003a; Neff 2003k) and has been found to be positively associated with personal growth. For example, self-compassion is positively associated with happiness, optimism, curiosity, and connectedness (Neff and Vonk 2009), which in turn function as mechanisms for enabling growth despite possible setbacks or negative events.

In a series of experiments, Leary, et al. (2007) found that self-compassion buffers people against the impact of negative events; that

[1] This is consistent with Chapter 6 where we explore emotion at the organizational level (see for review, Huy 1999).

is, more self-compassionate participants provided more accurate self-evaluations that were less tainted by *both* self-criticism and defensive self-enhancement than those who were less self-compassionate. After a negative event, individuals are at higher risk of either overly criticizing themselves – resulting in adverse outcomes, such as depression – or of avoiding key signals that preceded the negative event because they instead focus on defensively enhancing their self-worth (Neff 2003k). In contrast to harsh self-criticism, Leary et al. (2007: 887) found that after experimentally inducing self-compassion, people were able to "acknowledge their role in negative events without feeling over-whelmed with negative emotions." Furthermore, the absence of feeling overwhelmed was not merely due to higher self-esteem or the avoidance of key signals of the failure, but was rather a healthy confrontation with negative events and their causes. Importantly, an individual's self-compassion is distinct from self-esteem. Neff and Vonk (2009) found that relative to self-esteem, self-compassion is more positively associated with stable feelings of self-worth and is more negatively associated with social comparison, public self-consciousness, self-ruination, anger, and the need for cognitive closure. Similarly, Neff (2003k) found that self-esteem (i.e., positive feelings about oneself and believing that one is valued by others (Leary and MacDonald 2003) correlates with characteristics like narcissism, hubris, and self-enhancing illusions, whereas self-compassion does not. These findings suggest that self-compassion is likely to facilitate a healthy recovery (including learning) from unpleasant events.

Based on the recognition that compassion exists at the organizational level (e.g. Dutton, Worline, Frost, and Lilius 2006) and that individuals can direct compassion toward the self, we offer the construct of organizational self-compassion. We define organizational self-compassion in the context of failure events as *the collective emotional response of organizational members to negative emotional reactions to organizational failures that involve collectively feeling care and kindness toward the organization and its members, recognizing that these negative emotions are part of organizational experiences, and understanding – in a non-judgmental way – the inadequacies and missteps of the organization and its members.* As indicated in Figure 3.1, we anticipate that both organizational- and individual-level self-compassion are represented by three components: (1) self-kindness, (2) common humanity, and (3) mindfulness.

Self-kindness

Self-kindness is the first component of self-compassion. At the individual level, self-kindness involves "extending kindness and understanding to oneself rather than harsh judgment and self-criticism" (Neff 2003a: 89) at the onset of a failure event. When faced with a failure, an individual high in self-kindness tries to be understanding and patient toward those aspects of his or her personality he or she does not like, gives him- or herself the caring and tenderness needed when going through a very hard time, is tolerant of his or her flaws and inadequacies, and tries to be loving toward him- or herself when feeling emotional pain (Neff 2003k: 231). Self-kindness does not mean that one is content with his or her flaws or is passive toward the learning needed to eliminate future failures and/or minimize the effect of failures. It encourages action but does so with gentleness and patience (Neff 2003a). This gentleness and patience is important despite the immediate changes necessitated by a failure event. Individuals who are less self-kind are more self-judgmental; intolerant of their own flaws; and tough on themselves when times are difficult (Neff 2003k), such as when experiencing project failure. Without self-kindness, the response to failure is harsh self-criticism for not meeting ideal standards, which in turn inhibits an individual's ability to achieve personal growth (e.g., learning from the experience). For example, harsh self-condemnation exacerbates the pain and sense of failure that an individual feels when things go wrong (Blatt, Quinlan, Chevron, McDonald, and Zuroff 1982). That is, it adds additional anxiety to an already emotional event. Harsh self-criticism can lead to ruminations that escalate negative emotions (Nolen-Hoeksema 1991) and increase grief over project loss.

Like individuals, organizations can direct kindness externally (to others) and internally. In terms of being kind to others, while there is some dispute over whether corporate social responsibility, corporate philanthropy, and/or corporate donations represent a strategy for enhancing firm performance (Godfrey 2005), it appears that at least some organizations do good above and beyond what is expected (Logsdon and Wood 2002). That is, some organizations are benevolent and kind to their employees (Lloyd 1990; Milliman, Czaplewski, and Ferguson 2001; Schulman 1999) and members of society (Cowton 1987; Edmondson and Carroll 1999; Shaw and Post 1993). Thus, we develop the concept of organizational self-kindness in the context of failure events, which refers to *the collective emotional response of organizational members to negative emotional reactions to organizational failures that involves collectively feeling care and kindness toward the organization and its members.*

Common humanity

Common humanity is the second component of self-compassion. Individual common humanity refers to *"perceiving one's experiences as part of the larger human experience rather than seeing them as separating and isolating"* (Neff 2003a: 85). Experiencing failure with a common-humanity perspective means that when feeling inadequate in some way, an individual reminds him- or herself that most people experience feelings of inadequacy, that one's failings are part of the human condition, that there are many other people in the world feeling the same way, and that these difficulties are a part of life that everyone goes through (Neff 2003k: 231). Without such a perspective, actors are likely to believe that they are the only individuals who feel bad after a negative event and ignore any interconnectedness with others (Neff 2003k). Feelings of isolation cause additional anxiety and exacerbate the negative emotions already generated by the failure event.

As is the case with individuals, organizations can recognize that they are part of a common humanity in response to others' negative emotions and, as we develop later, their own failings. Indeed, the notion of being a corporate citizen acknowledges an organization's sense of belonging to a community (Logsdon and Wood 2002; Matten, Crane, and Chapple 2003). Recognition of common humanity may result in a feeling of social duty to help others, an ethical obligation to help others, and/or a recognition that the organization depends on society for its continued existence (Garriga and Melé 2004). Common humanity creates a feeling that the organization must look after its stakeholders (Emshoff and Freeman 1978) and members of the larger community (Donaldson and Dunfee 2000; Logsdon and Wood 2002). To the extent that organizations acknowledge common humanity in relation to their own (collective) negative reaction to failure, they demonstrate organizational common humanity. Thus, we develop the concept of organizational common humanity in the context of failure events, which refers to *the collective emotional response of organizational members to negative emotional reactions to organizational failures that involve collectively recognizing that these negative feelings are part of organizations' experiences.* For example, when facing a major project failure, an organization with common humanity can emphasize that most organizations face such conditions at some time in their lives and that when this happens, most organizations have a collective negative emotional reaction. That is, when an organization is able to recognize its current position and grief as part of normal "organizational life," it is able to remain connected to others despite a failure event. As another example, an organization might emphasize how it overcame similar events in its past and how it is resilient and can defy temporary failures in pursuit of broader successes or accomplishments.

Mindfulness

Mindfulness, in the context of self-compassion at the individual level, refers to "holding painful thoughts and feelings in balanced awareness rather than over-identifying with them" (Neff 2003a: 85). While mindfulness is often considered to involve "directing attention toward the *present moment* in an *open-minded* (non-judgmental) way," mindfulness as a dimension of self-compassion involves directing attention in an *open-hearted* way (Fredrickson, Cohn, Coffey, Pek, and Finkel 2008: 1096, emphasis added). Open-hearted mindfulness centers on the emotions involved in the present moment with a focus on increasing feelings of caring, warmth, and positivity toward the self and others (see also Fredrickson et al. 2008; Salzberg 1997). Those who are mindful try to keep their emotions in balance when facing a negative event, approach their feelings with curiosity and openness, and maintain a balanced view of the negative situation even when something painful happens (Neff 2003k: 232). In contrast, those who are less mindful "tend to obsess and fixate on everything that is wrong," "blow the incident out of proportion," generally become "carried away" with their feelings arising from a negative event, and are "consumed by feelings of inadequacy" (Neff 2003k: 232). Mindfulness does not involve self-evaluation or considerations of self-worth. Indeed, when one is mindful, the sense of self "softens or disappears" (Martin 1997: 292) to provide the sort of psychological distance between self-worth and the adversity that enables the non-judgmental acceptance of present-moment experiences (Bishop et al. 2004). This is not to say that mindfulness denies or eliminates the generation of negative emotions over project failure. On the contrary, painful thoughts and emotions generated by project failure are accepted and approached with curiosity as part of an open-hearted awareness.

Mindfulness at the organizational level is well documented in the organizing literature, particularly as it relates to high-reliability organizations (Weick, Sutcliffe, and Obstfeld 1999; Weick and Sutcliffe 2011). Although the notion of mindfulness represented in the organizing literature has focused on its cognitive aspects (e.g., Fiol and O'Connor 2003; Krieger 2005; Langer 1989), there has been some recognition of the potential role of the emotional side of organizational mindfulness. As it relates to self-compassion in the context of failure events, we offer the following definition of organizational (emotional) mindfulness: *the collective emotional response of*

organizational members to negative emotional reactions to organiza-
tional failures that involves collectively understanding – in a non-
judgmental way – the inadequacies and mis-steps of the organization
and its members. We anticipate that just as individual mindfulness
following a failure event can result in the generation of positive
emotions, organizations that systematically cultivate an environment
of open-hearted mindfulness are more likely to enhance positive emotions within the organization, which will in turn influence responses
(i.e., learning) to failures or setbacks. This reasoning is consistent with
the broaden-and-build theory of positive emotions (Fredrickson 2001)
and recent empirical research (Arimitsu and Hofmann 2015;
Fredrickson et al. 2008).

SELF-COMPASSION AND LEARNING FROM FAILURE

Self-compassion (i.e., self-kindness, common humanity, and mindfulness) likely contributes to learning from failure experiences. Although
there are many learning mechanisms, we focus on two in particular
because they capture many of the common aspects in both the psychological and organizational literature. Specifically, learning is
enhanced by a broad perception and a broad array of resources. In
the next sections, we first substantiate these learning mechanisms
at the individual and organizational levels, and then detail how these
learning mechanisms are influenced by self-compassion.

Self-compassion and learning from failure through broad perception

Broad perception of individuals: A broad perception refers to individuals' ability to make higher-level connections, widen their range of
percepts or ideas, and extend the attention and/or thinking that
enhances their outlook on events or issues (Fredrickson 1998;
Fredrickson et al. 2008). A broader perception of the environment
and failure events enhances learning from the experience. Rather than
having bounded awareness that blinds them to the signals and information available to them (Chugh and Bazerman 2007), individuals

with broader perception have greater situational awareness (Dane 2010; Weick et al. 1999), which contributes to their deeper comprehension of the situation and makes them more able to inform and predict the nature of possible future states (Endsley 1995). That is, they are in a better position to learn and apply that learning in subsequent projects.

First, an individual's self-kindness can broaden his or her perception about a failure event. Researchers have found that people high in self-knowledge pay increased attention to "unflattering self-relevant information" (Aspinwall 1998), which helps them build a more accurate picture of the situation (Leary et al. 2007; Sedikides 1993). Self-kindness helps separate self-worth from a failure event, thus making it unnecessary to hide shortcomings from oneself. In turn, the recognition of these shortcomings generates less anxiety (Leary et al. 2007). When an individual avoids harsh self-criticism, the protective functions of the ego are not triggered by failure. This is vital as these ego-protective functions can screen out signals to maintain high self-esteem (Horney 1950; Reich 1949), such as the signals of the underlying causes of failure. However, while one's self-esteem may remain high, the limited self-awareness caused by these ego functions allow weaknesses and mistakes to go unnoticed (Neff 2003a). Furthermore, individuals with less self-kindness engage in harsh self-criticism and often become carried away with their negative emotional reactions to loss events, which can lead to rumination and a narrowing of attention (Nolen-Hoeksema 1991). As a result, people with low levels of self-kindness typically develop an overly narrow perception of their current situation (Leary et al. 2007; Sedikides 1993) and are therefore less able to learn from their failure experiences.

Second, individuals' common humanity broadens perception of failure by allowing them to acknowledge their experiences in the broader human context (Goldstein and Michaels 1985; Scheff 1981). By putting failures in this broader context, individuals are less likely to engage ego-protective mechanisms (Baumeister, Smart, and

Boden 1996; Twenge and Campbell 2003) that lead to a rigid closed mindset that does not allow alternate viewpoints (Jost et al. 2003; Taris 2000). With greater common humanity, individuals can maintain a more open mindset that broadens their perception of the events leading up to failure, which facilitates learning from the experience.

Finally, more emotionally mindful individuals can develop a broader perception of a negative situation (Slagter et al. 2007) because their sense of self is softened (Martin 1997), and their attention is shifted away from the elaborate cognitive processing necessary for creating a story that protects the self but is instead shifted toward the nonjudgmental acceptance of present-moment experience (Bishop et al. 2004; Neff and Vonk 2009). That is, mindfulness involves experiencing loss without clinging to it (e.g., ruminating [Nolen-Hoeksema 1991]) or rejecting it (Leary and Tate 2007). Thus, more mindful individuals are able to maintain attentional sensitivity to internal and external signals (Baumeister, Heatherton, and Tice 1993; Carver and Scheier 1999; Dane 2010), which in turn provides a "quality of consciousness that is characterized by clarity and vividness of current experience and functioning" (Brown and Ryan 2003: 825). This new consciousness can reveal information about the failure that would otherwise remain hidden from view (cf. Brown, Ryan, and Creswell 2007; Hayes, Wilson, Gifford, Follette, and Strosahl 1996; Slagter et al. 2007).

Broad perception in organizations: Organizations can also have broader perceptions that increase their ability to understand the situation (Ocasio 1997; Weick et al. 1999) surrounding or leading up to a failure event. In turn, these perceptions inform organizations' actions that maintain or enhance organizational functioning. For example, conceptual slack represents the diversity among organizational members' perspectives about their organization's processes (Schulman 1993; Weick 1993), which increases the organization's ability to identify problems that need to be solved (Sutcliffe and Vogus 2003). Conceptual slack is more often promoted in organizations that value new perspectives; share information; and encourage the questioning of existing norms, procedures, and routines (Bogner and Barr 2000; Cho and Hambrick 2006). Such organizations encourage members to report failures and near misses (Edmondson 1996; Rochlin 1989) because such feedback provides more data points for learning and informs subsequent action (Weick et al. 1999; Weick and Sutcliffe 2006). Therefore, an organization's perception is likely broadened by self-compassion via three distinct mechanisms – self-kindness, common humanity, and mindfulness.

First, organizational self-kindness can contribute to a culture that encourages its members to report failures and near misses by protecting those who do the reporting and thereby increasing understanding of the causes underlying failure events. Internally directed reports can acknowledge failures, inadequacies, and flaws within the organizational system but have the potential to do so with caring and tenderness. These reports are likely to reflect discriminating wisdom by clearly evaluating the positive and negative quality of actions while maintaining a compassionate understanding of the complex, dynamic situational factors that impact these actions; as a result, particular performances are not taken as indicators of self-worth (Neff, Hsieh, and Dejitterat 2005: 264). Without the worth of the organization or its members being threatened, organizational members are likely to be more open to reporting failures, and these reports are likely to be more trusted.

Organizational self-kindness also acknowledges acceptable and unacceptable behaviors, and organizational members trust the managers' apportionment of blame for the failure to the organization's system and/or routines without undermining the worth of the organization as a whole. In contrast, harsh self-criticism over a failed project is likely to trigger mechanisms for protecting the organization's worth, and one means of doing this is to attribute blame externally – that is, to blame actors external to the organization for causing the failure rather than blaming the organization's internal routines and systems. The external attribution of blame can send a signal of inappropriately apportioning blame and undermining a just culture. In a more self-compassionate organization, failures and flaws do not need to be hidden in order to avoid harsh self-judgment; rather, organizational self-kindness helps members adopt a more objective perspective of a failure event, which enhances their ability to learn from the experience.

Second, recognizing that all organizations make mistakes and have flaws (i.e., common humanity) helps provide individuals a feeling of security when reporting the mistakes and flaws that led to the failure event. It also helps organizations maintain connections with external actors who may be important information sources about the organization's current situation. For example, patient complaints about physicians can be important information sources regarding any mistakes, flaws, or other inadequacies in the system to deliver adequate medical care, but hospitals often feel threatened by such information and are therefore less open to it (Allsop and Mulcahy 1998; Lupton 2012). Furthermore, individuals' emotional reactions to project failure are likely to be less negative when the event is positioned in terms of "organizational life" in general. This frees the organization's cognitive capacity, thereby facilitating greater awareness and processing of weak signals of the underlying causes of project failure. By making it clear that errors and flaws are something all organizations face at some time, project failure is less likely to challenge the overall worth of the organization. Additionally, organizational members are less likely to feel that they need to defend their worth (to themselves and to others) by unjustly apportioning blame. Similarly, by maintaining connections with outsiders (as a result of common humanity), the organization (i.e., the collective of organizational members) is less likely to unjustly blame these outsiders for the failure.[2] In contrast, with less common humanity, an organization is

---

[2] While providing an environment that is open to failure is important, this in and of itself does not guarantee positive results, including a broadened perception. As we discuss in Chapter 6, organizations must balance the acceptance of failure for learning with a tendency to normalize failure. When failure is normalized, it ceases to generate adequate attention and the emotional responses needed to generate substantive change.

already isolated from others and its members are more likely to unjustly attribute blame to those with which it is no longer connected. Furthermore, as negative emotions are exacerbated by isolation (Wood, Saltzberg, Neale, Stone, and Rachmiel 1990), the organization becomes increasingly motivated to reduce the negative emotions generated by project failure by shifting blame even when such a shift is unjust. Thus, the isolation itself removes the organization from others as a potentially important source of information for learning from the failure experience.

Finally, an organization's emotional mindfulness contributes to reports of information that are important in detecting signals for making sense of project failure. When organizational members as a collective hold painful thoughts in balanced awareness, their attention can remain "stable and vivid," thereby providing a clearer view of the situation (Weick and Sutcliffe 2006: 521), which in turn forms the basis of reporting. Given the non-judgmental nature of this kind of assessment, the organization's worth is not attacked, and this more fact-based report of failures, near misses, and flaws is likely to be more trusted by organizational members. Such an environment of trust allows individuals to express negative emotions as well as widen their perspective of the event (and associated emotions), which helps broaden their perspective and opens a pathway to more positive emotions.

While reports of an organization's failings are not distorted by organizational members' negative emotions, this does not mean that negative emotions are ignored. Rather organizational mindfulness helps members detect, understand, and report on their emotions so they can be regulated to promote resilience. Further, by separating assessments of negative events (and emotional reactions to them) from maintaining notions of self-worth, mindful organizations reduce the likelihood that their members will employ ego-defensive strategies (Leary et al. 2007; Neff, Kirkpatrick, and Rude 2007), such as unjustly apportioning blame (Lazarus 1991; Miller 1976). Indeed, more mindful organizations explore failures and flaws (and the negative emotions that result from them) with a non-judgmental curiosity that justly attributes causes and explores possible courses of action, which helps create the atmosphere of trust necessary to learn from project failures.

Self-compassion and learning from failure through a broad array of resources

Learning from failure is enhanced by taking actions based on beliefs about what caused the project failure, which itself provides feedback for subsequent learning and action. Therefore, learning from failure is likely enhanced by a broader array of resources that facilitate subsequent action. In this section, we discuss how individual and organizational resources for learning from failure are likely broadened and/or extended in the presence of individual and organizational self-compassion. We begin with individual resources.

Individual array of resources: For individuals, the "presence of latent resources that can be activated, combined, and recombined in new situations" (Sutcliffe and Vogus 2003: 97) enhances one's ability to take action to further make sense of project failure. These resources can be internal, such as, competence, coping skills, and self-efficacy (Fergus and Zimmerman 2005), or external to the individual, such as social support, role models, and mentoring (Brook, Whiteman, Gordon, and Cohen 1989; Zimmerman, Bingenheimer, and Notaro 2002). An individual's array of resources for learning from failure and moving forward is likely broadened by self-compassion in three primary ways.

First, an individual's self-kindness can increase his or her breadth of resources for dealing with failure and the flexibility to redeploy them effectively to new or existing projects. Self-kindness provides individuals with a more stable "feeling of self-worth over time" (Neff and Vonk 2009) and a greater focus on mastery goals than on performance-outcome goals (Neff et al. 2005). That is, by separating feelings of self-worth from failures, individuals can maintain a consistent notion of self-esteem from which to draw upon during failure experiences and to approach (rather than avoid) such experiences as learning situations. Self-kindness does not mean giving oneself a "free pass"; rather, out of a sense of caring and kindness to oneself, an individual is motivated to rectify a failure and improve so as to avoid repeating similar errors in the future. Indeed, self-kindness has been found to be linked to problem-focused coping (Neff et al. 2005) and adaptive responses (Leary et al. 2007) to failure. Because self-kindness eliminates harsh self-criticism, individuals are "freer" to take personal initiative, modify unproductive behaviors, and take on new challenges (for a review, see Neff and Vonk 2009).

Second, with greater common humanity, individuals can maintain a more open mindset and remain connected with others as sources of information who can inform their understanding of failure events. Further, with greater common humanity, individuals are less likely to exaggerate feelings of separation from others (Goldstein and Kornfield 1987; Neff 2003a) after experiencing project failure. This enables them to feel more related and secure (Gilbert and Irons 2005), and to maintain and build relationships (Campbell and Baumeister 2001). These relationships provide access to resources that may be useful to learn (Huy 1999; Shepherd 2009) from failure experiences and provide the emotional support needed to take proactive adaptive actions in subsequent projects.

Finally, mindfulness can contribute to an individual's resources for learning from failure and moving forward on subsequent projects. In fact, mindfulness has been described as the "capacity to be aware of internal and external events and occurrences as phenomena, rather than as objects of a conceptually constructed world" (Brown et al. 2007: 212; Olendzki 2005: 253) and as the ability to remain engaged when facing negative events (Eifert and Heffner 2003; Levitt, Brown, Orsillo, and Barlow 2004), such as project failure. An individual develops this ability because mindfulness leads to less emotional reactivity to adverse events (Hayes, Strosahl, and Wilson 1999; Leary et al. 2007) and the ability to predict (Dunn, Brackett, Ashton-James, Schneiderman, and Salovey 2007) and control (Leary and Tate 2007) emotional reactions to such events. This particular characteristic of mindfulness enables one to feel less cognitive and emotional disturbance (Brown and Ryan 2003) and greater social connectedness (Brown and Ryan 2003, 2004; Brown and Kasser 2005) after project failure, which is useful for the generation of and access to additional resources for learning from the experience and moving forward with new projects.

Organizational array of resources: Organizations also possess resources that are useful for addressing threats and can have processes that recombine resources and redeploy them in new ways (Eisenhardt and Martin 2000). This process of redeploying organizational resources increases the array of possible action repertoires (Weick et al. 1999) for enacting what is learned from failure experiences, which in turn opens the organization to additional feedback and learning. Social capital and relationships are also a source of resources, insight, and assistance (Leana and Van Buren 1999) that facilitate organizations' sensemaking (Weick, Sutcliffe, and Obstfeld 2005) from failure experiences. Similar to individuals, an organization's ability to make sense of project failure and act upon that understanding is likely broadened by self-compassion in three primary ways.

First, in a more self-kind organization, errors and flaws do not need to be hidden in order to avoid harsh self-judgment; rather, organizational self-kindness helps members adopt a more objective perspective of failure events. When an organization reduces the negative emotional reactions individuals feel toward a failure event (e.g., the additional anxiety generated by an organization's disapproving judgment of mistakes and flaws), there is less of a need for them to avoid attending to and thinking about those mistakes and flaws. Attending to mistakes and flaws provides a basis for learning from failure. Further, organizational self-kindness helps prevent members from being carried away by negative emotions from a loss and thus, reduces ruminations that can escalate grief (cf. Nolen-Hoeksema 1991). Such emotions and anxiety have been found to interfere with individuals' learning processes by consuming their information-processing capacity (Weick 1990).

Second, organizational common humanity can also contribute to a learning culture. It helps an organization avert its members from having a collective feeling that they are the only ones suffering, and it helps the organization avert its members from being carried away and becoming absorbed by their own feelings. As such, reducing the escalation of negative emotions and anxiety reduces obstacles to learning and adaptation (Huy,1999; Shepherd 2009; Weick 1990). As discussed earlier, because organizational common humanity helps organizations maintain their connections with others, it also allows them to maintain information sources that are critical for learning. Further, accepting that failures may occur in the future (as they do in all organizations), an organization with high common humanity is more willing to act despite the possibility of failure as well as to use the feedback from these actions (and possible failures) to learn. In addition, organizational members are able to approach failed projects with curiosity instead of fear.

Finally, organizational mindfulness can also amplify resources that contribute to a learning culture. Mindfulness enables a culture in which organizational members can explore – with curiosity – the collective emotional reaction to failure and failure events themselves without creating ego-protective obstacles to learning. It can also help reduce the anxiety associated with the generation of negative emotions, which leads to a reduced number of obstacles to learning (Huy 1999; Weick 1990). That is, by maintaining a balanced awareness of the collective emotional reaction to project failure, an organization is more likely to harness the benefits of negative emotions (i.e., affect as information [Forgas 1995; Gasper and Clore 2002], e.g., signaling the importance of situational cues [Clore 1992; Schwarz and Clore 1988]) without some of the associated costs (e.g., constricted information processing [Gladstein and Reilly 1985; Sutton and D'Aunno 1989]) to learn more about why a project failed and enact that learning in subsequent projects. Therefore, through emotional mindfulness, organizations can gather and process more salient information to learn about (and from) failure events.

Self-compassion, positive emotions, and learning from failure

In the previous sections, we argued for a direct relationship between self-compassion and learning from failure. In the following sections, we build on the broaden-and-build theory of emotions to propose that self-compassion also has an indirect path to learning from failure through the generation of positive emotions. In the next sub-section, we establish the link between the components of self-compassion and positive emotions at both the individual and organizational level. Then, we link these generated positive emotions to learning from failure.

SELF-COMPASSION AND POSITIVE EMOTIONS

Self-compassion can generate positive emotions, such as love, contentment, and interest, which can help reduce grief over project failure through a number of important mechanisms. First, self-kindness involves being understanding and tolerant of one's errors, flaws, and inadequacies and being kind, caring, tender, and loving toward oneself (Neff 2003k). In turn, these feelings of warmth and caring can generate positive emotions (Fredrickson 1998; Salzberg 2002). Indeed, induced kindness has been found to result in increased positive emotions (Otake, Shimai, Tanaka-Matsumi, Otsui, and Fredrickson 2006; Seligman, Steen, Park, and Peterson 2005). For example, one study (Lyubomirsky, King, and Diener 2005) found that participants who were asked to perform five acts of kindness in one day were happier than both those who were asked to perform five acts of kindness over seven days and those who were not asked to engage in any acts of kindness. An organization's kindness can also generate collective positive emotions. For instance, organizations can demonstrate kindness, such as through benevolence, that promotes happiness and other positive emotions among their employees and stakeholders (Jurkiewicz and Giacalone 2004; Milliman et al. 2001).

Second, common humanity can generate positive emotions. The common-humanity dimension of self-compassion involves putting one's failures, flaws, and inadequacies in perspective by acknowledging that most people face similar difficulties, make mistakes, and also have feelings of inadequacy (Neff 2003k). In this way, greater self-compassion can lead people to feel (and remain) connected to others. For example, Neff (2003k) found that self-compassion was positively associated with social connectedness. This social connectedness and the corresponding feelings of belonging are viewed as basic psychological needs (Baumeister and Leary 1995; Ryan 1991) that can generate positive emotions (Argyle 1987; McAdams 1985; McAdams and Bryant 1987). For example, the feeling of being accepted by others can lead to the positive emotion of contentment (De Rivera, Possell, Verette, and Weiner 1989; Izard 1997; Markus and Kitayama 1991). Indeed, this form of self-compassion can alter the "felt connection" between organizational members (Frost, Dutton, Worline, and Wilson 2000), which can generate a range of positive feelings (Dutton, Frost, Worline, Lilius, and Kanov 2002; Lilius et al. 2003). For instance, organizational values that facilitate a sense of being connected with others generate a collective feeling of completeness and joy (Giacalone and Jurkiewicz 2003).

Finally, mindfulness can generate positive emotions. The mindfulness dimension of self-compassion involves keeping emotions in balance, which leads one to approach his or her feelings with "curiosity and openness" (Neff 2003k: 232). Approaching feelings, including negative emotions, with curiosity and openness can itself generate the positive emotion of interest (Fredrickson 2000). Indeed, curiosity is "taking an interest in all of the ongoing experience" in one's life (Peterson and Seligman 2003, 2004; Seligman et al. 2005: 412) and is related to *thriving* on "novel, complex and challenging" tasks (Izard 1997; Kashdan and Steger 2007: 159). Curiosity can also lead to feelings of excitement, an urge to explore (Izard, 1997; Tomkins, 1962). This organizational curiosity and these feelings of interest and excitement discourage complacency and encourage organizational members to tolerate ambiguity and continue to engage in experimentation (Hedberg 1981; Steensma 1996; Vera and Crossan 2004) even after failure events.

POSITIVE EMOTIONS AND LEARNING
FROM FAILURE

Based on the "undo" principle (Fredrickson 1998, 2001), the positive emotions generated by self-compassion can help undo some of the negative consequences of emotions triggered by an adverse event (Fredrickson and Levenson 1998; Fredrickson, Mancuso, Branigan, and Tugade 2000) and can broaden the actor's "momentary thought-action repertoire" (Fredrickson 2001: 220). An expanded momentary thought–action repertoire broadens an individual's scope of attention for learning about the underlying causes of failure and offers a larger set of possible actions (Fredrickson 1998; Fredrickson and Branigan 2001) in response to that learning. For example, while negative emotions have been found to narrow focused attention (such that individuals cannot see the forest for the trees, so to speak), positive emotions have been found to broaden the scope of attention (Derryberry and Tucker 1994; Fredrickson and Branigan 2005; Isen and Daubman 1984). Positive emotions have also been found to be associated with cognitive processes that are more creative (George 1991; Isen, Daubman, and Nowicki 1987) and more flexible (Baumann and Kuhl 2005; Isen and Daubman 1984) and result in a greater variety of action alternatives (Isen 2001; Kahn and Isen 1993). Therefore, "the ability to harness positive emotions in the midst of negative experiences" (Tugade and Fredrickson 2004: 331) provides a basis for learning and moving forward.

To the extent that self-compassion can generate positive emotions during (or after) failure events, it can help broaden individuals' momentary thought–action repertoires that are likely to enable them to adapt to new situations or projects. For example, an organization's acts of kindness have been found to generate positive emotions that help organizational members deal with work-related stressors (Edwards and Cooper 1988; Simmons and Nelson 2001). Indeed, it has been proposed that organizational curiosity (and the resulting generation of positive emotion) is central to an actor's ability to detect "the weak signals that make or break" an organization (Day and

Schoemaker 2006). Collectively felt positive emotions likely help organizational members move forward after project failure because they are apt to increase their range of possible response options, maintain a creative perspective for problem solving, and generate energy (Avey, Wernsing, and Luthans 2008; Baumeister, Gailliot, DeWall, and Oaten 2006) to implement what they learn from the failure experience in subsequent projects. Although it is important to consider the factors that assist individuals in learning and moving on after experiencing failure, it is also important to understand how prolonging the failure event itself can prove influential in assisting with the coping process, which will be the focal topic of the next chapter.

DISCUSSION

Implications for research on learning from failure and mindfulness

Although the cognitive aspects of learning from the individual level of analysis have been used to build the current understanding of organizational learning, this has not been the case for the emotional aspects of learning (or at least to the same extent). That is, while emotions have been acknowledged in this line of research, it has typically been in terms of how negative emotions obstruct learning. Although we also acknowledged the generation of negative emotions and how they can undermine learning from failure, we offered a positive-psychology perspective of emotions. Specifically, individuals, alone and as a collective, can develop self-compassion that can directly enhance learning from failure by broadening an organization's attention and increasing its array of resources for action. However, self-compassion can also indirectly enhance learning from failure by generating positive emotions that undo negative emotions, broaden attention, and build resources. By focusing only on the negative emotions generated by adversity, cognitive approaches to learning miss out on the emotional sources of learning (i.e., self-compassion and the other positive emotions generated by it). Therefore, future research on responding to failure will be well served by investigating the organizing of self-kindness, common humanity, and mindfulness and the organizing of positive emotions in terms of organizational attention and the generation (i.e., access to and recombination of) resources.

The implications of our model for the current research on learning from failure are further heightened by our treatment of mindfulness. Although the organizational theory literature has acknowledged the importance of mindfulness, it has focused on its cognitive dimensions and has relatively ignored its emotional dimensions. We took an initial step into this emotional domain, and in doing so, we complemented the importance of facing negative events with an open mind. with the importance of facing negative events with an open heart. While we recognize there are different definitions of mindfulness and that some may exclude the emotional mindfulness offered here, it is important to note that our notion of mindfulness has been established conceptually (Neff 2003a) and empirically (Arimitsu and Hofmann 2015; Fredrickson et al. 2008; Neff 2003k) in the psychology literature building on Buddhist philosophy. Whether they are two dimensions of the same construct or two different constructs altogether, we believe that it is important to investigate approaching failure with an open heart to gain a deeper understanding of learning from failure experiences. We believe future contributions to the organizational learning literature will come from finer-grained research on the interrelationship between cognitive mindfulness and emotional mindfulness.

Implications for research on the psychology of self-compassion

Psychology studies have built on Buddhist philosophies to introduce the notion of self-compassion (self-compassion at the individual level) (Neff 2003a; for a review, see Neff, 2009). We complemented and extended this literature in three primary ways. First, we focused on learning from failure as the outcome of self-compassion. Although adding another dependent variable to a long list of dependent variables at the individual level of analysis (e.g., positively associated with happiness, optimism, wisdom, curiosity, personal initiative [Neff, et al. 2007], and interpersonal relationships [Neff 2006] and negatively associated with anxiety, depression, and rumination [Neff et al. 2005; Neff et al. 2007]) is not a contribution, the "learning from failure" construct is sufficiently broad so as to encapsulate many of these previously investigated outcome variables. That is, by theorizing about self-compassion and learning from failure, we were able to offer both a broad and parsimonious model – one that has the potential of integrating or reconciling numerous studies under a more general theoretical framework (Bacharach 1989; Whetten 1989).

Second, we highlighted the mediating role of positive emotions in the relationship between self-compassion and learning from failure. Previous research has focused on how compassion minimizes the generation of negative emotions. We acknowledged these same mechanisms but added an additional concept – self-compassion – that can generate positive emotions and undo negative emotional reactions generated from project failure. This focus is important as the role of self-compassion in generating positive emotions that undo negative emotions has received little attention in past research. Furthermore, the mechanisms by which self-compassion influences various well-being outcomes have often remained implicit. We make explicit how self-compassion can enhance learning from failure by building on the broaden-and-build principle of positive emotions. We hope future empirical research will investigate the nature of these relationships.

Finally, we considered the construct of self-compassion at the organizational level as well as at the individual level. Although the notion of compassion has been applied at the organizational level, the notion of self-compassion has not. By extending self-compassion to the organizational level, we were able to connect it to organizational learning and collective emotions. We hopefully provide a bridge from the self-compassion literature to the organizational literature on learning from failure and emotion (both positive and negative) and more generally to positive organizational scholarship. While we have taken the initial step of conceptualizing self-compassion at the organizational level and theorizing on the organizing mechanisms that enhance organizational learning from failure and generate positive emotions, there are ample opportunities for future research in this area. These include a finer-grained investigation of these mechanisms and the antecedents of organizational self-compassion.

Implications for research on positive emotions

We built on the broaden-and-build principle of positive emotions in the psychology literature to gain a deeper understanding of how self-compassion indirectly influences resilience. However, our theorizing has several implications for the literature on positive emotions as well. First, we investigated the broaden-and-build principle at the organizational level, which helped explain why some organizations learn more from their failure experiences than others. This complements the research on emotions in organizations that has primarily focused on negative emotions interfering with learning or change (Huy 1999; Shepherd, Covin, and Kuratko 2009) and on positive emotions as part of emotional labor (Ashforth and Humphrey 1993; Hochschild 1979). Therefore, rather than focus on the negative role emotions play in cognitions or the role employees' emotional displays play in the emotions of customers, consistent with a positive-psychology perspective of organizational research, we highlighted the role of positive emotions in broadening attention and increasing the array of resources for moving forward after failure events.

Second, we offered self-compassion as a source of positive emotions. Although the literature has recognized the potential benefits of positive emotions, there has been little research on the antecedents of these positive emotions, especially when individuals face adversity. At the individual level, research on positive emotions has investigated traits (Ekman 1994), genuine (Duchenne) smiling (Papa and Bonanno 2008), laughter (Bonanno and Keltner 1997), and the use of humor (Weick and Westley 1996). At the organizational level, research has focused on superficial and deep acting to generate displays that generate positive emotions in others (Grandey 2003). We added the

construct of self-compassion to these lists. Individuals and organizations with greater self-compassion are able to generate more positive
emotions, especially during the period of adversity surrounding failure
events. Future research can investigate the relationship between these
different mechanisms that promote self-compassion. Perhaps, humor
and laughter are more effective at generating positive emotions in
individuals who are higher in self-compassion; humor might even be
an effective tool for generating self-compassion. In addition, perhaps
self-compassion is further developed in an organization whose culture
encourages the "deep acting" of self-compassion, which becomes
heartfelt after time.

Finally, our model focused on how self-compassion generates
positive emotions because we were interested in explaining how self-
compassion indirectly influences learning from failure. However,
future research can explore the possible feedback loop for the relationship between self-compassion and positive emotions. That is,
although we proposed that self-compassion generates positive emotions, perhaps, positive emotions also enhance self-compassion. As
positive emotions help to broaden momentary thought–action repertoires so that thought patterns are more flexible and creative and offer
a broader array of action alternatives in response to failure events,
these thought patterns may lead to a broader array of self-compassion
repertories. That is, a broader, more flexible, and more creative
thought process can enhance organizational self-kindness, common
humanity, and/or emotional mindfulness. In turn, this may generate
even more positive emotions as part of a virtuous learning spiral.

Managerial implications

Beyond the theoretical contributions discussed earlier, this study also
has implications that could influence practicing managers. All organizations experience failure at least to some degree, and they do so at
multiple levels (i.e., individuals failing at their jobs, project teams failing
to achieve objectives, and organization failing overall). We anticipate
three primary managerial implications that address key concerns

associated with learning from failure. First, managers should consider the various benefits their organizations can receive by understanding individual and organizational self-compassion. By incorporating the principles explained here, managers might generate more value from exploratory projects, instill a culture of learning in their organizations, and avoid or reduce the negative outcomes associated with failure. Similarly, managers might explore opportunities to develop self-compassion in their organizations, proactively shaping a culture of positivity and growth, which is likely to have a positive influence on key employee activities (e.g., engagement, productivity, satisfaction) (Arimitsu and Hofmann 2015). Thus, creating a culture of self-compassion should provide more positive outcomes than just learning from failure.

Second, managers should be aware of the different levels of self-compassion and how they interact in shaping individual- and organizational-level responses to failure. Organizational members come to the organization with diverse backgrounds and skill sets, including their ability to experience self-compassion. By recognizing these differences, managers might develop methods for identifying self-compassionate employees as well as cultivating individual-level self-compassion once individuals are employed. Combined with this effort, managers can develop an organizational culture of self-compassion that can then be replicated at the project, team, and (hopefully) individual levels, further reinforcing the overall objectives of the firm. By understanding the different levels of self-compassion, managers have a number of resources at hand to help their organizations manage failure and learning from failure.

Finally, beyond cultivating self-compassion, this study also identified the importance of positive emotions and its influence on resources that serve as mechanisms for learning. As suggested earlier, positive emotions provide a number of benefits for organizations and their members. Managers should consider how to cultivate positive emotions, specifically in response to negative events, such as project failure. In addition, managers should tie efforts to generate positive emotions to the resource they have at hand to facilitate learning.

That is, positive emotions should be directed toward attending to causes of a failure and taking action to overcome those issues, moving forward as opposed to simply offering an escape from errors. Both organizations and individuals have resources at hand when dealing with failure events; the key takeaway for managers is the need to understand how to enhance the effectiveness or scale of those resources to facilitate learning from failure events.

CONCLUSION

In this chapter, we offered a model of self-compassion as a source of learning from failure. We investigated the role of self-compassion (rather than other-related compassion) on learning from failure and its indirect role in the generation of positive emotions. This model provided a parsimonious explanation of these relationships that is applicable at both the individual and organizational levels of analysis. We believe that our model provides new insights into the role of self-compassion in dealing with failure events.

REFERENCES

Allsop, J. and Mulcahy, L. 1998. Maintaining professional identity: Doctors' responses to complaints. *Sociology of Health & Illness*, 20(6): 802–824.

Argyle, M. 1987. *The Psychology of Happiness*. London: Methuen.

Arimitsu, K. and Hofmann, S. G. 2015. Cognitions as mediators in the relationship between self-compassion and affect. *Personality and Individual Differences*, 74: 41–48.

Ashforth, B. E. and Humphrey, R. H. 1993. Emotional labor in service roles: The influence of identity. *Academy of Management Review*, 18(1): 88–115.

Aspinwall, L. G. 1998. Rethinking the role of positive affect in self-regulation. *Motivation and Emotion*, 22(1): 1–32.

Avey, J. B., Wernsing, T. S., and Luthans, F. 2008. Can positive employees help positive organizational change? Impact of psychological capital and emotions on relevant attitudes and behaviors. *The Journal of Applied Behavioral Science*, 44(1): 48–70.

Bacharach, S. B. 1989. Organizational theories: Some criteria for evaluation. *Academy of Management Review*, 14(4): 496–515.

Baumann, N. and Kuhl, J. 2005. Positive affect and flexibility: Overcoming the precedence of global over local processing of visual information. *Motivation and Emotion*, 29(2): 123–134.

Baumeister, R. F., Heatherton, T. F., and Tice, D. M. 1993. When ego threats lead to self-regulation failure: Negative consequences of high self-esteem. *Journal of Personality and Social Psychology*, 64(1): 141.

Baumeister, R. F. and Leary, M. R. 1995. The need to belong: Desire for interpersonal attachments as a fundamental human motivation. *Psychological bulletin*, 117(3): 497.

Baumeister, R. F., Smart, L., and Boden, J. M. 1996. Relation of threatened egotism to violence and aggression: the dark side of high self-esteem. *Psychological Review*, 103(1): 5.

Baumeister, R. F., Gailliot, M., DeWall, C. N., and Oaten, M. 2006. Self-regulation and personality: How interventions increase regulatory success, and how depletion moderates the effects of traits on behavior. *Journal of Personality*, 74(6): 1773–1802.

Bennett-Goleman, T. 2002. *Emotional Alchemy: How the Mind can Heal the Heart: Harmony*. New York: Three Rivers Press.

Bishop, S. R., Lau, M., Shapiro, S., Carlson, L., Anderson, N. D., Carmody, J., Segal, Z. V., Abbey, S., Speca, M., and Velting, D. 2004. Mindfulness: A proposed operational definition. *Clinical Psychology: Science and Practice*, 11(3): 230–241.

Blaine, B. and Crocker, J. 1993. Self-esteem and self-serving biases in reactions to positive and negative events: An integrative review, *Self-esteem*: 55–85: Springer.

Blatt, S. J., Quinlan, D. M., Chevron, E. S., McDonald, C., and Zuroff, D. 1982. Dependency and self-criticism: Psychological dimensions of depression. *Journal of Consulting and Clinical Psychology*, 50(1): 113–124.

Bogner, W. C. and Barr, P. S. 2000. Making sense in hypercompetitive environments: A cognitive explanation for the persistence of high velocity competition. *Organization Science*, 11(2): 212–226.

Bonanno, G. A. and Keltner, D. 1997. Facial expressions of emotion and the course of conjugal bereavement. *Journal of Abnormal Psychology*, 106(1): 126–137.

Brook, J. S., Whiteman, M., Gordon, A. S., and Cohen, P. 1989. Changes in drug involvement: A longitudinal study of childhood and adolescent determinants. *Psychological Reports*, 65(3): 707–726.

Brown, K. W. and Ryan, R. M. 2003. The benefits of being present: Mindfulness and its role in psychological well-being. *Journal of Personality and Social Psychology*, 84(4): 822.

Brown, K. W. and Ryan, R. M. 2004. Perils and promise in defining and measuring mindfulness: Observations from experience. *Clinical Psychology: Science and Practice*, 11(3): 242–248.

Brown, K. W. and Kasser, T. 2005. Are psychological and ecological well-being compatible? The role of values, mindfulness, and lifestyle. *Social Indicators Research*, 74(2): 349–368.

Brown, K. W., Ryan, R. M., and Creswell, J. D. 2007. Mindfulness: Theoretical foundations and evidence for its salutary effects. *Psychological Inquiry*, 18(4): 211–237.

Campbell, W. K. and Baumeister, R. F. 2001. Chapter Seventeen, *Blackwell Handbook of Social Psychology: Interpersonal Processes*: 437. Oxford, UK: Blackwell Publishing.

Carver, C. S. and Scheier, M. F. 1999. Stress, coping, and self-regulatory processes.

Cho, T. S. and Hambrick, D. C. 2006. Attention as the mediator between top management team characteristics and strategic change: The case of airline deregulation. *Organization Science*, 17(4): 453–469.

Chugh, D. and Bazerman, M. H. 2007. Bounded awareness: What you fail to see can hurt you. *Mind & Society*, 6(1): 1–18.

Clore, G. L. 1992. Cognitive phenomenology: Feelings and the construction of judgment. *The Construction of Social Judgments*, 10: 133–163.

Cowton, C. J. 1987. Corporate philanthropy in the United Kingdom. *Journal of Business Ethics*, 6(7): 553–558.

Crocker, J. and Park, L. E. 2004. The costly pursuit of self-esteem. *Psychological Bulletin*, 130(3): 392.

Dane, E. 2010. Paying attention to mindfulness and its effects on task performance in the workplace. *Journal of Management* July 2011, 37(4): 997–1018.

Day, G. S. and Schoemaker, P. J. 2006. *Peripheral Vision: Detecting the Weak Signals That Will Make or Break Your Company*. Boston, USA: Harvard Business School Press.

De Rivera, J., Possell, L., Verette, J. A., and Weiner, B. 1989. Distinguishing elation, gladness, and joy. *Journal of Personality and Social Psychology*, 57(6): 1015.

Derryberry, D. and Tucker, D. M. 1994. Motivating the focus of attention. In P. M. Niedenthal, and S. Kitayama (eds.), *The Heart's Eye: Emotional Influences in Perception and Attention*: 167–196. San Diego, CA, USA: Academic Press.

Diener, E. and Lucas, R. E. 1999. Personality and subjective well-being. In D. Kahneman, E. Diener, and N. Schwarz (eds.), *Well-being: The Foundations of Hedonic Psychology*: 213–229. New York: Russell Sage Foundation.

Donaldson, T. and Dunfee, T. W. 2000. Precis for ties that bind. *Business and Society Review*, 105(4): 436–443.

Dunn, E. W., Brackett, M. A., Ashton-James, C., Schneiderman, E., and Salovey, P. 2007. On emotionally intelligent time travel: Individual differences in affective forecasting ability. *Personality and Social Psychology Bulletin*, 33(1): 85–93.

Dutton, J. E., Frost, P. J., Worline, M. C., Lilius, J. M., and Kanov, J. M. 2002. Leading in times of trauma. *Harvard Business Review*, 80(1): 54–61, 125.

Dutton, J. E., Worline, M. C., Frost, P. J., and Lilius, J. 2006. Explaining compassion organizing. *Administrative Science Quarterly*, 51(1): 59–96.

Edmondson, A. C. 1996. Learning from mistakes is easier said than done: Group and organizational influences on the detection and correction of human error. *The Journal of Applied Behavioral Science*, 32(1): 5–28.

Edmondson, V. C. and Carroll, A. B. 1999. Giving back: An examination of the philanthropic motivations, orientations and activities of large black-owned businesses. *Journal of Business Ethics*, 19(2): 171–179.

Edwards, J. R. and Cooper, C. L. 1988. Research in stress, coping, and health: Theoretical and methodological issues. *Psychological Medicine*, 18(1): 15–20.

Eifert, G. H. and Heffner, M. 2003. The effects of acceptance versus control contexts on avoidance of panic-related symptoms. *Journal of Behavior Therapy and Experimental Psychiatry*, 34(3): 293–312.

Eisenhardt, K. M. and Martin, J. A. 2000. Dynamic capabilities: What are they? *Strategic Management Journal*, 21(1): 1105–1121.

Ekman, P. 1994. Strong evidence for universals in facial expressions: A reply to Russell's mistaken critique. *Psychological Bulletin*, Mar 1994, 115(2): 268–287.

Emshoff, J. R. and Freeman, R. E. 1978. *Stakeholder Management*, Wharton Applied Research Center *Working Paper*, 3–78.

Endsley, M. R. 1995. Toward a theory of situation awareness in dynamic systems. *Human Factors: The Journal of the Human Factors and Ergonomics Society*, 37(1): 32–64.

Fergus, S. and Zimmerman, M. A. 2005. Adolescent resilience: A framework for understanding healthy development in the face of risk. *Annual Review Public Health*, 26: 399–419.

Fiol, C. M. and O'Connor, E. J. 2003. Waking up! Mindfulness in the face of bandwagons. *Academy of Management Review*, 28(1): 54–70.

Forgas, J. P. 1995. Mood and judgment: The affect infusion model (AIM). *Psychological Bulletin*, 117(1): 39.

Fredrickson, B. L. 1998. What good are positive emotions? *Review of General Psychology*, 2(3): 300.

Fredrickson, B. L. and Levenson, R. W. 1998. Positive emotions speed recovery from the cardiovascular sequelae of negative emotions. *Cognition & Emotion*, 12(2): 191–220.

Fredrickson, B. L. 2000. Cultivating positive emotions to optimize health and well-being. *Prevention & Treatment*, 3(1): 1a.

Fredrickson, B. L., Mancuso, R. A., Branigan, C., and Tugade, M. M. 2000. The undoing effect of positive emotions. *Motivation and Emotion*, 24(4): 237–258.

Fredrickson, B. L. 2001. The role of positive emotions in positive psychology: The broaden-and-build theory of positive emotions. *American Psychologist*, 56(3): 218.

Fredrickson, B. L. and Branigan, C. 2001. Positive emotions. In T. Mayne and G. A. Bonanno (eds.), *Emotions: Current Issues and Future Directions*. New York City, USA: Guilford Press.

Fredrickson, B. L. and Branigan, C. 2005. Positive emotions broaden the scope of attention and thought-action repertoires. *Cognition & Emotion*, 19(3): 313–332.

Fredrickson, B. L., Cohn, M. A., Coffey, K. A., Pek, J., and Finkel, S. M. 2008. Open hearts build lives: Positive emotions, induced through loving-kindness meditation, build consequential personal resources. *Journal of Personality and Social Psychology*, 95(5): 1045.

Frost, P. J., Dutton, J. E., Worline, M. C., and Wilson, A. 2000. Narratives of compassion in organizations. *Emotion in Organizations*, 2: 25–45.

Garriga, E. and Melé, D. 2004. Corporate social responsibility theories: Mapping the territory. *Journal of Business Ethics*, 53(1–2): 51–71.

Gasper, K. and Clore, G. L. 2002. Attending to the big picture: Mood and global versus local processing of visual information. *Psychological Science*, 13(1): 34–40.

George, R. 1991. *A field evaluation of the cognitive interview*. Unpublished master's thesis, Polytechnic of East London.

Giacalone, R. A. and Jurkiewicz, C. L. 2003. *Handbook of Workplace Spirituality and Organizational Performance*. London, England: Me Sharpe.

Gilbert, P. and Irons, C. 2005. Focused therapies and compassionate mind training for shame and self-attacking. In P. Gilbert (ed.), *Compassion: Conceptualisations, Research and Use in Psychotherapy*: 263–325. New York, USA: Routledge.

Gladstein, D. L. and Reilly, N. P. 1985. Group decision making under threat: The tycoon game. *Academy of Management Journal*, 28(3): 613–627.

Godfrey, P. C. 2005. The relationship between corporate philanthropy and shareholder wealth: A risk management perspective. *Academy of Management Review*, 30(4): 777–798.

Goldstein, A. P. and Michaels, G. Y. 1985. *Empathy: Development, Training, and Consequences*. Hillsdale, NJ: Lawrence Erlbaum.

Goldstein, J. and Kornfield, J. 1987. *Seeking the Heart of Wisdom*. Boston: Shambhala Publications.

Grandey, A. A. 2003. When "the show must go on": Surface acting and deep acting as determinants of emotional exhaustion and peer-rated service delivery. *Academy of Management Journal*, 46(1): 86–96.

Hayes, S. C., Wilson, K. G., Gifford, E. V., Follette, V. M., and Strosahl, K. 1996. Experiential avoidance and behavioral disorders: A functional dimensional approach to diagnosis and treatment. *Journal of Consulting and Clinical Psychology*, 64(6): 1152–1168.

Hayes, S. C., Strosahl, K. D., and Wilson, K. G. 1999. *Acceptance and Commitment Therapy: An Experiential Approach to Behavior Change*. New York City: Guilford Press.

Hedberg, B. 1981. How organizations learn and unlearn. In Nystrom, P. C., Starbucks, W. H. (eds.), *Handbook of Organizational Design*. Oxford: Oxford University Press.

Hochschild, A. R. 1979. Emotion work, feeling rules, and social structure. *American Journal of Sociology*, 85(3): 551–575.

Horney, K. 1950. *The Collected Works of Karen Horney: Self analysis*. New York City: WW Norton.

House, R., Rousseau, D. M., and Thomashunt, M. 1995. The meso paradigm-A framework for the integration of micro and macro organizational-behavior. *Research in Organizational Behavior: An Annual Series of Analytical Essays and Critical Reviews*, 17: 71–114.

Huy, Q. N. 1999. Emotional capability, emotional intelligence, and radical change. *Academy of Management Review*, 24(2): 325–345.

Isen, A. M. and Daubman, K. A. 1984. The influence of affect on categorization. *Journal of Personality and Social Psychology*, 47(6): 1206.

Isen, A. M., Daubman, K. A., and Nowicki, G. P. 1987. Positive affect facilitates creative problem solving. *Journal of Personality and Social Psychology*, 52(6): 1122.

Isen, A. M. 2001. An influence of positive affect on decision making in complex situations: Theoretical issues with practical implications. *Journal of Consumer Psychology*, 11(2): 75–85.

Izard, C. E. 1997. Emotions and facial expressions: A perspective from differential emotions theory. *The Psychology of Facial Expression*: 57–77.

Jost, J. T., Glaser, J., Kruglanski, A. W., and Sulloway, F. J. 2003. Political conservatism as motivated social cognition. *Psychological Bulletin*, 129(3): 339–375.

Jurkiewicz, C. L. and Giacalone, R. A. 2004. A values framework for measuring the impact of workplace spirituality on organizational performance. *Journal of Business Ethics*, 49(2): 129–142.

70 SELF-COMPASSION AND LEARNING FROM FAILURE

Kahn, B. E. and Isen, A. M. 1993. The influence of positive affect on variety seeking among safe, enjoyable products. *Journal of Consumer Research*: 257–270.

Kahneman, D., Diener, E., and Schwarz, N. 1999. *Well-being: Foundations of Hedonic Psychology*. New York: Russell Sage Foundation.

Kanov, J. M., Maitlis, S., Worline, M. C., Dutton, J. E., Frost, P. J., and Lilius, J. M. 2004. Compassion in organizational life. *American Behavioral Scientist*, 47(6): 808–827.

Kashdan, T. B. and Steger, M. F. 2007. Curiosity and pathways to well-being and meaning in life: Traits, states, and everyday behaviors. *Motivation and Emotion*, 31(3): 159–173.

Krieger, J. L. 2005. Shared mindfulness in cockpit crisis situations: An exploratory analysis. *Journal of Business Communication*, 42(2): 135–167.

Langer, E. J. 1989. Minding matters: The consequences of mindlessness–mindfulness. *Advances in Experimental Social Psychology*, 22: 137–173.

Lazarus, R. S. 1991. *Emotion and Adaptation*: Oxford University Press, New York.

Leana, C. R. and Van Buren, H. J. 1999. Organizational social capital and employment practices. *Academy of Management Review*, 24(3): 538–555.

Leary, M. R. and MacDonald, G. 2003. Individual differences in self-esteem: A review and theoretical integration. In M. R. Leary and J. P. Tangney (eds.), *Handbook of Self and Identity*: 401–418. New York: Guilford Press.

Leary, M. R. and Tate, E. B. 2007. The multi-faceted nature of mindfulness. *Psychological Inquiry*, 18(4): 251–255.

Leary, M. R., Tate, E. B., Adams, C. E., Batts Allen, A., and Hancock, J. 2007. Self-compassion and reactions to unpleasant self-relevant events: The implications of treating oneself kindly. *Journal of Personality and Social Psychology*, 92(5): 887–904.

Levitt, J. T., Brown, T. A., Orsillo, S. M., and Barlow, D. H. 2004. The effects of acceptance versus suppression of emotion on subjective and psychophysiological response to carbon dioxide challenge in patients with panic disorder. *Behavior Therapy*, 35(4): 747–766.

Lilius, J. M., Worline, M. C., Dutton, J. E., Kanov, J., Frost, P. J., and Maitlis, S. 2003. What good is compassion at work? *Ann Arbor*, 1001: 808–827.

Lloyd, T. 1990. *The 'Nice' Company: Why 'Nice' Companies Make More Profits*. London: Bloomsbury.

Logsdon, J. M. and Wood, D. J. 2002. Business citizenship. *Business Ethics Quarterly*, 12(2): 155–187.

Lupton, D. 2012. *Medicine as Culture: Illness, Disease and the Body*. London: Sage.

Lyubomirsky, S., King, L., and Diener, E. 2005. The benefits of frequent positive affect: Does happiness lead to success? *Psychological Bulletin*, 131(6): 803–855.

Markus, H. R. and Kitayama, S. 1991. Culture and the self: Implications for cognition, emotion, and motivation. *Psychological Review*, 98(2): 224.

Martin, J. R. 1997. Mindfulness: A proposed common factor. *Journal of Psychotherapy Integration*, 7(4): 291–312.

Matten, D., Crane, A., and Chapple, W. 2003. Behind the mask: Revealing the true face of corporate citizenship. *Journal of Business Ethics*, 45(1–2): 109–120.

McAdams, D. P. 1985. *Power, Intimacy, and the Life Story*. Homewood, IL: Dorsey.

McAdams, D. P. and Bryant, F. B. 1987. Intimacy motivation and subjective mental health in a nationwide sample. *Journal of Personality*, 55(3): 395–413.

McGregor, I. and Little, B. R. 1998. Personal projects, happiness, and meaning: On doing well and being yourself. *Journal of Personality and Social Psychology*, 74(2): 494.

Miller, D. T. 1976. Ego involvement and attributions for success and failure. *Journal of Personality and Social Psychology*, 34(5): 901.

Milliman, J. F., Czaplewski, A. J., and Ferguson, J. M. 2001. *An exploratory empirical assessment of the relationship between spirituality and employee work attitudes.* Paper presented at the Academy of Management proceedings Washington, D.C.

Neff, K. 2003a. Self-compassion: An alternative conceptualization of a healthy attitude toward oneself. *Self and Identity*, 2(2): 85–101.

Neff, K. D. 2003k. The development and validation of a scale to measure self-compassion. *Self and Identity*, 2(3): 223–250.

Neff, K. D., Hsieh, Y.-P., and Dejitterat, K. 2005. Self-compassion, achievement goals, and coping with academic failure. *Self and Identity*, 4(3): 263–287.

Neff, K. D. and Suizzo, M.-A. 2006. Culture, power, authenticity and psychological well-being within romantic relationships: A comparison of European American and Mexican Americans. *Cognitive Development*, 21(4): 441–457.

Neff, K. D., Kirkpatrick, K. L., and Rude, S. S. 2007. Self-compassion and adaptive psychological functioning. *Journal of Research in Personality*, 41(1): 139–154.

Neff, K. D. 2009. The role of self-compassion in development: A healthier way to relate to oneself. *Human Development*, 52(4): 211.

Neff, K. D. and Vonk, R. 2009. Self-compassion versus global self-esteem: Two different ways of relating to oneself. *Journal of Personality*, 77(1): 23–50.

Nolen-Hoeksema, S. 1991. Responses to depression and their effects on the duration of depressive episodes. *Journal of Abnormal Psychology*, 100(4): 569–582.

Ocasio, W. 1997. Towards an attention-based view of the firm. *Strategic Management Journal*, 18: 187–206.

Olendzki, A. (2005). The roots of mindfulness. In Germer, C. K., Siegel, R. D., & Fulton, P. R. (Eds.), *Mindfulness and psy- chotherapy*: 241–261. New York: Guilford.

Otake, K., Shimai, S., Tanaka-Matsumi, J., Otsui, K., and Fredrickson, B. L. 2006. Happy people become happier through kindness: A counting kindnesses intervention. *Journal of Happiness Studies*, 7(3): 361–375.

Papa, A. and Bonanno, G. A. 2008. Smiling in the face of adversity: The interpersonal and intrapersonal functions of smiling. *Emotion*, 8(1): 1.

Peterson, C. and Seligman, M. E. 2003. Character strengths before and after September 11. *Psychological Science*, 14(4): 381–384.

Peterson, C. and Seligman, M. E. 2004. *Character Strengths and Virtues: A Handbook and Classification*. New York: Oxford University Press.

Reich, W. 1949. *Character Analysis*. New York: Oregon Institute Press.

Rochlin, G. I. 1989. Informal organizational networking as a crisis-avoidance strategy: US naval flight operations as a case study. *Organization & Environment*, 3(2): 159–176.

Rosenberg, M. B. 1999. *Nonviolent Communication: A Language of Compassion*. Encinitas, CA: PuddleDancer Press.

Ryan, R. M. and Deci, E. L. 1991. A motivational approach to self: Integration in Personality. *Perspectives on Motivation*, 38: 237.

Ryan, R. M. and Deci, E. L. 2001. On happiness and human potentials: A review of research on hedonic and eudaimonic well-being. *Annual Review of Psychology*, 52(1): 141–166.

Salzberg, S. 1997. *Loving-kindness: The Revolutionary Art of Happiness*. Boston, MA: Shambhala.

Salzberg, S. 2002. *Lovingkindness: The Revolutionary Art of Happiness*. Boston, MA: Shambhala.

Salzberg, S. 2004. *Lovingkindness: The Revolutionary Art of Happiness*. Boston, MA: Shambhala Publications.

Scheff, T. J. 1981. The distancing of emotion in psychotherapy. *Psychotherapy: Theory, Research & Practice*, 18(1): 46–53.

Schulman, P. 1999. Applying learned optimism to increase sales productivity. *Journal of Personal Selling & Sales Management*, 19(1): 31–37.

Schulman, P. R. 1993. The negotiated order of organizational reliability. *Administration & Society*, 25(3): 353–372.

Schwarz, N. and Clore, G. L. 1988. How do I feel about it? The informative function of affective states. In K. Fiedler, J. Forgas (eds.), *Affect, Cognition, and Social Behavior*: 44–62. Toronto: Hogrefe International.

Sedikides, C. 1993. Assessment, enhancement, and verification determinants of the self-evaluation process. *Journal of Personality and Social Psychology*, 65(2): 317.

Seligman, M. E., Steen, T. A., Park, N., and Peterson, C. 2005. Positive psychology progress: empirical validation of interventions. *American Psychologist*, 60(5): 410.

Shaw, B. and Post, F. R. 1993. A moral basis for corporate philanthropy. *Journal of Business Ethics*, 12(10): 745–751.

Shepherd, D. A. 2009. Grief recovery from the loss of a family business: A multi- and meso-level theory. *Journal of Business Venturing*, 24(1): 81–97.

Shepherd, D. A., Covin, J. G., and Kuratko, D. F. 2009. Project failure from corporate entrepreneurship: Managing the grief process. *Journal of Business Venturing*, 24(6): 588–600.

Simmons, B. L. and Nelson, D. L. 2001. Eustress at work: The relationship between hope and health in hospital nurses. *Health Care Management Review*, 26(4): 7–18.

Slagter, H. A., Lutz, A., Greischar, L. L., Francis, A. D., Nieuwenhuis, S., Davis, J. M., and Davidson, R. J. 2007. Mental training affects distribution of limited brain resources. *PLoS Biology*, 5(6): e138.

Steensma, H. K. 1996. Acquiring technological competencies through inter-organizational collaboration: An organizational learning perspective. *Journal of Engineering and Technology Management*, 12(4): 267–286.

Sutcliffe, K. and Vogus, T. J. 2003. Organizing for resilience. *Positive Organizational Scholarship: Foundations of a New Discipline*, 94: 110.

Sutcliffe, K. M. and Weick, K. E. 2003. Hospitals as cultures of entrapment: A re-analysis of the Bristol Royal Infirmary. *California Management Review*, 45(2): 73–84.

Sutton, R. I. and D'Aunno, T. 1989. Decreasing organizational size: Untangling the effects of money and people. *Academy of management Review*, 14(2): 194–212.

Taris, T. W. 2000. *A Primer in Longitudinal Data Analysis* California: Sage Thousand Oaks.

Tomkins, S. S. 1962. *Affect, Imagery, Consciousness*: Vol. I. The positive affects New York: Springer.

Tugade, M. M. and Fredrickson, B. L. 2004. Resilient individuals use positive emotions to bounce back from negative emotional experiences. *Journal of Personality and Social Psychology*, 86(2): 320–333.

Twenge, J. M. and Campbell, W. K. 2003. "Isn't it fun to get the respect that we're going to deserve?" Narcissism, social rejection, and aggression. *Personality and Social Psychology Bulletin*, 29(2): 261–272.

Vera, D. and Crossan, M. 2004. Strategic leadership and organizational learning. *Academy of Management Review*, 29(2): 222–240.

Wallace, B. A. and Shapiro, S. L. 2006. Mental balance and well-being: Building bridges between Buddhism and Western psychology. *American Psychologist*, 61(7): 690.

Weick, K. and Westley, F. 1996. Organizational learning: Affirming an Oxymoron In S. Clegg, C. Hardy, and W. Nord (eds.), *Handbook of Organization Studies*. London: Sage.

Weick, K. E. 1990. The vulnerable system: An analysis of the Tenerife air disaster. *Journal of Management*, 16(3): 571–593.

Weick, K. E. 1993. The collapse of sensemaking in organizations: The Mann Gulch disaster. *Administrative Science Quarterly*, 38: 628–652.

Weick, K. E., Sutcliffe, K. M., and Obstfeld, D. 1999. Organizing for high reliability: Processes of collective mindfulness. *Research in Organizational Behavior*, 21: 81–123.

Weick, K. E., Sutcliffe, K. M., & Obstfeld, D. 2005. Organizing and the process of sensemaking. *Organization Science*, 16(4): 409–421.

Weick, K. E. and Sutcliffe, K. M. 2006. Mindfulness and the quality of organizational attention. *Organization Science*, 17(4): 514–524.

Weick, K. E. and Sutcliffe, K. M. 2011. *Managing the Unexpected: Resilient Performance in an Age of Uncertainty*. New Jersey: John Wiley & Sons.

Whetten, D. A. 1989. What constitutes a theoretical contribution?*Academy of Management Review*, 14(4): 490–495.

Wood, J. V., Saltzberg, J. A., Neale, J. M., Stone, A. A., and Rachmiel, T. B. 1990. Self-focused attention, coping responses, and distressed mood in everyday life. *Journal of Personality and Social Psychology*, 58(6): 1027.

Zimmerman, M. A., Bingenheimer, J. B., and Notaro, P. C. 2002. Natural mentors and adolescent resiliency: A study with urban youth. *American Journal of Community Psychology*, 30(2): 221–243.

4 Anticipatory grief, persistence, and recovery

We have established that failure is an experience that is an ever-present possibility facing those who engage in entrepreneurship. However, although most (if not all) entrepreneurs will eventually be forced to face failure, these experiences are not homogeneous in nature, and in fact, individuals will vary substantially with regard to how they endure failure (in particular, see Chapter 2). In this chapter, we focus on an area of particular interest with regard to how individuals experience failure – namely, the amount of time and effort entrepreneurs spend prolonging the failure experience. Specifically, we examine what factors – both intrinsic and extrinsic – cause entrepreneurs to delay the decision to terminate their business ventures even when presented with evidence that failure will most likely be the ultimate decision. We will also see how these delays can both help and hinder entrepreneurs in their subsequent efforts to move on after failure.

Although we may expect that underperforming firms will be selected out of an economy, the evidence suggests that performance often does not explain survival (Baden-Fuller 1989; Karakaya 2000; van Witteloostuijn 1998). Indeed, Meyer and Zucker (1989) pointed out that "efficient performance is only one—and not necessarily the most important—determinant of organizational survival." It has been argued that an economy suffers when underperforming firms persist rather than fail (McGrath and Cardon 1997); they are seen to squander resources, occupy market positions better filled by others, and increase uncertainty for stakeholders of entrepreneurial firms (Karakaya 2000; McGrath and Cardon 1997; Ruhnka, Feldman, and Dean 1992). These firms have been labeled as living dead (Bourgeois and Eisenhardt, 1987; Ruhnka et al., 1992), underperforming (Gimeno, Folta, Cooper, and Woo 1997), permanently failing organizations

(Meyer and Zucker 1989), and chronic failures (van Witteloostuijn 1998). These underperforming firms – "organizations whose performance, by any standard, falls short of expectations … yet whose existence continues" (Meyer and Zucker 1989: 19) – can exist over an extended period (Gimeno et al. 1997; Karakaya 2000; van Witteloostuijn 1998).

Considerable scholarly effort has been invested in trying to explain why some entrepreneurs delay closing their poorly performing businesses. In Figure 4.1, we offer a model of the causes and consequences of the delayed decision to terminate a failing firm (based largely on (DeTienne, Shepherd, and De Castro) [2008], (Gimeno et al.) [1997], and (Shepherd, Wiklund, and Haynie) [2009]). In the center of the figure is the delayed decision to terminate a failing business, which can be exacerbated by procrastination and/or the entrepreneur's performance threshold. The performance threshold is influenced by expectations of firm performance turnaround, motivation to justify previous entrepreneurial decisions, and the desire to be consistent with previous entrepreneurial decisions. The nature of these relationships depends on the entrepreneur's extrinsic motivation and values. A delayed decision to terminate a failing business

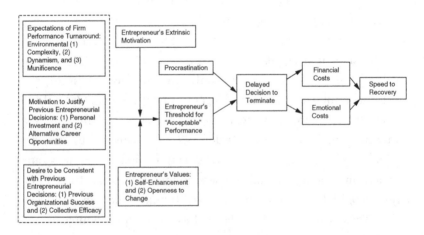

FIGURE 4.1: Conceptual model of entrepreneurial persistence and its consequence

has consequences for the financial and emotional costs borne by the entrepreneur, and in turn, impact his or her speed of recovery. In the sections that follow, we develop the nature of these relationships.

PROCRASTINATION AND PERSISTING WITH A POORLY PERFORMING FIRM

Procrastination refers to the deferment of an action or activity that could be interpreted as emotionally unpleasant but that is important from a cognitive perspective since it will likely produce positive future outcomes (van Eerde 2003). It happens when these emotionally unpleasant hazards are avoided, resulting in the suspension of further activity (Lazarus and Folkman 1984). In these instances, the expectation of the threat produces a negative emotional response (e.g., anxiety, fear, sadness, etc.). By evading these situations, entrepreneurs can reduce these negative emotions, which signify a negative reinforcement that further perpetuates these types of behaviors (Anderson 2003e; Milgram, Sroloff, and Rosenbaum 1988). For example, entrepreneurs may engage in procrastination because it delays the decision to declare their business bankrupt, thereby forcing them to cease ownership or management of their venture. Although this decision can be emotionally overwhelming, it is an essential duty because the sooner it is completed, the lower the financial cost of venture failure. Additionally, previous research has indicated that tasks associated with higher levels of anticipated negative emotions are more likely to invoke procrastination than those associated with lower levels of anticipated negative emotions (Anderson 2003a).

Based on this perspective, it seems as if procrastination is a particularly salient factor to consider in the context of entrepreneurship. It is possible that entrepreneurs could engage in procrastination as a way to delay the decision to take action and formally declare their ventures insolvent, which would result in the cessation of their active involvement as owners and managers of the business. Although the decision to terminate a business can be emotionally overwhelming (Byrne and Shepherd 2015), it is an important action to take because doing so will stop an entrepreneur from "throwing good money after bad" – that is, to stop investing resources into the business that will not receive a sufficient return and will likely be lost when the business fails.

There are several possible mechanisms underlying this procrastination, one of which is the notion that it is more difficult to learn and easier to ignore or forget negative information. Research has indicated that under certain conditions, individuals find it more difficult to learn negative information (Amir, Coles, Brigidi, and Foa 2001). Additionally, investigations into the mechanism involved in forgetting have uncovered that negative information is indeed more easily forgotten than neutral or positive information (Myers, Brewin, and Power 1998). Taken together, these findings suggest that one of the reasons why procrastination might occur is that the negative information that should be considered when deciding to terminate a failing business might be easier to ignore and more difficult to remember, therefore providing a convenient cognitive side step in the decision-making process. For instance, entrepreneurs who are presented with information that sales for their venture have increased but that they are still losing money at an alarming rate could potentially register and focus on the positive information regarding sales and not learn or quickly forget that the business is still failing in terms of overall performance. This could in turn substantially increase the likelihood for procrastination.

There are a number of factors that might influence the anticipated negative emotions associated with a given task, thereby enhancing the likelihood of procrastination. First, decisions that are perceived as irreversible tend to result in producing higher levels of negative emotions (Anderson 2003a). In an excellent review of the factors that influence decision avoidance, Anderson (2003a) discussed the mechanism underlying the relationship between the perceived irreversibility of decisions and the likelihood of decision avoidance. In his review, Anderson noted that when individuals are presented with decisions they believe will be irreversible, they are much more likely to experience anticipated regret over making those decisions. That is, when thinking about the possibility of making a decision that cannot be reversed, individuals tend to focus on the potential negative outcomes of making an incorrect choice and, as a result, experience anticipated regret over that choice, which can in turn cause them to prolong the decision-making process. As an example, consider entrepreneurs who are faced with the decision to terminate one business in order to pursue a new and promising opportunity. While it is possible for entrepreneurs who dissolve one venture to begin another, the decision to end the first business is final and irreversible. When analyzing the termination decision, such entrepreneurs will likely consider how they will feel if their new enterprise does not end up being successful, leading them to experience feelings of anticipated regret over a decision they have not actually made yet.

Second, the likelihood of procrastination can be substantially influenced by what entrepreneurs attribute the actual cause of the failure to be. If entrepreneurs feel that they are personally responsible for the failure outcome, it is likely that they will expect to experience higher levels of negative emotions as a result of the final decision. Entrepreneurs often perceive their ventures as extensions of their own identities (Bruno, McQuarrie, and Torgrimson 1992; Cova and Svanfeldt 1993) and are thus more likely to assign personal responsibility to the ultimate failure of their firms.

Finally, when entrepreneurs perceive that their own actions have caused the negative outcome (compared to situations in which they perceive others' actions to have caused the failure), it is likely that they will generate higher levels of negative emotions, which could in turn increase the likelihood that they will postpone business failure. When considered together, there are likely a number of factors involved in the decision to declare that a business has failed that might enhance the possibility of procrastination.

Thus, although the negative financial consequences of persistence can be substantial (Garland, Sandefur, and Rogers 1990; Ross and Staw 1986, 1993), from a procrastination perspective, the emotional byproducts of persistence remain comparatively unexplored. This point is illustrated by Anderson who, after a thorough review of the literature, concluded that "it is interesting to note that the vast majority of [procrastination] studies support the conclusion that emotional goals influence decision avoidance but that post-decisional emotions are infrequently measured.... It is reasonable to assume that people make choices that reduce negative emotions" (Anderson 2003a: 142). This consideration of the potential emotional consequences of failure can be very influential in prolonging the decision to terminate. Next, we shift our attention to how developing acceptable performance thresholds and evaluating actual performance relative to those thresholds can also influence the decision to delay terminating a failing business.

PERFORMANCE THRESHOLDS IN THE DECISION TO TERMINATE

Gimeno and colleagues (Gimeno et al. 1997) found that firm performance relative to a performance threshold plays a role in explaining organizational survival (or, said differently, in delaying failure decisions). A firm performance threshold refers to "the level of performance below which the dominant organizational constituents will act to dissolve the organization" (Gimeno et al. 1997: 750). This notion of a threshold for performance is consistent with pain thresholds (Forys and Dahlquist 2007), risk thresholds (Monahan and Silver 2003), and aspiration levels (Kahneman and Tversky 1979). More specifically, pain thresholds represent levels of physical discomfort individuals utilize to determine acceptable versus unacceptable experiences of pain. When an individual experiences pain below his or her threshold, he or she is unlikely to disengage in or retreat from the stimulus responsible for that pain. However, once this threshold has been exceeded, it is highly likely that the individual will seek to disengage from the pain-producing activity. Similarly, risk thresholds are of common interest, particularly within the field of forensic sciences and the study of judicial decision making regarding potential violent criminals. In this context, individuals tasked with making decisions regarding the potential violent risk posed by those brought before them most often employ a risk threshold. Individuals deemed to be below this threshold are usually determined not to pose a significant risk for violence, whereas individuals who exceed this perceived threshold are deemed potential violent threats and are thus often subjected to containment in either mental or prison facilities. Finally, aspiration levels represent "the smallest outcome that would be deemed satisfactory by the decision maker" (Schneider 1992: 1053). These aspiration thresholds provide a convenient cognitive heuristic that allows for the simplification of decision making: change happens when results are below the perceived threshold, and persistence happens when performance exceeds this level (Greve 2002).

The notion of a threshold for firm performance explains why Firm A that is performing worse than Firm B may survive while Firm B fails. That is, the entrepreneur of Firm A has a threshold for firm performance that is lower than the entrepreneur of Firm B. As Figure 4.2 shows, Firm B is in fact outperforming Firm A from an objective performance perspective, but the threshold used to determine acceptable performance levels for Entrepreneur A is

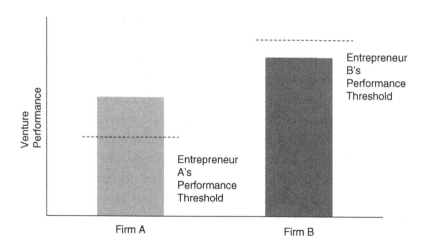

FIGURE 4.2: Subjective threshold evaluation

substantially lower than that employed by Entrepreneur B. Therefore, based upon this comparison, it is more likely that Entrepreneur B would ultimately determine that Firm B's performance is unacceptable, thereby deciding to terminate the firm, than it would be for Entrepreneur A to come to a similar conclusion. This situation is primarily due to the fact that the subjective thresholds that each has assigned as criteria to make this decision are substantially different from one another. The question then becomes what explains why some entrepreneurs have a lower threshold for performance and thus delay failure decisions.

HETEROGENEITY IN ENTREPRENEURS' PERFORMANCE THRESHOLDS

An explanation for variance in entrepreneurs' firm performance thresholds appears to depend on the (1) expectations of (or hopes for) firm performance turnaround, (2) motivation to justify previous entrepreneurial decisions, (3) desire to be consistent with previous entrepreneurial decisions, and (4) individual differences in extrinsic motivation (DeTienne et al. 2008).

Expectations of (or hopes for) firm performance turnaround

An entrepreneur's expectation about the future performance of his or her firm (including a turnaround in current poor performance) is heavily influenced by the nature of the external environment. The nature of the external environment can be captured by the dimensions of complexity, dynamism, and munificence (Aldrich 1979; Dess and Beard 1984). When the environment is highly complex, there is considerable heterogeneity in the environment, and there are many factors for decision makers to consider (Wiersema and Bantel 1993). This greater complexity increases entrepreneurs' uncertainty over the environment and increases their cognitive load for collecting and processing information (Dess and Beard 1984; Rauch, Wiklund, Lumpkin, and Frese 2009). Both higher uncertainty and the cognitive load of collecting and processing information increases doubt over the accuracy of information suggesting that current performance is poor. Furthermore, opportunities are more prevalent in complex environments (Brown and Eisenhardt 1997). Given that prior knowledge in the industry may facilitate the identification of these opportunities (Shepherd and DeTienne 2005) and that entrepreneurs are typically overconfident (Busenitz and Barney 1997; Forbes 2005; Hayward, Shepherd, and Griffin 2005), entrepreneurs may delay failure decisions because they believe they are well positioned to take advantage of the complex environment to exploit new opportunities and thereby turnaround firm performance.

Environmental dynamism refers to the level of instability in the environment and involves frequent changes that are difficult to predict in advance (Beard and Dess 1979; Bluedorn 1993). From a management perspective, environmental dynamism has been shown to influence a number of important processes and outcomes ranging from decision making (Priem, Rasheed, and Kotulic 1995) to innovation (Baron and Tang 2011) to overall firm performance (Simerly and Li 2000). Additionally, environmental dynamism can moderate the relationship between leadership behaviors and new venture performance (Ensley, Pearce, and Hmieleski 2006) as well as influence the relationship between entrepreneurial orientation and venture performance (Wiklund and Shepherd 2005). Interestingly, although dynamic environments are characterized by instability and change, they have also been shown to be fertile breeding grounds for entrepreneurial opportunity and success. Because dynamic environments are ever changing, they are continuously presenting new potential opportunities for individuals who have the vision and motivation to exploit them. Indeed, evidence has shown that new ventures led by individuals with a promotion focus (e.g., those who actively seek to achieve positive results) perform much better in highly dynamic environments than those led by individuals with a prevention focus (e.g., those who actively seek to avoid negative results) (Hmieleski and Baron 2008). Again, although environmental dynamism places greater cognitive strain on the entrepreneur (Li and Simerly 1998; Waldman,

Ramirez, House, and Puranam 2001), opportunities are created in environments that are rapidly changing (Brown and Eisenhardt 1997), and given their prior knowledge of this particular market, these entrepreneurs likely feel well positioned to quickly identify and act on these opportunities (Shepherd, McMullen, and Jennings 2007). This belief, whether based on overconfidence (Forbes 2005; Hayward, Forster, Sarasvathy, and Fredrickson 2009) or not, encourages the entrepreneur to delay the failure decision in the hopes of being able to eventually succeed when environmental conditions shift.

As an example of how environmental dynamism might delay the decision to terminate a venture, consider the following scenario. Entrepreneur A is the founder of a new venture in a rapidly developing technology-based industry, whereas Entrepreneur B is the founder of a more traditional manufacturing-based industry. It is likely that both Entrepreneur A and Entrepreneur B will experience issues with initial performance as well as continued viability. If, upon evaluation, Entrepreneur B determines that his or her performance does not meet acceptable thresholds, it is likely that the decision to "cut one's losses" and terminate the venture will occur after a relatively short period of time. This choice is in no small part influenced by Entrepreneur B's perception that the conditions within the environment are relatively stable, so if the firm is unable to compete under the current conditions, it is unlikely that the competitive landscape will be altered substantially enough in the future to allow for higher levels of competitiveness. However, this might not be the case with Entrepreneur A. Because the environment in this situation is highly dynamic, it is possible that rapid shifts and alterations could occur in the competitive landscape, essentially changing the environment so as to place Entrepreneur A's firm in a much more competitive position. The knowledge that such an environmental shift is possible could motivate Entrepreneur A to prolong the decision to terminate the venture in the hopes of being able to eventually achieve a successful, sustainable competitive position.

The final dimension of the external environment is environmental munificence (Starbuck 1976), which represents the extent to which the environment is capable of supporting prolonged growth (Dess and Beard 1984). A munificent environment has been described as a tide that raises all boats (Wasserman 2003). Munificence not only expedites an entrepreneur's ability to acquire resources but also assists in opportunity identification (Hitt, Ireland, Sirmon, and Trahms 2011). Having relatively easy access to resources also helps free up cognitive load, which can in turn be utilized for dealing with other important decision-making tasks that must be completed in day-to-day firm operation. Indeed, environmental munificence has been found to moderate the relationship between rational decision making and new venture performance, with rational decision making having a more positive influence on venture performance under conditions of high munificence (Goll and Rasheed 2005). Therefore, it is possible that entrepreneurs operating in munificent environments could prolong the decision to terminate their venture in the hopes that the abundance of resources and opportunities present within the environment will eventually enhance their firm's performance.

Consider the following hypothetical situations faced by entrepreneurs in various levels of environmental munificence. For those with ventures operating in environments that are relatively low in munificence, when firm performance falters, it is unlikely that they will have access to the necessary resources required to keep the firm afloat until performance improves. Additionally, in environments low in munificence, it is unlikely that alternative opportunities are available in abundance, essentially reducing or eliminating any option the entrepreneur might have of switching focus to a more desirable opportunity.

However, this is not likely the case in highly munificent environments. In munificent environments, even when firm performance is below the desired threshold, additional resources are available to supplement the firm's operations, thereby enabling the entrepreneur to delay the decision to terminate the venture. Furthermore, because munificent environments are characterized by more opportunities, it is possible that faltering ventures within such environments could decide to abandon their original business model in lieu of focusing on a newly discovered alternative opportunity within the environment. In summary, it is likely that entrepreneurs will delay failure decisions in environments they believe may eventually lift firm performance.

For example, in a metric conjoint study of 2,848 decisions nested within 89 entrepreneurs, DeTienne and colleagues (2008) found that entrepreneurs are more likely to persist with their poorly performing firms in munificent environments. They also found an effect for environmental complexity and dynamism, but this effect depended on the extrinsic motivation of the entrepreneur (which we discuss later). Thus, it is not just the attributes of the external environment that impact persistence; entrepreneurs (as all people) (Staw and Fox 1977; Staw 1981) are often motivated to justify previous positions, and this motivation can also lead to delaying the failure decision, to which we now turn.

Motivation to justify previous entrepreneurial decisions

In addition to external factors that can contribute to prolonging the failure decision, internal factors also likely motivate individuals in this decision. In other words, individuals could be intrinsically motivated to delay the failure decision for reasons that may not provide financial benefits but could result in important emotional and psychological rewards.

First, such motivation can come from the entrepreneur's personal investment in the business (e.g., sunk costs [Northcraft et al. 1984]). Personal investments of time, money, and energy lead to the formation of a strong psychological bond between an entrepreneur and his or her business (Pierce, Kostova, and Dirks 2001; Wagner, Parker, and Christiansen 2003). This personal investment may be so great that the entrepreneur perceives the business as an extension (or reflection) of his or her individual identity (Dobrev and Barnett 2005; Phillips 2002). For example, entrepreneurs have been known to refer to their business as "their baby" or "their child" (Cardon, Zietsma,

Saparito, Matherne, and Davis 2005; Dodd 2002). The decision to terminate the business (i.e., institute the failure event) would break this valuable (psychological) bond; the greater the personal investment of an entrepreneur into his or her business, the greater the likely persistence despite poor performance (DeTienne et al. 2008; Gimeno et al. 1997).

Second, the motivation to justify previous decisions and thereby delay business termination is enhanced by the scarcity of other personal career opportunities. That is, an entrepreneur's decision to terminate a business is likely considered alongside his or her other career-related options. (e.g., for employee turnover, see [Jackofsky and Peters 1983; March and Simon 1958]). If there are many attractive alternatives, the entrepreneur is less likely to persist with the current underperforming firm and terminate it, but if there are few (if any) other alternatives, the entrepreneur will decide to persist with the current firm (DeTienne et al. 2008; Gimeno et al. 1997). These findings are further supported by evidence regarding the factors that individuals consider prior to starting their own ventures. Studies have shown that opportunity costs are an important factor influencing the decision to switch from a wage-earning employment position to being a self-employed business owner/operator (Campbell 1995; O'Brien, Folta, and Johnson 2003). Therefore, it would stand to reason that similar considerations are made when deciding to transition back from being self-employed to again working a more traditional salaried/wage-earning position.

Take for example Entrepreneur A, who for our purposes we will name "Joe." Joe decided to forego completing his college degree in order to pursue his dream of starting his own landscaping and lawn-maintenance company. Although his venture had substantial initial success, the recent downturn in the economy coupled with rising fuel and labor prices have placed Joe's firm in danger of dissolution. Now consider Entrepreneur B, who we will refer to as "Jane." Jane has an advanced degree in electrical engineering and left a lucrative position as a senior systems engineer with a Fortune 500 company to start her own venture based on a new product technology she had conceived during her graduate studies. While Jane's idea held promise, she has reached a point where further business operations will require substantial external funding, and she has exhausted almost all avenues available for her to acquire the necessary funds to keep her business operating. Essentially, both Joe and Jane are at a crossroads in their ventures and must decide whether to terminate their ventures and move on to more traditional employment or to delay the termination decision in hopes that their fortunes might change dramatically and allow for them to continue operating their respective businesses. However, while the decision is technically the same for each, the relative likelihood of the decision that will be made by either is dramatically different in no small part due to the potential alternatives each has regarding their other employment options.

For Jane, these options are substantial. She is likely to obtain a similar position to the one she left offering a six-figure salary plus the benefits and security associated with employment in a large, stable company. These options are likely to provide ample temptations to persuade Jane to dissolve her business quickly so as to lessen the opportunity costs associated with not only continuing her failing business but also in not collecting compensation from her new position as quickly as possible. This is not the case for Joe. Without a college degree or advanced technical training and with little to no applicable experience in a more traditional employment role, Joe's alternatives for employment upon the termination of his business are decidedly less appealing. When considering both examples, it becomes evident that Jane is likely to make the decision to terminate her venture quickly as a result of her other employment options, whereas Joe – because his alternatives to self-employment are limited at best – is more apt to prolong the failure decision in the hopes that the situation will improve, thereby allowing him to remain in business.

Norms for consistency

The decision to persist with a poorly performing firm is also influenced by individuals' need to be perceived (by others and themselves) as consistent. Even in the presence of disconfirming evidence, people may see consistency as the best course of action (Caldini 1993; Staw and Ross 1980). Caldini (1993: 53) described the norm for consistency in the following way: "Because it is a preprogrammed and mindless method of responding, automatic consistency can supply a safe hiding place from troubling realizations." In this way, entrepreneurs may look for evidence that confirms consistency through persistence and ignore or discount information that points to the opposite. For example, consistency (i.e., persistence) may be encouraged by previous organizational success (Audia, Locke, and Smith 2000) – it worked out in the past, so if I persist it will eventually be successful in the future (Levinthal and March 1993).

In a similar way, perceived collective efficacy can promote consistency in decisions, which is persisting with a poorly performing firm in this case. We know that self-efficacy is associated with persistence at a task (for a meta-analysis, see [Multon, Brown, and Lent 1991]), and it appears that collective efficacy is also related to persistence (Hodges and Carron 1992; Little and Madigan 1997). Perceived self-efficacy can be conceptualized as the "judgments of how well one can execute courses of action required to deal with prospective situations" (Bandura 1982) and as an extension of this logic, entrepreneurial self-efficacy "refers to the strength of a person's belief that he or she is capable of successfully performing the various roles and tasks of entrepreneurship" (Chen, Greene, and Crick 1998). Individual self-efficacy has been linked to increased levels of persistence in a number of categories, including academic achievement (Lent, Brown, and Larkin 1984), work performance (Gist 1987), and entrepreneurial endeavors (McCarthy, Schoorman, and Cooper 1993).

Building off this concept of individual self-efficacy, researchers have applied beliefs concerning the ability to perform specific tasks to the group level, creating the concept of collective self-efficacy. Unlike individual self-efficacy, collective self-efficacy is defined as "the group's beliefs in their collective power to produce desired results" (Bandura 2000). It is important to note that collective self-efficacy "is not merely the sum of the efficacy beliefs of the individual (group) members.... rather, it is an emergent group-level property" (Bandura 2000). This collective self-efficacy has also been shown to have a positive relationship with persistence (Goddard, Hoy, and Hoy 2004; Little and Madigan 1997), demonstrating how group-level factors can influence individual behaviors and actions. To the extent that an individual is influenced by the collective belief within his or her organization, high collective efficacy is also likely to encourage persistence. High levels of collective efficacy can translate the belief that the group is capable of performing specific tasks irrespective of whether or not individuals within that group have adequate levels of individual self-efficacy regarding their abilities to achieve the desired outcomes. Therefore, it is possible that high levels of collective self-efficacy can supersede individual perceptions of self-efficacy, thereby motivating individuals to persist with the group's chosen course of action. Indeed, DeTienne and colleagues (2008) found that entrepreneurs are more likely to decide to persist with their poorly performing firms when they have previously experienced high organizational success and are embedded in a group with high collective efficacy than when they have experienced low previous organizational success and low collective efficacy.

Entrepreneurs' extrinsic motivation

Not all entrepreneurs are subject to the aforementioned forces that promote persistence. Entrepreneurs are likely heterogeneous in extrinsic motivation. Extrinsic motivation is "a cognitive state reflecting the extent to which an individual factors the force of his or her task behaviors to some extrinsic outcome" (Brief and Aldag 1977). In entrepreneurship, we often think of extrinsic rewards in terms of financial outcomes (Campbell 1992; Kuratko, Hornsby, and Naffziger 1997; Shepherd and DeTienne 2005), which include (but are not necessarily limited to) monetary rewards, acquisition of personal wealth, and individual entrepreneurial income (Kuratko et al. 1997). It has been well established that the potential for financial reward can provide an important motivational influence on entrepreneurial behavior (Campbell 1992; Kuratko et al. 1997; Schumpeter 1961). Scholars as far back as Schumpeter (1961) have proposed that the construction of a business empire in the hopes of achieving financial gains represents an important motivation to engage in entrepreneurial activities. Similarly, Campbell postulated that individuals decide to become entrepreneurs if the value of rewards achieved from entrepreneurship exceeds the expected value of rewards obtained from being an employee (Campbell 1992). Additionally, recent research has found that potential financial rewards provide an important motivation for both recognizing opportunities (Shepherd and DeTienne 2005) and sustaining entrepreneurial activities (Kuratko et al. 1997).

While relatively little research has examined the role extrinsic motivation plays in regard to persistence, a parallel stream of research can be found in the job-pay satisfaction and turnover literatures. Substantial amounts of research has supported the notion that there is a negative relationship between job-pay satisfaction and employee turnover (Cotton and Tuttle 1986) as well as a positive relationship between job-pay satisfaction and employee commitment to the organization (Johnston, Parasuraman, Futrell, and Black 1990). This evidence implies that lower levels of satisfaction with monetary compensation from work translates to lower levels of organizational commitment, thereby increasing the likelihood that individuals experiencing such dissatisfaction will ultimately leave the organization. Mapping these findings onto the field of entrepreneurship, we propose that it is possible that entrepreneurs who are more extrinsically motivated will be less likely to be swayed by factors that influence persistence. Therefore, to the extent that entrepreneurs are extrinsically motivated, they are less likely to be influenced by the other factors (e.g., the environment, motivation to justify, and norms for consistency) to delay terminating poorly performing firms, a proposition

largely supported by DeTienne and colleagues' (2008) study of entrepreneurs' decision policies.[1] Entrepreneurs not only differ in their
extrinsic motivation but also in their values, and these values can
influence the decision to persist – that is, the decision to delay the
voluntary termination of poorly performing firms (e.g., failure event).

ENTREPRENEURS' VALUES

Values are "enduring perspectives of what is fundamentally right or
wrong ... can be thought of as preference or need for a particular
outcome" (Judge and Bretz 1992: 264), and are central to decision
making (Judge and Bretz 1992) because they inform assessments of
outcomes as more or less desirable (Feather 1995; Rohan 2000). Building on Schwartz's (1992) universal types, Holland and Shepherd (2013)
found that these higher-order values – self-enhancement and openness
to change – influence entrepreneurs' decision making on whether to
persist with underperforming ventures in a number of ways.

First, in their study of 3,200 decisions nested within 100 entrepreneurs, Holland and Shepherd (2013) found that the greater the
expectations of future financial returns, the more likely the entrepreneur is to delay failure, but the strength of this relationship depends on
the entrepreneur's self-enhancement values. Self-enhancement values
"focus on the development of personal interests, even at the expense of
others if necessary" (Holland and Shepherd 2013). These personal interests are typically satisfied by the prominence gained through the firm's
financial success and subsequent wealth for the entrepreneur. In regard
to the nature of how self-enhancement values influence the decision to
persist, Holland and Shepherd's (2013) results suggest that future financial returns have a greater influence on the decision making of entrepreneurs who place high value on self-enhancement as a prominent
attribute in their life than they do for entrepreneurs who place less

---

[1] Entrepreneurs who were more extrinsically motivated were more likely to persist
based on personal investment, but this could be largely because personal investment
was represented in financial terms.

value on self-enhancement. Essentially, entrepreneurs with high levels of self-enhancement values will be more motivated by the potential for future financial returns to persist in their underperforming ventures than entrepreneurs with low levels of self-enhancement values.

Second, Holland and Shepherd (2013) also found that the value of openness to change impacts persistence decisions, but this time through its impact on the anticipation of non-financial benefits. Openness to change includes the values of stimulation, self-directing, and hedonism such that individuals high in openness to change "appreciate through action and thrive on the excitement and challenge of life" (Holland and Shepherd 2013: 339); they seek out experiences that are novel (Bardi, Calogero, and Mullen 2008) and give them freedom and autonomy (Amit, MacCrimmon, Zietsma, and Oesch 2001; Carter, Gartner, Shaver, and Gatewood 2003). Therefore, they are likely to focus on these attributes of the business when deciding to persist (despite poor performance). Evidence provided by Holland and Shepherd (2013) support the relationship between valuing openness to change and the influence of non-financial rewards on entrepreneurs' decisions to persist. Specifically, entrepreneurs who place higher value on openness to change as an important facet of their lives are more likely to place greater weight on non-financial returns when determining their decisions to persist with an underperforming venture. Therefore, even if the venture is underperforming from a financial perspective, as long as it still provides them with acceptable levels of non-financial benefits, entrepreneurs with higher values of openness to change will be more likely to persist rather than dissolve the venture.

CONSEQUENCES OF PERSISTING WITH A POORLY PERFORMING FIRM

Financial costs

Under the traditional economic model of persistence (Ansic and Pugh 1999), entrepreneurs should "persist only until the point of time when the current losses exceed the present value of expected profits"

(Shepherd et al. 2009: 136). The notion here is that if the business is performing this poorly, then investing additional resources is like "throwing good money after bad." It increases the amount of the loss when failure eventually occurs. Because entrepreneurs also often put their own personal funds at risk (Thorne 1989) – including personal guarantees for debt – the greater the loss, the deeper the financial hole the entrepreneur must climb out of to recover from the failure. The longer the entrepreneur persists with a poorly performing firm, the longer it will take him or her to recover from the failure when it eventually occurs (Shepherd et al. 2009).

Therefore, all the factors we discussed earlier that encourage procrastination and a lower performance threshold for "acceptable" performance are largely categorized (in the literature) as negative factors because they make financial recovery more difficult. However, there is more to recovery than solely the financial. Throughout the book, we have highlighted how grief can be generated by the death of a business and that this grief can obstruct learning from the experience and also decrease one's motivation to try again by starting a subsequent business. Recovery can be enhanced by emotion regulation that reduces grief. Interestingly, this process of reducing grief over the loss of a business can occur before the business is terminated. To understand this process, we return to the psychology literature on loss to explore the notion of anticipatory grief and the role it may play in promoting recovery from business failure (Shepherd et al. 2009).

Emotional costs

Anticipatory grief occurs before the loss event and will influence the level of grief one experiences after a loss actually occurs (Lindemann 1944; Parkes and Weiss 1983; Rando 1986). That is, the processes of mourning, coping, and psychosocial reorganization can be stimulated by the realization that a loss will occur despite the fact that it has not yet occurred (Rando 1986). These processes allow the individual to emotionally prepare for a loss by beginning to withdraw from the soon-to-be loss as a safeguard for the eventuality (Lindemann 1944;

Parkes and Weiss 1983). The individual can start to make sense of the loss because it is seen as a predictable outcome (Parkes and Weiss 1983), which helps him or her further break emotional bonds to what is being lost and make emotional investments elsewhere (Shepherd et al. 2009). For the entrepreneur, this may set up conflicting pulls. On one side, the entrepreneur must begin to withdraw from the business, such as by disentangling his or her personal identity from that of the business (Major and Schmader 1998; Major, Spencer, Schmader, Wolfe, and Crocker 1998). However, the business situation is one that draws the entrepreneur in to "put out the many fires" that arise in a failing business (Shepherd et al. 2009: 140).

Despite these conflicting pulls, evidence from the psychology literature suggests that some delay in termination gives the individual a chance to prepare for the loss, but interestingly, too much time appears to lead to poor psychological outcomes. For example, in a study of parents whose children died of cancer, those whose children experienced a moderate time of illness fared better than parents whose children had a short or long illness (Rando 1986). Presumably, the parents whose children only had a short illness did not have sufficient time to prepare for the loss. While those whose children had a long illness had time to prepare; yet, this extended period was emotionally exhausting, and the resulting resource depletion made post-death recovery difficult. Again, it is worth noting that we are in no way saying that the death of a child is the same as a business failure; we are simply saying that our knowledge of the psychological processes of one likely provide insight into the other.

Although entrepreneurs can be in denial that their business will fail right up until the event (and therefore have no anticipatory grieving), many appear to know that failure will eventually occur. Indeed, there are bankruptcy-prediction models based on standard accounting ratings. The breaching of these ratings thresholds signal that business failure will occur (at least with a very high probability) (Altman 1968; Ohlson 1980; Zmijewski 1984). Realizing that their business will eventually fail, entrepreneurs can grieve over things that have been lost now – for example, the dream of handing the business on to the next generation of the family – and can gain some insight into what that future will look like. This period of anticipation gives entrepreneurs the ability to prepare emotionally for the upcoming loss (Parkes and Weiss 1983), thereby allowing them to gradually extract their emotional energy from the failing venture. By providing the entrepreneur the opportunity to prepare to cope with the impending failure, this period of anticipatory grief can help mitigate the overall emotional costs eventually associated with the decision to terminate a failed venture. Therefore, this time between the realization that failure will occur and the time the business actually dies can be valuable in preparing for the loss.

Preparation involves some grief work – starting the processing of the loss experience (Bonanno and Keltner 1997; Prigerson et al. 1996; Wortman and Silver 1989, 1992) – but can also involve periods of a restoration orientation to gain the benefits of oscillation (Shepherd 2003; Stroebe and Schut 1999). Preparation helps reduce the level of grief once the loss occurs and therefore likely helps with the emotional recovery from business failure. This emotional recovery is important to remove obstacles to learning from the experience. To a large extent, this learning will be lost if the individual is unwilling to pursue a subsequent entrepreneurial business. To the extent that an individual experiences grief and/or can quickly eliminate that grief, he or she will be more motivated to try again. Therefore, although under the traditional economic model of termination, any persistence beyond a "rational" financial threshold is detrimental to recovery and decisions to persist are so-called "biased," overall recovery likely involves both financial and emotional recovery, to which we now turn.

OPTIMIZING RECOVERY FROM FIRM FAILURE

The proposed anticipatory grief model for prolonging the decision to terminate a failed venture centers on the need to balance the entrepreneur's financial and emotional expenditures with the hope of speeding the recovery from the failure experience. It is important to note that striking this balance is likely a heterogeneous experience both between individual entrepreneurs as well as within failures experienced by a single individual. From a financial wealth perspective, while it is possible that some entrepreneurs might have their personal wealth reduced substantially as a result of the failed venture, other entrepreneurs may have a large portion of their individual net worth protected from the failure event. For example, they might find that failure is a somewhat necessary "badge of honor" required in the eyes of venture capitalists in a certain industry, they might not have secured debt financing with personal guarantees throughout the course of developing their business, or they might simply operate a large diversified portfolio of business investments. All these factors would reduce the costs associated with failure assuming it happened without any attempts to prolong the termination decision. Nevertheless, despite minimization of the financial costs of business failure, if there is no delay in the decision to terminate, there is likely variance in the rate financial costs accumulate as a result of ever-longer delays in termination. Simply put, the financial costs of prolonging the failure decision are likely greater for some entrepreneurs than for others. For example, ventures with higher capital burn rates will require more substantial financial resources to prolong business failure than those with lower capital burn rates. Additionally, some industry-specific assets might depreciate more rapidly, translating to a faster depletion of the entrepreneur's residual claim on those business assets.

While the financial costs associated with prolonging failure are an important component to our anticipatory grief model, we have also argued that the grief entrepreneurs experience as a result of failure also influences their decisions to delay failure. Just as it is likely that the financial costs associated with failure are not uniform across all entrepreneurs, so too are the emotional costs related to failure; that is, entrepreneurs are heterogeneous in the emotional costs they experience from failure (for examples, see Chapter 2). Research has indicated that individuals experience higher levels of grief when they lose objects they perceive they have made considerable emotional investments to attain. This association between higher levels of grief and the loss of objects perceived to have higher emotional investments has most often been studied with regard to the loss of loved ones (e.g., significant others, parents, children, etc.) (Jacobs, Mazure, and Prigerson 2000; Robinson, Baker, and Nackerud 1999). These studies have revealed that individuals with strong emotional connections to objects of loss are more likely to experience more intense feelings of grief regarding the loss. Building off of this, it is likely that entrepreneurs will experience greater levels of grief regarding the failure of ventures they have owned and operated for a long period of time (consistent with the endowment effect [Van Boven, Dunning, and Loewenstein 2000]). Additionally, it is possible that experiencing numerous losses in rapid succession could result in an accumulation of grief for those involved in the losses (Nord 1996). Therefore, entrepreneurs of ventures that fail after several other similar failures will likely experience greater grief. Finally, evidence has shown that the greater the level of importance assigned to the failure, the higher the emotional response resulting from that event (Archer 1999). When entrepreneurs perceive that their businesses constitute an important component of their own self-identity, the failure of that business will often produce higher levels of grief. Consequently, it is possible that while some entrepreneurs will experience considerable grief as a result of their failed businesses, for others, this grief could be substantially less.

While our model proposes that a certain amount of delay in the decision to terminate a firm might result in reducing the levels of grief entrepreneurs experience as a result of business failure, it is possible that variance exists in both the extent to which entrepreneurs leverage this time period to actively engage in anticipatory grieving as well as the overall effectiveness of their efforts at accomplishing this task. For some entrepreneurs, this period of delay might be spent in denial about the overwhelming evidence suggesting that the business is destined to fail. These entrepreneurs engage in little or no anticipatory grieving, and so the delay does not provide the proposed benefits in terms of lessening subsequent grief. Additionally, some entrepreneurs might utilize this period to engage in anticipatory grieving, but they might not have the necessary skills required to accomplish this activity successfully.

Recent research has suggested that recovering from grief is optimized when individuals oscillate between periods focusing on the loss and working through the events leading up to the experience and periods of distraction, whereby individuals cease thinking about the loss and instead take time to address other sources of stress (Archer 1999; Shepherd, Patzelt, and Wolfe 2011). Therefore, while it is likely that a certain amount of persistence can enhance an entrepreneur's eventual recovery from business failure, the duration of this time period must be carefully considered to strike a balance between the emotional benefits and financial costs associated with such a delay in making the failure decision.

A graphical depiction of the financial, emotional, and total costs associated with the delay of business failure can be seen in Figure 4.3.

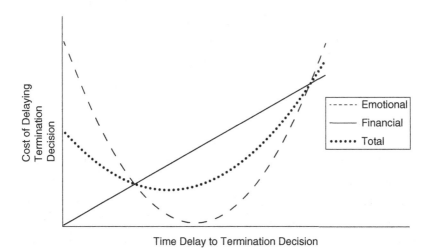

FIGURE 4.3: Costs associated with termination delay

DISCUSSION

Scholarly implications

What causes entrepreneurs to postpone the decision to terminate a business venture, knowing that such a delay will be financially costly? The most common rationale presented in the existing literature suggests that such a delay is merely the result of biased decision making and that engaging in such procrastination represents a simple error in entrepreneurial judgment. We offered an alternative perspective, suggesting that some amount of procrastination can actually be beneficial in assisting entrepreneurs in the recovery process. We recognized that venture failure is undoubtedly costly from a financial perspective and that higher financial losses equate to more challenging financial recoveries. However, we supplemented this purely financial rationale by discussing the role negative emotions regarding venture failure play as well as the significance of emotional recovery. It is to be expected that entrepreneurs might suffer grief over venture failure, which can in turn impede recovery. In detailing the concept of anticipatory grief, we theorized that a certain period of procrastination with regard to the termination of a failing business could in fact reduce the amount of grief experienced as a result of the failure event. Therefore, if overall recovery is conceptualized as a combination of both financial and emotional costs that occur as a result of business failure, our model of anticipatory grief offers a plausible explanation for the benefits of prolonging business failure – one based on considering the financial and emotional costs of failure in an attempt to optimize subsequent recovery. It is our belief that this anticipatory grief perspective regarding business failure provides several important implications for researchers.

First, this model provides an important counterpoint to both the economic and escalation research, which account for persistence in terms of biases and errors in judgment. We proposed that under certain conditions, some persistence prior to business failure can prove to be beneficial to entrepreneurs. This perspective could possibly reveal new areas of research regarding escalation of commitment. For instance, it alludes to the potential importance of extending the span of such studies beyond the scope of an individual project. It is possible that what is interpreted as a bias for one project could well prove beneficial to the individual over the course of a number of projects. Extending past the outcomes of a single project emphasizes the need to investigate dependent variables other than basic financial costs associated with persistence. We chose to focus on the potential emotional costs associated with business failure as well as the ramifications such costs might have on future emotional investments.

Second, although emotion is recognized as a potential cause of persistence throughout the procrastination literature, this persistence is almost uniformly viewed in the long run as a detriment to the individual. We proposed that given the roles emotion and emotional processing (e.g., anticipatory grief and grief) play in eventual recovery from failure, persistence could actually provide some long-term benefits. As a result, while certain entrepreneurs' persistence could be classified as procrastination, in other instances, this might be an improper characterization that is more appropriately rationalized by our anticipatory grief model. Specifically, prolonging business failure could provide a better balance between the financial and emotional costs associated with that failure, thereby optimizing eventual recovery. In order to distinguish between procrastination and anticipatory grief as the underlying cause of entrepreneurial persistence, it is necessary to consider the emotional inputs and outputs associated with the process. Our efforts along this front represent a small step in addressing the relative paucity of research on how the desire to reduce negative emotions can influence entrepreneurial activities.

Third, while it is not astonishing that business scholars have traditionally fixated on the financial costs of delaying business failure whereas scholars interested in grief have concentrated on the emotional aspects of loss, neither of these divergent streams of research has made much of an attempt to combine both aspects to provide a more comprehensive perspective of the consequences of business failure. Our anticipatory grief model highlights the importance of taking both into consideration in order to better understand how entrepreneurs recover after business failure. While the concepts of anticipatory grief and grief have been applied to situations of loss rather than just the loss of a loved one (Christopherson 1976; Roach and Kitson 1989), the emphasis of such research has remained almost exclusively on the emotional outcomes of such loss. With substantial care, we argued that perhaps there is an important financial element to consider in some loss situations. For instance, what factors do individuals consider when deciding to delay divorce? Does this decision have consequences on both their financial and their emotional recovery from such an occurrence? Research has suggested that some individuals do grieve in anticipation of divorce (Roach and Kitson 1989), and it is possible that some benefits can be gained by persisting for a certain period prior to divorce, essentially allowing for emotional preparation for when the actual event occurs. Regardless, we recognized there is a substantial amount of work to be done investigating the financial and emotional consequences of undergoing an important loss.

Fourth, our anticipatory grief model provides an important complement to the existing literature regarding grief experienced as a result of business failure. The seminal model proposed by Shepherd (2003) starts with the failure event and details how this event can elicit negative emotional responses. Our model introduces the idea that grief can occur in anticipation of venture failure, and this anticipatory grief can in turn impact the amount of grief experienced as a result of the business failure event. Moreover, Shepherd (2003) emphasized the importance of improving the grief-recovery process as a crucial component to maximizing the amount of learning that could be accomplished as a result of the failure event. Our model concentrates on how anticipatory grieving can serve to balance the financial and emotional costs of failure in order to optimize entrepreneurs' subsequent recovery.

Finally, recent research has called attention to the importance of the emotional bonds entrepreneurs form with their businesses. Evidence suggests that entrepreneurs make substantial emotional investments in their ventures (Cardon et al. 2005) and that entrepreneurs consider their businesses to be an important component of their individual identities (Downing 2005). For example, Cardon and colleagues (2005) invoked a renewed interest in the study of entrepreneurial passion and the role it plays in the entrepreneurial process. Although our research investigates the converse of passion (i.e., grief), it is our desire that future research continues to delve into the influence that both positive emotions (e.g., passion) and negative emotions (e.g., grief) can have on the entire entrepreneurial process.

Managerial implications

There are a number of important managerial implications that can be drawn from this chapter and offer critical insight into the entrepreneurial process of deciding to complete or delay the termination of an underperforming or failing business. First, it is important to note that the decision-making process involved in coming to the termination conclusion is non-uniform for both different entrepreneurs and for the same entrepreneur facing different situational contexts. Whereas failure and the decision to cease a failing business have most often been classified as simply a question of financial or economic losses, we provided a more nuanced representation of the various facets involved with this particular decision. There are in fact numerous factors that influence the decision to delay the termination of an underperforming venture, and while continued financial losses naturally factor into this equation, they are by no means the only – or in many cases the most significant – inputs that entrepreneurs must consider when making their ultimate failure decision.

Second, and building off of the previous notion that decisions to terminate businesses involve heterogeneous contexts, variations in terms of environmental landscapes are important factors to consider when facing the decision to delay business termination. Aspects of the external environment, such as complexity, dynamism, and munificence, can all substantially influence individuals' understanding of why they might consider delaying terminating a failed venture. Because the certainty of eventual outcomes is lower in complex environments, it is possible that individuals might forego the immediate termination of a failing business operating in such an environment in the hopes that their assessment of the eventual outcome was incorrect. Additionally, complex environments might offer greater levels of potential opportunities, which could in turn encourage entrepreneurs to delay business termination in the hopes of capitalizing on one of these alternative opportunities.

Environmental dynamism might also factor into the decision-making process when one is determining whether to end or delay terminating an entrepreneurial venture. Because dynamic environments are ever changing, it is possible that if an entrepreneur was to delay terminating a poorly performing venture, rapid future environmental shifts might result in a competitive landscape that is much more amenable for the struggling business. Therefore, it is possible that entrepreneurs operating firms in highly dynamic environments might be more apt to delay failure decisions. Similarly, highly munificent environments could also cause entrepreneurs to delay their decisions to terminate. Because munificent environments are rich in resources, it is possible that individuals operating ventures within such environments could be able to supplement their venture's poor performance with external resources, allowing them to delay the decision to terminate the venture.

Third, although environmental factors are important to consider when deciding whether or not to delay business termination, there are other intrinsic motivations that influence this process that can vary between individuals. Specifically, the need to justify previous decisions, the need to conform to norms for consistency, and perceptions of collective self-efficacy are all factors that affect this decision-making process. Because entrepreneurs invest substantial amounts of time, energy, and resources when establishing a new venture, it is likely that they form strong emotional and psychological connections between their personal identities and the new venture. As a result of these connections, it is possible that they view a failing business as a manifestation of their own failure that resulted from prior decisions they made while beginning and running the business. Therefore, in an attempt to justify their previous efforts and investments, entrepreneurs may delay making failure decisions, and the duration of this delay is likely enhanced with greater levels of personal investments (e.g., time, energy, money, etc.).

Likewise, the decision to delay terminating a failing business can also be affected by individuals' need to be perceived (by both themselves and by others) as being consistent. This need for consistency might lead entrepreneurs to place greater weight on information that reinforces the validity of continuing with their previous actions and activities while simultaneously discounting information suggesting that consistency might not lead to desired results. The results of this desire for consistency can produce bias, leading entrepreneurs to believe that if consistency produced the desired results in the past, then continued persistence will eventually result in similar outcomes. This overly optimistic perspective can also be influenced by the perceived collective self-efficacy that the entrepreneur has regarding the organization as a whole. If the entrepreneur senses that the organization's overall collective self-efficacy is relatively high, this might lead her or him to continue to operate the business in the face of counterfactual evidence. In other words, the prevailing logic that the business will eventually turn around simply because "the organizational team is good" can also result in an entrepreneur delaying the decision to terminate the venture in the hopes that future performance results will be different than historical evidence might suggest.

Fourth, the levels of specific types of extrinsic motivation can also affect the decision to delay the termination of a failing business. Perhaps the most obvious form of extrinsic motivation associated with entrepreneurial ventures is satisfaction with monetary compensation. The level of motivation provided by monetary compensation varies across individuals. However, individuals who are more highly motivated by monetary compensation are more likely to place greater weight on this factor above other environmental and intrinsic motivations when determining whether to persist with a failing venture.

Specifically, individuals with higher levels of motivation for monetary compensation are less likely to persist with ventures that do not provide them with sufficient returns in this area regardless of the other environmental (e.g., complexity, dynamism, and munificence) or intrinsic (e.g., need to justify previous decisions, norms for consistency, and collective self-efficacy) motivations present within the decision-making context.

Extrinsic motivation is also related to individuals' values regarding what they perceive as "right or wrong" as well as their preference for a particular outcome. Because the value of self-enhancement focuses on the accumulation and development of personal rewards, it is likely that entrepreneurs with higher levels of this value will persist with endeavors that they perceive have greater potential to provide them with future financial rewards. In other words, if an entrepreneur highly values self-enhancement and perceives that his or her business could provide substantial future financial rewards, he or she will likely delay the decision to terminate the business even if it is currently failing to meet the desired performance threshold. In a similar manner, individuals who value openness to change are motivated by non-financial rewards and are likely to persist with ventures they perceive as granting them higher levels of these non-financial benefits regardless of the ventures' current or future financial performance.

Fifth, although research has recognized that there are potential emotional consequences associated with persistence, the prevailing logic is that such persistence is ultimately detrimental to individuals in the long run. We took a slightly different perspective and proposed that persistence could in fact afford individuals some long-term benefits as a result of the role it plays in emotional coping and the processing of grief (both anticipatory and experiential). As a result, while some entrepreneurs' persistence might fall into the category of procrastination, thereby ultimately proving to be detrimental, others might utilize this delay in a more beneficial manner through anticipatory grief. This utilization of persistence could result in a better balance between the emotional and the financial costs associated with failure, allowing for better recovery from failure. In order to differentiate between procrastination and anticipatory grief, it is important to understand both the emotional inputs and outcomes associated with the entrepreneurial process.

Sixth, while business scholars have primarily focused on the financial consequences of failure and bereavement scholars tend to emphasize the emotional consequences that failure can produce, in this chapter, we hoped to stress the importance of considering and balancing both in order to maximize recovery from business failure. How much financial loss can be realized as a result of persisting with a failing venture? What are the emotional benefits reaped as a result of delaying termination, thereby allowing individuals to engage in anticipatory grieving, which reduces the overall emotional consequences associated with such failures? These are important questions to consider, and the attempt entrepreneurs make to strike a balance between these two factors is important to consider as it influences the decision-making process.

Finally, although the majority of the research regarding entrepreneurial failure centers on coping with the emotional consequences experienced after a failure event, this chapter offers a complementary perspective – looking at how emotions can be influenced by processes entrepreneurs engaged in prior to the actual failure event. By persisting in a failing venture, it is possible that entrepreneurs gain time to engage in anticipatory grieving. This process of anticipatory grief can be a vital component in mitigating the overall emotional consequences associated with failure and can therefore be crucial in optimizing entrepreneurs' ability to eventually cope with and recover from failure experiences.

REFERENCES

Aldrich, H. E. 1979. *Organizations and Environments*. Englewood Cliffs, NJ: Prentice-Hall.
Altman, E. I. 1968. Financial ratios, discriminant analysis and the prediction of corporate bankruptcy. *The Journal of Finance*, 23(4): 589–609.

Amir, N., Coles, M. E., Brigidi, B., and Foa, E. B. 2001. The effect of practice on recall of emotional information in individuals with generalized social phobia. *Journal of Abnormal Psychology*, 110(1): 76–82.

Amit, R., MacCrimmon, K. R., Zietsma, C., and Oesch, J. M. 2001. Does money matter?: Wealth attainment as the motive for initiating growth-oriented technology ventures. *Journal of Business Venturing*, 16(2): 119–143.

Anderson, C. J. 2003a. The psychology of doing nothing: Forms of decision avoidance result from reason and emotion. *Psychological Bulletin*, 129(1): 139–167.

Anderson, M. C. 2003e. Rethinking interference theory: Executive control and the mechanisms of forgetting. *Journal of Memory and Language*, 49: 415–445.

Ansic, D. and Pugh, G. 1999. An experimental test of trade hysteresis: Market exit and entry decisions in the presence of sunk costs and exchange rate uncertainty. *Applied Economics*, 31(4): 427–436.

Archer, J. 1999. *The Nature of Grief: The Evolution and Psychology of Reactions to Loss*. New York: Routledge.

Audia, P. G., Locke, E. A., and Smith, K. G. 2000. The paradox of success: An archival and a laboratory study of strategic persistence following radical environmental change. *Academy of Management Journal*, 43(5): 837–853.

Baden-Fuller, C. W. F. 1989. Exit from declining industries and the case of steel castings. *The Economic Journal*, 99(398): 949–961.

Bandura, A. 1982. Self-efficacy mechanism in human agency. *American Psychologist*, 37: 122–147.

Bandura, A. 2000. Exercise of human agency through collective efficacy. *Current Directions in Psychological Science*, 9(3): 75–78.

Bardi, A., Calogero, R. M., and Mullen, B. 2008. A new archival approach to the study of values and value – Behavior relations: Validation of the value lexicon. *Journal of Applied Psychology*, 93(3): 483–497.

Baron, R. A. and Tang, J. 2011. The role of entrepreneurs in firm-level innovation: Joint effects of positive affect, creativity, and environmental dynamism. *Journal of Business Venturing*, 26(1): 49–60.

Beard, D. W. and Dess, G. G. 1979. Industry profitability and firm performance: A preliminary analysis of the business portfolio question. *Academy of Management Proceedings*: 123–127.

Bluedorn, A. C. 1993. Pilgrim's progress: Trends and convergence in research on organizational size and environments. *Journal of Management*, 19(2): 163–191.

Bonanno, G. A. and Keltner, D. 1997. Facial expressions of emotion and the course of conjugal bereavement. *Journal of Abnormal Psychology*, 106(1): 126–137.

Bourgeois, L. J., III and Eisenhardt, K. M. 1987. Strategic decision processes in Silicon Valley: The anatomy of a "living dead". *California Management Review*, 30(1): 143–159.

Brief, A. P. and Aldag, R. J. 1977. The intrinsic-extrinsic dichotomy: Toward conceptual clarity. *Academy of Management Review*, 2(3): 496.

Brown, S. L. and Eisenhardt, K. M. 1997. The art of continuous change: Linking complexity theory and time-paced evolution in relentlessly shifting organizations. *Administrative Science Quarterly*, 42(1): 1–34.

Bruno, A. V., McQuarrie, E. F., and Torgrimson, C. G. 1992. The evolution of new technology ventures over 20 years: Patterns of failure, merger, and survival. *Journal of Business Venturing*, 7: 291–302.

Busenitz, L. W. and Barney, J. B. 1997. Differences between entrepreneurs and managers in large organizations: Biases and heuristics in strategic decision-making. *Journal of Business Venturing*, 12(1): 9–30.

Byrne, O. and Shepherd, D. A. 2015. Different strokes for different folks: Entrepreneurial narratives of emotion, cognition, and making sense of business failure. *Entrepreneurship Theory and Practice*, 39(2): 375–405.

Caldini, R. B. 1993. *Influence: Science and Practice* (3rd ed.). New York: Harper-Collins College Publishers.

Campbell, C. A. 1992. A decision theory model for entrepreneurial acts. *Entrepreneurship Theory and Practice*, 17(1): 21–27.

Campbell, C. A. 1995. An empirical test of a decision theory model for entrepreneurial acts. *Entrepreneurship and Regional Development*, 7: 95–103.

Cardon, M. S., Zietsma, C., Saparito, P., Matherne, B. P., and Davis, C. 2005. A tale of passion: New insights into entrepreneurship from a parenthood metaphor. *Journal of Business Venturing*, 20(1): 23–45.

Carter, N. M., Gartner, W. B., Shaver, K. G., and Gatewood, E. J. 2003. The career reasons of nascent entrepreneurs. *Journal of Business Venturing*, 18(1): 13–39.

Chen, C. C., Greene, P. G., and Crick, A. 1998. Does entrepreneurial self-efficacy distinguish entrepreneurs from managers? *Journal of Business Venturing*, 13(4): 295–316.

Christopherson, L. K. 1976. Cardiac transplant: Preparation for dying or for living. *Health and Social Work*, 1(1): 58–72.

Cotton, J. L. and Tuttle, J. M. 1986. Employee turnover: A meta-analysis and review with implications for research. *Academy of Management Review*, 11(1): 55–70.

Cova, B. and Svanfeldt, C. 1993. Societal innovations and the postmodern aestheticization of everyday life. *International Journal of Research in Marketing*, 10: 297–310.

Dess, G. G. and Beard, D. W. 1984. Dimensions of organizational task environments. *Administrative Science Quarterly*, 29(1): 52–73.

DeTienne, D. R., Shepherd, D. A., and De Castro, J. O. 2008. The fallacy of "only the strong survive": The effects of extrinsic motivation on the persistence decisions for under-performing firms. *Journal of Business Venturing*, 23(5): 528–546.

Dobrev, S. D. and Barnett, W. P. 2005. Organizational roles and transition to entrepreneurship. *Academy of Management Journal*, 48(3): 433–449.

Dodd, S. D. 2002. Metaphors and meaning: A grounded cultural model of US entrepreneurship. *Journal of Business Venturing*, 17(5): 519–535.

Downing, S. 2005. The social construction of entrepreneurship: Narrative and dramatic processes in the coproduction of organizations and identities. *Entrepreneurship Theory and Practice*, 29(2): 185–204.

Ensley, M. D., Pearce, C. L., and Hmieleski, K. M. 2006. The moderating effect of environmental dynamism on the relationship between entrepreneur leadership behavior and new venture performance. *Journal of Business Venturing*, 21(2): 243–263.

Feather, N. T. 1995. Values, valences, and choice: The influences of values on the perceived attractiveness and choice of alternatives. *Journal of Personality and Social Psychology*, 68(6): 1135–1151.

Forbes, D. P. 2005. Managerial determinants of decision speed in new ventures. *Strategic Management Journal*, 26(4): 355–366.

Forys, K. L. and Dahlquist, L. M. 2007. The influence of preferred coping style and cognitive strategy on laboratory-induced pain. *Health Psychology*, 26(1): 22–29.

Garland, H., Sandefur, C., and Rogers, A. 1990. De-escalation of commitment in oil exploration: When sunk losses and negative feedback coincide. *Journal of Applied Psychology*, 75: 721–727.

Gimeno, J., Folta, T. B., Cooper, A. C., and Woo, C. Y. 1997. Survival of the fittest? Entrepreneurial human capital and the persistence of underperforming firms. *Administrative Science Quarterly*, 42(4): 750–783.

Gist, M. E. 1987. Self-efficacy: Implications for organizational behavior and human resource management. *Academy of Management Review*, 12(3): 472–485.

Goddard, R. D., Hoy, W. K., and Hoy, A. W. 2004. Collective efficacy beliefs: Theoretical developments, empirical evidence, and future directions. *Educational Researcher*, 33(3): 3–13.

Goll, I. and Rasheed, A. A. 2005. The relationships between top management demographic characteristics, rational decision making, environmental munificence, and firm performance. *Organization Studies*, 26(7): 999–1023.

Greve, H. R. 2002. Sticky aspirations: Organizational time perspective and competitiveness. *Organization Science*, 13(1): 1–17.

Hayward, M. L. A., Shepherd, D. A., and Griffin, D. 2005. A hubris theory of entrepreneurship. *Management Science*, 52(2): 160–172.

Hayward, M. L. A., Forster, W. R., Sarasvathy, S. D., and Fredrickson, B. L. 2009. Beyond hubris: How highly confident entrepreneurs rebound to venture again. *Journal of Business Venturing*, 25(6): 569–578.

Hitt, M. A., Ireland, R. D., Sirmon, D. G., and Trahms, C. A. 2011. Strategic entrepreneurship: Creating value for individuals, organizations, and society. *Academy of Management Perspectives*, 25(2): 57–75.

Hmieleski, K. M. and Baron, R. A. 2008. Regulatory focus and new venture performance: A study of entrepreneurial opportunity exploitation under conditions of risk versus uncertainty. *Strategic Entrepreneurship Journal*, 2(4): 285–299.

Hodges, L. and Carron, A. V. 1992. Collective efficacy and group performance. *International Journal of Sport Psychology*, 23(1): 48–59.

Holland, D. V. and Shepherd, D. A. 2013. Deciding to persist: Adversity, values, and entrepreneurs' decision policies. *Entrepreneurship Theory and Practice*, 37(2): 331–358.

Jackofsky, E. F. and Peters, L. H. 1983. The hypothesized effects of ability in the turnover process. *Academy of Management Review*, 8(1): 46–49.

Jacobs, S., Mazure, C., and Prigerson, H. 2000. Diagnostic criteria for traumatic grief. *Death Studies*, 24(3): 185–199.

Johnston, M. W., Parasuraman, A., Futrell, C. M., and Black, W. C. 1990. A longitudinal assessment of the impact of selected organizational influences on salespeople's organizational commitment during early employment. *Journal of Marketing Research*, 17: 333–334.

Judge, T. A. and Bretz, R. D. 1992. Effects of work values on job choice decisions. *Journal of Applied Psychology*, 77(3): 261–271.

Kahneman, D. and Tversky, A. 1979. Prospect theory: An analysis of decision under risk. *Econometrica*, 47(2): 263–291.

Karakaya, F. 2000. Market exit and barriers to exit: Theory and practice. *Psychology and Marketing*, 17(8): 651–668.

Kuratko, D. F., Hornsby, J. S., and Naffziger, D. W. 1997. An examination of owner's goals in sustaining entrepreneurship. *Journal of Small Business Management*, 35(1): 24–33.

Lazarus, R. S. and Folkman, S. 1984. *Stress, Appraisal, and Coping*. New York: Springer.

Lent, R. W., Brown, S. D., and Larkin, K. C. 1984. Relation of self-efficacy expectations to academic achievement and persistence. *Journal of Counseling Psychology*, 31(3): 356–362.

Levinthal, D. A. and March, J. G. 1993. The myopia of learning. *Strategic Management Journal*, 14: 95–112.

Li, M. and Simerly, R. L. 1998. The moderating effect of environmental dynamism on the ownership and performance relationship. *Strategic Management Journal,* 19(2): 169–179.

Lindemann, E. 1944. Symptomatology and management of acute grief. *American Journal of Psychiatry,* 101: 141–148.

Little, B. L. and Madigan, R. M. 1997. The relationship between collective efficacy and performance in manufacturing work teams. *Small Group Research,* 28(4): 517–534.

Major, B. and Schmader, T. 1998. Coping with stigma through psychological disengagement. In J. Swim and C. Stangor (eds.), *Prejudice: The Target's Perspective:* 219–241. New York: Academic.

Major, B., Spencer, S., Schmader, T., Wolfe, C., and Crocker, J. 1998. Coping with negative stereotypes about intellectual performance: The role of psychological disengagement. *Personality and Social Psychology Bulletin,* 24(1): 34–50.

March, J. G. and Simon, H. A. 1958. *Organizations.* Oxford, England: Wiley.

McCarthy, A. M., Schoorman, F. D., and Cooper, A. C. 1993. Reinvestment decisions by entrepreneurs: Rational decision-making or escalation of commitment? *Journal of Business Venturing,* 8(1): 9–24.

McGrath, R. G. and Cardon, M. S. 1997. *Entrepreneurship and the Functionality of Failure.* Seventh Annual Global Entrepreneurship Research Conference. Montreal, Canada.

Meyer, M. W. and Zucker, L. G. 1989. *Permanently Failing Organizations.* Newbury Park, CA: Sage.

Milgram, N. A., Sroloff, B., and Rosenbaum, M. 1988. The procrastination of everyday life. *Journal of Research in Personality,* 22: 197–212.

Monahan, J. and Silver, E. 2003. Judicial decision thresholds for violence risk management. *International Journal of Forensic Mental Health,* 2(1): 1–6.

Multon, K. D., Brown, S. D., and Lent, R. W. 1991. Relation of self-efficacy beliefs to academic outcomes: A meta-analytic investigation. *Journal of Counseling Psychology,* 38: 30–38.

Myers, L. B., Brewin, C. R., and Power, M. J. 1998. Repressive coping and the directed forgetting of emotional material. *Journal of Abnormal Psychology,* 107(1): 141–148.

Nord, D. 1996. Issues and implications in the counseling of survivors of multiple AIDS-related loss. *Death Studies,* 20: 389–413.

Northcraft, G. B. and Wolf, G. 1984. Dollars, sense, and sunk costs: A life cycle model of resource allocation decisions. *Academy of Management Review,* 9(2): 225–234.

O'Brien, J. P., Folta, T. B., and Johnson, D. R. 2003. A real options perspective on entrepreneurial entry in the face of uncertainty. *Managerial and Decision Economics*, 24(8): 515–533.

Ohlson, J. A. 1980. Financial ratios and the probabilistic prediction of bankruptcy. *Journal of Accounting Research*, 18(1): 109–131.

Parkes, C. and Weiss, R. 1983. *Recovery from Bereavement*. New York: Basic Books.

Phillips, D. J. 2002. A genealogical approach to organizational life chances: The parent-progeny transfer among Silicon Valley law firms, 1946–1996. *Administrative Science Quarterly*, 47: 474–506.

Pierce, J. L., Kostova, T., and Dirks, K. T. 2001. Toward a theory of psychological ownership in organizations. *Academy of Management Review*, 26(2): 298–310.

Priem, R. L., Rasheed, A. M. A., and Kotulic, A. G. 1995. Rationality in strategic decision processes, environmental dynamism and firm performance. *Journal of Management*, 21(5): 913–929.

Prigerson, H. G., Shear, M. K., Newsom, J. T., Frank, E., III, C. F. R., Maciejewski, P. K., Houck, P. R., Bierhals, A. J., and Kupfer, D. J. 1996. Anxiety among widowed elders: Is it distinct from depression and grief?*Anxiety*, 2(1): 1–12.

Rando, T. A. 1986. *Loss and Anticipatory Grief*. Lexington, MA: D. C. Heath.

Rauch, A., Wiklund, J., Lumpkin, G. T., and Frese, M. 2009. Entrepreneurial orientation and business performance: An assessment of past research and suggestions for the future. *Entrepreneurship Theory and Practice*, 33(3): 761–787.

Roach, M. J. and Kitson, G. C. 1989. Impact of forewarning on adjustment to widowhood and divorce. In Dale A. Lund (ed.), *Older Bereaved Spouses: Research with Practical Applications*: 185–200. New York: Hemisphere.

Robinson, M., Baker, L., and Nackerud, L. 1999. The relationship of attachment theory and perinatal loss. *Death Studies*, 23(3): 297–304.

Rohan, M. J. 2000. A rose by any name? The values construct. *Personality and Social Psychology Review*, 4(3): 255–277.

Ross, J. and Staw, B. M. 1986. Expo 86: An escalation prototype. *Administrative Science Quarterly*, 31(2): 274–297.

Ross, J. and Staw, B. M. 1993. Organizational escalation and exit: Lessons from the Shoreham Nuclear Power Plan. *Academy of Management Journal*, 36(4): 701–732.

Ruhnka, J. C., Feldman, H. D., and Dean, T. J. 1992. The "living dead" phenomenon in venture capital investments. *Journal of Business Venturing*, 7(2): 137–155.

Schneider, S. K. 1992. Governmental response to disasters: The conflict between bureaucratic procedures and emergent norms. *Public Administration Review*, 52(2): 135–145.

Schumpeter, J. A. 1961. *The Theory of Economic Development: An Inquiry into Profits, Capital, Credit, Interest and the Business Cycle.* New York: Oxford Press.

Schwartz, S. H. 1992. Universals in the content and structure of values: Theoretical advances and empirical tests in 20 countries. In M. P. Zanna (ed.), *Advances in Experimental Social Psychology*, Vol. 25: 1–65. Orlando, FL: Academic.

Shepherd, D. A. 2003. Learning from business failure: Propositions of grief recovery for the self-employed. *Academy of Management Review*, 28(2): 318–328.

Shepherd, D. A. and DeTienne, D. R. 2005. The impact of prior knowledge and potential financial reward on the identification of opportunities. *Entrepreneurship Theory and Practice*, 29(1): 91–112.

Shepherd, D. A., McMullen, J. S., and Jennings, P. D. 2007. The formation of opportunity beliefs: Overcoming ignorance and reducing doubt. *Strategic Entrepreneurship Journal*, 1(1–2): 75–95.

Shepherd, D. A., Wiklund, J., and Haynie, J. M. 2009. Moving forward: Balancing the financial and emotional costs of business failure. *Journal of Business Venturing*, 24(2): 134–148.

Shepherd, D. A., Patzelt, H., and Wolfe, M. T. 2011. Moving forward from project failure: Negative emotions, affective commitment and learning from the experience. *Academy of Management Journal*, 54(6): 1229–1259.

Simerly, R. L. and Li, M. 2000. Environmental dynamism, capital structure and performance: A theoretical integration and an empirical test. *Strategic Management Journal*, 21(1): 31–49.

Starbuck, W. H. 1976. Organizations and their environments. In M. D. Dunnette (ed.), *Handbook of Industrial and Organizational Psychology*: 1069–1123. Chicago, IL: Rand McNally.

Staw, B. M. and Fox, F. V. 1977. Escalation: The determinants of commitment to a chosen course of action. *Human Relations*, 30(5): 431–450.

Staw, B. M. and Ross, J. 1980. Commitment in an experimenting society: An experiment on the attribution of leadership from administrative scenarios. *Journal of Applied Psychology*, 65: 249–260.

Staw, B. M. 1981. The escalation of commitment to a course of action. *The Academy of Management Review*, 6(4): 577–587.

Stroebe, M. and Schut, H. 1999. The dual process model of coping with bereavement: Rationale and description. *Death Studies*, 23(3): 197–224.

Thorne, J. R. 1989. Alternative financing for entrepreneurial ventures. *Entrepreneurship Theory and Practice*, Spring: 7–9.

Van Boven, L., Dunning, D., and Loewenstein, G. 2000. Egocentric empathy gaps between owners and buyers: Misperceptions of the endowment effect. *Journal of Personality and Social Psychology*, 79(1): 66–76.

van Eerde, W. 2003. A meta-analytically derived nomological network of procrastination. *Personality and Individual Differences*, 35(6): 1401–1418.

van Witteloostuijn, A. 1998. Bridging behavioral and economic theories of decline: Organizational inertia, strategic competition, and chronic failure. *Management Science*, 44(4): 501–519.

Wagner, S. H., Parker, C. P., and Christiansen, N. D. 2003. Employees that think and act like owners: Effects of ownership beliefs and behaviors on organizational effectiveness. *Personnel Psychology*, 56(4): 847–871.

Waldman, D. A., Ramirez, G. G., House, R. J., and Puranam, P. 2001. Does leadership matter? CEO leadership attributes and profitability under conditions of perceived environmental uncertainty. *Academy of Management Journal*, 44(1): 134–143.

Wasserman, N. 2003. Founder-CEO succession and the paradox of entrepreneurial success. *Organization Science*, 14(2): 149–172.

Wiersema, M. F. and Bantel, K. A. 1993. Top management team turnover as an adaptation mechanism: The role of the environment. *Strategic Management Journal*, 14(7): 485–504.

Wiklund, J. and Shepherd, D. A. 2005. Entrepreneurial orientation and small business performance: A configurational approach. *Journal of Business Venturing*, 20(1): 71–91.

Wortman, C. B. and Silver, R. C. 1989. The myths of coping with loss. *Journal of Consulting and Clinical Psychology*, 57(3): 349–357.

Wortman, C. B. and Silver, R. C. 1992. Reconsidering assumptions about coping with loss: An overview of current research. In L. Montada, S. H. Filipp, and M. S. Lerner (eds.), *Life Crises and Experiences of Loss in Adulthood*: 341–365. Hillsdale, NJ: Erlbaum.

Zmijewski, M. E. 1984. Methodological issues related to the estimation of financial distress prediction models. *Journal of Accounting Research*, 22: 59–82.

5   Delaying project failure as creeping death

In the previous chapter, we explained persistence (and its flipside, delay) with a failing business. We now turn our attention to the decision to terminate entrepreneurial projects within an organization. Central to the notion of entrepreneurship is the pursuit of potential opportunities, and these potential opportunities exist (or are created) in environments of high uncertainty (McMullen and Shepherd 2006). Entrepreneurial organizations manage this uncertainty (Brown and Eisenhardt 1997; McGrath 1999) by using experiments to probe the environment in order to reveal information about the "potential" of an entrepreneurial project. This information can be used to terminate poorly performing projects quickly and redeploy resources to those projects that show promise.

Although failure refers to "the termination of an initiative to create value that has fallen short of its goals" (Hoang and Rothaermel 2005; McGrath 1999; Shepherd, Patzelt, and Wolfe 2011), these failed projects are a valuable source of information from which organizational members (and the organization as a whole) can learn (McGrath 1999; Shepherd and Cardon 2009; Sitkin 1992). Project failures signal that there was something wrong with the initial conjecture and that there is therefore a need to adjust one's belief system (Chuang and Baum 2003; Sitkin 1992). Failures also tend to motivate individuals to find their underlying cause as a basis for a solution (Ginsberg 1988; McGrath 2001; Morrison 2002; Petroski 1985). It is for these reasons that it is often argued that individuals learn more from their failures than their successes (Petroski 1985; Popper 1959).

However, despite the importance of learning from failure and the potential to do so, most organizational members (and organizations) find it difficult (Cannon and Edmondson 2005). Indeed, in this book, we have highlighted many of the cognitive and emotional obstacles to learning from failure. We have also provided some recommendations on how these obstacles can be reduced or eliminated. In the previous chapter, we explored how the timing of business termination can influence an entrepreneur's emotional recovery – namely, some delay provides emotional preparation that enhances recovery, but too much delay likely contributes to emotional exhaustion that hinders recovery. In this chapter, we build on an inductive study of projects in a large multinational organization (Shepherd, Patzelt, Williams, and Warnecke 2014) to explore the role of termination timing.

In exploring new insights into the emotions of failure and the implications for learning from the failure experience, we highlight differences in reactions and learning responses to failure. Specifically, we explore differences in reactions to failure for those working on a terminated project (i.e., those who "are the option") as opposed to those who make the decision to terminate a project (i.e., those who "own the option") (McGrath, Ferrier, and Mendelow 2004: 96). By doing so, we gain a deeper understanding of the mechanisms connecting the speed of a project's termination to team members' learning from the failure experience. Prior studies have paid primary attention to those who own the option; however, in this chapter, we build on recent research that has begun to address the research question regarding those who are the option.

Research on learning from failure and project-termination timing have advanced on relatively independent tracks (the exception being from the cognitive perspective of the decision maker or owner of the option [see Corbett et al. 2007]). This is interesting as both research streams are viewed as critical in explaining how entrepreneurial organizations function successfully under uncertainty (McGrath 1999; Meyer and Zucker 1989; vanWitteloostuijn 1998). In this section of the chapter, we briefly review each of these literature streams.

LEARNING FROM FAILURE

Failure is an important signal that can generate action in that it suggests a disconnect between one's beliefs and reality (Chuang and Baum 2003; Sitkin 1992) and can drive exploration for solutions to address this disconnect (Ginsberg 1988; McGrath 2001; Morrison 2002; Petroski 1985). Given the salience of a failure event, it is believed that failure can uniquely motivate individuals to acquire new knowledge and that individuals gain greater insights from failure than successes (Petroski 1985; Popper 1959). In a project setting, learning from failure likely occurs when projects "(1) result from thoughtfully planned actions, (2) have uncertain outcomes, (3) are of modest scale, (4) are executed and responded to with alacrity, and (5) take place in domains that are familiar enough to permit effective learning" (Sitkin 1992: 243).

While learning from failure is nearly universally accepted as critical for growth and development, most organizations and individuals within organizations find learning from failure to be difficult (Cannon and Edmondson 2005). Information revealed in a failure event can be difficult to process effectively, thereby reducing learning (Weick 1990; Weick and Sutcliffe 2007). While research has provided a deeper understanding of the organizational challenges associated with learning from failure (e.g., reward systems that punish [Sitkin 1992] or even stigmatize [Cannon and Edmondson 2005] failure), additional research has highlighted individual obstacles to learning from failure events. Within this stream of research, attribution theory is frequently used to explain cognitive reactions to failure (Sitkin 1992). Attribution theory suggests that when an individual succeeds, he or she attributes that success to internal or personal actions, whereas when a failure event occurs, the individual attributes that failure to other sources, such as the environment or uncontrollable external factors (Wagner and Gooding 1997). These types of attributions (i.e., success to the self and failure to others) enable individuals to protect and maintain high self-esteem; however, this attribution bias obstructs learning as individuals distance themselves from failure events, considering the causes of those events to be beyond their influence (Reich 1949). Despite this bias, some research has found that over time (i.e., sometime subsequent to the failure event), individuals are more likely to come to attribute failures to internal causes (Frank and Gilovich 1989), taking more responsibility for the failure (Pronin and Ross 2006) and thus potentially removing key obstacles to learning.

While cognitive factors like the external attribution of failure provide one set of obstacles to learning, research has also focused on emotions associated with failure and how they impose obstacles to learning. Research and development (R&D) projects can be incredibly important to team members, and if it is important to an individual, the project's failure can generate negative emotional reactions – namely, grief (Shepherd and Cardon 2009; Shepherd, Covin, and Kuratko 2009; Shepherd et al. 2011: see also Chapters 1, 2, and 3 in this book). While not all negative emotions produce undesirable outcomes (e.g., negative emotions can drive individuals to seek an explanation for why the failure occurred, which is a critical step for learning) (Cyert and March 1963; Kiesler and Sproull 1982), they can disrupt or interfere with the information processing or attention allocation needed for learning to occur from the failure experience (consistent with Bower 1992; Fredrickson 2001).

Specifically, prior research has identified three adverse learning outcomes associated with negative emotions. First, negative emotions "narrow individuals' momentary thought-action repertoire by calling forth specific action tendencies (e.g., attack, flee) ... [whereas] many positive emotions broaden individuals' momentary thought-action repertoires, prompting them to pursue a wider range of thoughts and actions than is typical" (Fredrickson and Branigan 2005: 314). In creative-minded groups, such as R&D departments, the "narrowing" effect of negative emotions could be extremely counterproductive in developing novel innovations (Fredrickson and Branigan 2005).

Second, negative emotions can adversely impact individuals' affective commitment to their organization, which in turn reduces their willingness to invest personal resources toward the realization of organization-specific goals (Allen and Meyer 1990; O'Reilly and Chatman 1986; Shepherd et al. 2011). Affective commitment is important as it can increase organizational performance (Gong, Law, Chang, and Xin 2009), but it must be balanced with other factors, such as learning from failure, as learning can also increase organizational performance (McGrath 1999).

Finally, negative emotions "narrow people's attention, making them miss the forest for the trees" (Fredrickson 2001: 222), thereby disrupting both their creative and integrative thinking (Estrada, Isen, and Young 1997; Fredrickson and Branigan 2005; Isen, Daubman, and Nowicki 1987) as well as learning (Fredrickson and Branigan 2005; Masters, Barden, and Ford, 1979). Focusing their attention on the loss, including the excruciating details of the loss, individuals have little attentional capacity left to focus on learning and improving.

In sum, the key conclusion from the literature on learning from failure is that negative emotions impose substantial obstacles to learning from project failure.

SPEED OF PROJECT TERMINATION

Just as it is important for individuals to find a balance when terminating a failing business, which we discussed in Chapter 3, so too is it important for organizations to manage the timing of terminating failing projects. For corporations investing in innovative projects, it is critical to balance when to advance such projects through a substantial commitment of resources and when to "cut one's losses" by terminating projects that do not live up to expectations (Brown and Eisenhardt 1997; Green and Welsh 2003; McGrath 1999; Pinto and Prescott 1990). As organizations consider whether, when, and how to terminate a failing project, they face the challenge of "bounding" the failure. Extant literature, specifically from economics, has suggested that failure (and its costs) is bounded by rapidly terminating projects that fail to achieve the desired objectives (i.e., rapid cessation of project activities) and quickly reassigning resources (e.g., personal, financial, etc.) to more promising endeavors (Ansic and Pugh 1999; Ohlson 1980).

The rapid termination of projects, however, is not always easy to achieve, especially when there is ambiguity surrounding current performance and future potential as well as surrounding the severity of the consequences of termination (Staw and Ross 1987). In addition, rapid termination can increase personal responsibility for the project initiator (Staw, Barsade, and Koput 1997) or can be held up by non-performance-related forces, such as political or institutional factors that "force" the continuation of a project (Guler 2007).

Similarly, delayed termination is often attributed to continued hope for future payout despite ongoing project underachievement (including sunk cost arguments) (Arkes and Blumer 1985; Dixit and Pindyck 2008), escalation of commitment (Brockner 1992; Garland, Sandefur, and Rogers 1990), and decision-making procrastination (Anderson 2003; Van Eerde 2000: also see Chapter 4). Key projects, especially important innovation projects that are considered "the future" of an organization, are thus often continued long after they are considered lost causes, holding up critical resources that could have otherwise been redeployed (Arkes and Blumer 1985). For example, the Long Island Lighting Company delayed the termination of a key project (Shoreham Nuclear Power Plant) for more than twenty-three years, with costs rising from an initial estimate of $75 million to more than $5 billion, at which point the project was finally abandoned (Ross and Staw 1993). While this example is shocking, the reasons are similar to those of smaller-scale projects that managers struggle to terminate, including managers' history of success, information-processing errors, institutionalization and politicization of the project within the organization, and external justification requirements (Ross and Staw 1993).

Given the risks associated with prolonging failing projects, organizations have introduced a variety of measures to assist with "pulling the plug" and facilitating rapid termination. For example, some organizations implement performance-monitoring systems that might include hitting key milestones as a means of assessing commercial or technical progress (Pinto and Prescott 1988). These "stage-gate" processes are designed to assist managers in shutting down projects that fall below predetermined performance thresholds (Cooper 2008). Despite the tools used to assist organizations in making decisions regarding projects, such decisions are still made by individual managers who are subject to political, psychological, social, and other contextual factors that might result in prolonging projects beyond what is reasonable or rational (Green, Welsh, and Dehler 2003; Schmidt and Calantone 1998).

To summarize, despite "rational" explanations for when and how projects should be terminated, there is considerable variance in how the termination process actually occurs (i.e., how quickly projects are terminated and resources are redeployed). A particularly poignant gap in the extant literature is a lack of understanding regarding the link between termination speed and its influence (if any) on individual team members, specifically their ability to learn from the failure event. In this chapter, we build on some of our recent research to address this gap and provide new insights regarding how the timing of termination influences both emotional and learning outcomes for individual team members.

TERMINATION TIMING AND LEARNING FROM FAILURE

This chapter is largely based on our recent study of eight failed projects across four subsidiaries of a large R&D-intensive multinational organization (Shepherd et al. 2014). The organization has more than 50,000 employees, has sales of more than $20 billion, and spends approximately $1 billion annually on R&D investments. Given its scope of R&D projects, many projects are terminated each year, which provides an ideal setting for gaining a deeper understanding of the nature of the relationship between learning from failure and termination speed.

In this study, we found that delaying the termination of an entrepreneurial project was like a double-edged sword. On one edge of the
sword, organizational members perceived delaying project termination
as "creeping death," which triggered a negative emotional reaction. On
the other edge of the sword, delaying project termination provided
organizational members the time to reflect, articulate, and codify their
learning from the project experience. In contrast, those organizational
members' whose projects were rapidly terminated had few negative
emotional reactions to the failure, but also learned little from the
experience because they quickly moved on, emotionally and cognitively, to new engineering challenges represented by the new projects
to which they were deployed. We now explore these issues in detail.

LEARNING FROM PROJECT EXPERIENCES

While research has shown that groups (i.e., organizations and teams)
are capable of learning (Fiol and Lyles 1985), we focused on the learning
outcomes of individual team members. We found that variance
occurred both between and within subsidiaries of this large multinational organization. We grouped cases initially based on the degree
of learning achieved on each project. For example, the manager of one
project learned important skills for organizing a team effectively:

> [In the future,] I would lead this project by keeping the team on a
> much "shorter leash." ... In such a project, I would bring people
> together as close as possible – in one place.... Also, I [learned] that
> we need to exchange people between sites more often. It simply
> doesn't work if you know people only by having phone contact –
> you must have a personal relationship.

Further, we heard from a conversation between a project manager and
one of his team members that as a result of terminated projects, the
subsidiary manager had established a lessons-learned database, and
they discussed specific lessons that had been entered in the database.
Similarly, a team member from a different project explained, "We have
learned a lesson. It cost the company a lot of money, but we

have learned some very important lessons. [Specifically what to] not do again." Consistent with this quote, our field notes and internal emails similarly demonstrated that team members from another project expressed hope that important lessons learned from their failure could be applied for the "greater good" in the future. Finally, one team member summarized his team's view of the failure this way: "I learned to avoid letting things really get to you. . . . I'm trying to assess the facts [what went wrong, etc.]. . . . These are simply experiences that are part of a professional life." This perspective was highly oriented toward learning from failure experiences, with the individual recognizing them as a pathway to longer-term professional success.

In contrast to the high level of learning found in team members of four specific projects, team members within four other projects experienced much lower levels of learning. For example, one team leader said the following: "Concerning how I relate to our company as an employee and how we do the projects, I would say no [whether he changed the way he worked on projects]. . . . So the recipe itself for how I perform projects will not change a lot." Similarly, all members of two other projects stated that specific learning regarding how to improve R&D projects did not emerge from the failure experience, again standing in stark contrast to those projects for which future-oriented learning was prevalent.

Another common theme for those who had lower levels of learning was a lack of recognition of the importance of the failure experience as a chance to learn. That is, team members from these projects expressed that any learning from the failure experience could have been obtained from any other circumstance. One team member even went so far as to say, "This project was terminated due to a decision of the top management, not due to our mistakes. We didn't make any mistakes [to learn from]; we are not bad engineers. We should be thanked." Similarly, one team leader explained, "I will do it [projects in the future] in exactly the same way," again suggesting that – according to these team members – no real mistakes were made; thus making the opportunity to learn irrelevant.

Given that the data led us to categorize projects based on learn-ing outcomes, we continued comparing the cases in accordance with this initial separation to help us understand why variance in learning levels occurred across these groups. We found that there was a clear difference in the speed with which projects were terminated. Specif-ically, we found that for project teams that experienced rapid and abrupt termination (i.e., rapid termination), individual team members appeared to have lower levels of learning than when a project's ter-mination was delayed over an extended period of time (i.e., delayed termination).

Team members were quite explicit as to how a project was terminated (and subsequently how that influenced their actions/reac-tions to the project). For example, team members who learned little from project failure, all described the process as rapid, calling the termination process "immediate" and a "hard stop" as opposed to a "soft stop" (i.e., rapid termination versus delayed transition) as well as "quickly decided ... and business oriented."

In contrast, for the projects team members who learned from their failure experience, there was an emphasis on delay in the termination process. For example, one team leader described the termination as a "slow descent," which was substantiated by a team member from a different project who described it as "a process ... not an event." Simi-larly, another team leader called the termination of his project a "slow starvation," or, as one team member called it, a "creeping death."

We next explore how project-termination speed impacted team members emotionally as well as how it shaped their engagement in learning activities.

CREEPING DEATH: NEGATIVE EMOTIONS FROM A STALLED DECISION, NOT LOSS OF A PROJECT

As indicated in the earlier section, team members from different projects experienced different termination processes for their respect-ive projects. We found that termination processes influenced team members' emotional reactions.

Individuals on teams that experienced delayed project termination appeared to have experienced higher levels of negative emotions, specifically compared to those with rapid project termination.
As mentioned earlier, one team member described his experience
with the delay as a "creeping death": "I guess it was good that at
some point, there was a definitive decision. To this day, it still causes
people to shake their heads [in disbelief] because it was such a creeping death." While not universally used across projects as a term to
convey the emotional and temporal sentiment of delayed termination, all team members in delayed projects expressed an emotional
reaction similar to the notion of creeping death.

Combining these descriptions, we define creeping death as "a
project that is on the path to being terminated, and while this likely
outcome is known, the steps along the path to termination are
small and slow, and the process is emotionally painful" (Shepherd
et al. 2014: 527). In the paragraphs that follow, we demonstrate our
conceptualization of creeping death from the team members'
perspectives.

First, in creeping death, failure of the project and its resulting
termination were anticipated well in advance and for an extended
period of time. One team member anticipated the termination of his
project for some time, explaining that it "was to be expected . . . , [and]
this discussion was in meetings for some time. . . . I had already
resigned myself [to the project's termination]." He noted that it was
"perhaps two or three months from when I saw signs the project
would fall until the decision actually came." Similarly, a team
member of a different project explained the following, "By the time
the announcement was made, we knew what was happening; there
was no surprise there, which is probably why I do not remember it [the
actual announcement]. I do not remember the particular meeting
[where the final decision was given] simply because it was an
inevitability."

Another team leader stated that the "shutdown was a kind of
slow descent." Indeed, one team member, frustrated by six months of

endless delays and missed deadlines, explained that "The configuration itself would have likely taken weeks. Errors were still present, and it would have been a miracle to convince any customer that it really could work!" It appears that knowing a project was failing but not being able to jump to a separate project or escape from the failing project resulted in frustration and distress.

Second, and as suggested in the first point, the delay in terminating a failing project generated negative emotions for project team members. Rather than rallying team members in hopes of pulling off a successful project despite the obstacles, delaying termination appeared to result in negative emotions. The team leader of one project expressed frustration with the uncertainty that resulted from stalled decision making:

> I personally fell in a real motivation gap.... [The six-month delay in the termination decision] hurt our development department very badly because we actually had finished development in the spring, and we wanted to know the new direction. We knew that we had the people here, and they could not be redeployed back to their home country [office], which would have been a waste of time and money anyway. This was a very, very bad situation.

A team member from the same project expressed frustration with the wasted use of human and material resources during the delay, "My frustration, if you will, is that the project members are really good. A lot of people do really a very, very good job, and they are very committed. The fact that we don't use them sufficiently and effectively and that we waste time with projects that drag on and ultimately we don't pursue [is very frustrating]."

Similarly, a team member from a different project explained that the delay generated "frustration" and that he experienced incredible "relief" when a decision was ultimately made to end the project: "We had an incredibly long time with no definitive decisions, and at least this was a decision." A team member from another project concurred, explaining, "Ultimately, if the decision is that a project is not flying, then I can accept that. But I need a clear explanation, which was lacking, and the late timing [of the termination] was frustrating."

Interestingly, these negative emotions appear to be connected primarily to the delay, not to sentiments regarding the project itself.

Indeed, the delay, or creeping death, generated worry, not regarding whether or not the project would succeed but, rather, worry about team members being held back from pursuing other activities or projects. The primary frustration was that key human resources (themselves and others) were unnecessarily "tied up." One team member explained, "As you can imagine, if you keep 20 of the best engineers you have and an extended team of 70 people occupied with such a project, they are not available for other problems and opportunities elsewhere in the organization."

In a broader organization constantly focused on novel and innovative ideas, the last place these individuals wanted to be was stuck on a failing project that was slowly limping toward termination. Field notes captured by our team corroborated this finding. Specifically, while engaging interviewees in side conversations, we discovered that a frequent topic was the extreme nature of the negative emotions participants experienced while enduring delayed termination. Furthermore, emails we obtained between team members confirmed that the primary source of negative emotion was indeed the delay (as opposed to the loss of the project).

Therefore, although we (somewhat surprisingly) found that the actual and final termination of a project (i.e., team members' redeployment to other tasks) was not the source of negative emotional responses, a delayed termination, or creeping death, did elicit negative emotions. Specifically, we found that team members valued the ability to pursue engineering challenges more so than the specific outcome of a particular project. For the team members, these engineering challenges referred to "the specific technical aspect of a project or job that the team member performs and that often relates to a team member's fascination with the science behind potential products"

(Shepherd et al. 2014: 530). Throughout all the interviews, team members repeatedly referenced their appreciation for engineering challenges. One project leader commented, "It was also satisfying when you design a machine and everything fits. So if the top was put on the machine, our machines are very large, several meters long and several meters in diameter, and you have gaps that are tolerated in tenths of millimeters ... and everything fits. This is a great feeling. Therefore, this project was really satisfying for me."

Despite the overall failure of the project, this comment highlights the positive aspects as viewed by the team: individual achievements on engineering challenges were valued more than the overall well-being of the project. As another example, one team member explained, "Ultimately, I believe that we have had a very good project here from a technical perspective: we have set a benchmark in the timeline we needed, we have gone through the product-development process appropriately, we have involved all necessary parties."

For this team member, the positive elements were related to the product timeline and development, specifically from a technical perspective (as opposed to successful commercialization of the technology).

Finally, while one team member expressed indifference to the success of any particular project, he was thrilled to move to a new project due to the engineering challenge. He explained, "[In my new project,] I get to focus on mathematics and developing algorithms.... This is a huge positive as I will be in my element." As Green and colleagues (2003: 423) noted, "innovators like to innovate; being on the leading edge of a technology can be both scientifically satisfying and ego gratifying."

Consistent with our discovery of just how important it was for workers to engage in an active engineering challenge rather than generate a specific outcome, we found that only when this challenge was removed did team members experience high levels of negative emotions. In the R&D environment of this study, team members were (typically) rapidly redeployed when official project termination occurred. In fact, most of the team members described their transition to a new project as immediate when official word of termination was received. This notion was supported by executives at both the corporate and subsidiary levels, where they put an emphasis on moving on as quickly as possible from failed projects. Team members appeared to appreciate moving on, especially as it allowed them to move to new engineering challenges. Therefore, it appears that the engineers in our sample who did not experience negative emotional reactions associated with project failure were able to avoid such emotions because they were able to continue doing that which they loved and valued – exploring technical solutions to complex and challenging problems – as opposed to staying in dead-end, failing projects.

In contrast to the delayed-termination projects discussed till now, four projects were terminated quickly – the decision to end the projects was unequivocal and final, and there was little time from expecting termination to actual termination. This type of termination was described by team members as "suddenly a reality," for which "the information [decision to terminate] was delivered abruptly to the team members – practically immediately. It was clear there was a decision to stop the project, so it meant that we should immediately stop spending money." When asked if he had anticipated a project shutdown, one team member responded, "Quite honestly, not directly.... I don't remember any signs or timeline [red flags] indicating a possible termination.... I did not expect the decision to be so abrupt. Suddenly there was nothing, and it was said, 'The project is stopped,' and that was it.... As a team, we were all surprised by the decision."

Similarly, when asked about anticipating project termination, a team member replied, "No, not until I had this meeting.... And then I thought 'Ok, then we have to terminate because we have no chance to get the material.' So we could not continue."

As another point of contrast, team members of rapidly-terminated projects did not experience negative emotions or worry even when we directly asked about it. As an example, one team leader explained that the rapid termination of his project cost him "One night's sleep, I think. That is because I think there were no implications to my working situation." Specifically, there were no implications because he was able to continue working on engineering challenges but on a separate project. Other project leaders noted, "I am not that hurt by it. I now have another really big project," and "It was not necessarily fun to terminate the project, but we had to do it, and it was 'business as usual' (laughs). . . . Really it was no problem." Indeed, one project leader explained, "I was also relieved," a sentiment shared by his fellow team members as the stress of the project (e.g., meeting deadlines, etc.) was substantial.

LEARNING BEFORE RATHER THAN AFTER THE TERMINATION EVENT

In contrast to the extant literature on negative emotions, our findings suggest that negative emotions stimulated rather than constrained learning from the failure experience (Shepherd et al. 2014). Given that lost access to an engineering challenge was the primary source of negative emotions (given expectations of its ultimate demise), these negative emotions motivated individuals to search for a new type of challenge while awaiting ultimate project termination, namely learning why the current project had failed to meet expectations. Team members were therefore motivated to understand and ultimately learn from the failing project (at least to some degree) because learning represented a challenge that was stimulating enough to compensate for the inability to move on to the next project. Team members, motivated to find a challenge, dedicated time and effort (including systems, spreadsheets, programs, etc.) to ensure that they learned from the failure for future reference despite the creeping death and its associated negative emotions.

For example, a team member explained that during the creeping death associated with the delay, he decided to take a "neutral position, a position of an observer" to reflect on what had happened.

A fellow team member went on to say, "I've been thinking a lot about the project. . . . I asked myself again and again how could it happen. . . . So I did learn [from this delayed termination]." This reflection on the loss, or search for a meaningful outcome despite the delay, was similarly expressed by team members of other creeping-death projects. Specifically, a team member searched for real engineering and hence business value from the experience in order to carry that new knowledge on to future projects. He explained, "I think you feel very isolated [due to the failure] . . . [but] we have to learn from this, capitalize on it, get value from it. . . . As long as people sweep it [project failure] under the carpet . . . we lose the opportunity to convert that bad experience into financial value, real business value. . . . [Normally,] we are not good at closing projects out."

A team member of another creeping-death project similarly emphasized that this learning had to take place during the delay (or at least the life of the project) because "once the job stops, the reviews stop." As a final example, one team member described creeping death as "endless misery" and would have preferred a "miserable end" so he could "be staffed immediately, anywhere!" to resume an engineering challenge. However, despite feeling "trapped," this team member spent time making sense of the project, its failings, and specifically how he could apply those learnings in the future. He explained that he "absorbed the termination" by "documenting all our results . . . in an ordered manner so it all wasn't just thrown away." As a result, he learned that the decision to terminate was "dead right." He explained that "if we really went, with the limited knowledge at that time, directly into a commercial project, then this would have cost our company, I think, a tremendous amount of money in the end." In this sense, he was able to identify meaning and value from the experience that, while painful to incur, provided similar benefits as did engaging in an engineering challenge.

Therefore, we found that the negative emotions generated by delay were also capable of producing a positive outcome – it drove individuals to allocate time and effort typically used on engaging in an engineering challenge toward learning from the experience of the failed project. Thus, the motivation (i.e., desire to work on something meaningful) became useful when combined with the time to work on the meaningful outcome (i.e., learning from failure).

We found that in general, team members lacked the time to reflect on failed projects after they were terminated. This occurred for three primary reasons. First, in nearly every situation, project team members were rapidly redeployed after the official termination, which led them to redirect attention and resources toward starting new assignments, understanding new problems, and connecting with new team members. These activities were given substantial priority over taking time to reflect on what went wrong with the previous project. For example, multiple individuals were redeployed to new assignments within hours of receiving news of their project's termination, while all others were redeployed within one to ten days (with the exception of one team leader who waited about one month). Given this rapid timeline, there was simply no time after the project had ended for these individuals to reflect on or implement change relating to the prior project.

Second, project members were motivated to reduce role uncertainty by moving onto a new role specifically relating to identifying a new problem or engineering challenge to address. For example, one team member explained that the most important thing for him following a project failure was "to get a new task." When asked how soon, he said without hesitation, "Immediately!" Similarly, subsidiary leaders all expressed the importance of getting the team to "move on" so that they would not dwell on the negative outcome.

Finally, the pressure to move on and the pull of interesting work elsewhere within the organization appeared to limit individual team members' ability to carve out time and attention for mentally processing the failed project. While some individuals mentioned filling out technical sheets or other generic forms, they put forth little mental capacity to making sense of the failed project once it was formally terminated. Given the rapid redeployment after project termination for all team members of every project, the period provided by delayed termination took on increasing importance in terms of processing learning opportunities from the failing project.

MECHANISMS FOR LEARNING FROM FAILURE

We found evidence connecting termination timing and learning from failure through the activation of three key learning mechanisms: reflect, articulate, and codify (Prencipe and Tell 2001; Zollo and Winter 2002).

First, delayed-project termination provided team members with time to reflect on their experience, which enabled learning. For example, a project leader stated, "I personally learned a lot on the project ... during the [six to eight months of the failing project]. . . . I was almost in the position of an observer, watching what we were doing and [reflecting] on what exactly did we do here." Notably, this project leader highlighted the fact that he was in a position to "observe" the failing project, allowing real-time assessments of what was going wrong given the delayed termination. In a similar statement, one of his team members explained that he engaged in "introspective reflection," helping him identify lessons to apply in future projects. He stated, "[During this period of delayed termination,] everyone evaluated his experiences and drew conclusions, for example, what he would do next time in the same way or what he would do differently. I personally learned that I would deal with the customer differently next time."

The delay provided an opportunity for reflection in that stalled team members redirected their desire to work on "interesting" projects to making sense of the failing project.

Second, the delayed termination also generated an opportunity for team members to articulate what they had learned with their fellow team members, an opportunity that might otherwise not have been possible given a culture of rapid redeployment following termination. Once a project is terminated, it may become difficult to establish forums for team members to come together, especially given the global nature of (some) teams. In addition, the motivation to work through project problems could be substantially reduced once team members move on to other assignments and there is no longer a profit-driven rationale for maintaining engagement in the project and its challenges. For example, one team leader explained how resource-intensive these meetings could be: "There were meetings where we looked intensively at the system, conducting an error analysis to improve our understanding of the details [of what was going wrong]." These meetings all occurred during a period of uncertainty regarding the status of the project, which while frustrating, provided time for team members to meet to articulate lessons learned. Similarly, a team member from a different project described a number of "intensive reviews" he and his team held during the delayed termination. During this delay, team members attempted to determine the "root cause" behind the product failure. He explained, "We held a whole series of reviews to talk about where the performance was going. Was it a build issue? Were we looking at leaks within the system? ... This probably went on for four to five months."

Finally, a delay in project termination also provided team members with an opportunity to codify (i.e., to reflect on and articulate) what they learned through formal means, including database uploads, spreadsheets, lessons-learned documents, and other methods of choice. Specifically, this type of learning differed from other post-project documentation activities conducted in low-learning projects. In high-learning scenarios, lessons-learned documentation focused on explanations of project outcomes (i.e., why project outcomes occurred as they did, what could have been done differently, etc.) as opposed to specific descriptions (i.e., technical features of the project, amount of money spent, etc.) of what happened during the project. For example, in one project that experienced a delayed termination, the team leader explained that articulating specific explanations for project outcomes was critical:

> We found that in essence, it [the time taken to capture lessons learned] is about facts that can be written down for why something

did not work. To document that we have used a specific design for the product, why it didn't work, and what we should have considered in our design. Thus, in the next design phase, colleagues can benefit from the learning and do not have to have the same experience themselves.

Project teams that experienced creeping death all had adequate time to reflect on, articulate, and codify their experiences associated with project failure, which appears to have resulted in increased learning.

In contrast, teams of projects that were rapidly terminated had little to no time for reflection on, articulation of, and codification of learning as they were immediately redeployed to new projects. For each of these projects, team members specifically expressed lack of time to reflect on the failure experience. For example, during a business lunch with several team members, one of the interviewees explained the following, "[I did not have] sufficient time to process and document the lessons learned from the terminated project because [after the rapid termination of the project,] I was immediately transitioned to a new project due to the large pipeline of development projects in the firm."

Given this limited warning time and immediate redeployment, team members appeared to apply their limited cognitive capacity toward making a good start on the new project rather than reflecting on what went wrong in the previous project. This finding was supported by a team member of a different project, who explained, "The day after [the termination], I just said, 'Ok, now my task has changed. I need to do this for that [new project], and this is what I am focusing on now.'" Starting a new project took a lot of energy and mental capacity, and leadership encouraged individuals to "jump in with both feet" to make sure that the new project was a success. However, an (perhaps) unintended consequence of these actions was that individuals never adequately reflected on what went wrong, resulting in fewer opportunities to learn from the failed project.

In addition to limited opportunities to reflect on learning from failed projects, individuals who experienced rapidly-terminated projects also expressed limited opportunities to articulate potential learning from their experiences. Highlighting what was a common theme among team members on these projects, one team leader succinctly explained, "I would say here at our location, we did not share [lessons learned]." It appears that the rapid termination of projects limited team members' ability to articulate what they had experienced, including what they had learned. Several interviewees specifically lamented the lack of opportunity to articulate learning during our discussions with them and suggested that this influenced their ability to learn. They even expressed gratitude for the chance to engage with us in the interview process, explaining that this was their first and most substantial opportunity to reflect on and articulate what had happened during the failed project and how things could have been different. Consistent with the majority of responses we received, when we asked one team member if he would have enjoyed holding a discussion like this earlier (i.e., closer to project termination and involving his team members in the process), he exclaimed, "Yes, absolutely!" From these interviews, it was clear that there was a missed opportunity to articulate learning due to the rapid termination and redeployment of team members following project failure.

Finally, members from projects that were rapidly terminated were also unable to effectively codify experiences and lessons learned from the failed project, again due to their rapid redeployment. While project documentation was not completely absent for these team members, the type of documentation they completed was substantially different from those teams that effectively codified learning. For example, some teams described a process for capturing the "basics" – a description (as opposed to an explanation) of the project for basic record-keeping/auditing purposes. These basic codification reports were expressly designed to track technical aspects of the project, including the budget and "mathematical results." Even these types of codification, however, appeared to be rare as most team members emphasized a complete lack of documentation given their intense focus on moving forward to a new project. For example, one team member noted, "I haven't really met anybody who said 'Well, make sure if something goes wrong that we document it, that we learn from it, and that we somehow inform others.' I have not seen that. . . . There is this saying that I have heard: 'If only our company knew what our company knows.'" While the team members acknowledged the presence of knowledge within the broader organization, they were also reluctant to try and access this knowledge given the need to move forward on to new projects. In particular, the draw of a new engineering challenge and the desire to put the failure behind them made mentally returning to the failed project undesirable and unfeasible.

The findings summarized here contribute to our understanding that failure events can trigger learning – perhaps more substantially than successes (Sitkin 1992) – as failure provides strong and (seemingly) undeniable signals that existing activities were inadequate. These signals can motivate and facilitate sensemaking and therefore learning activities (Ginsberg 1988; Morrison 2002). That is, in the aftermath of a termination event, individual team members can reflect on the failure event (i.e., what led up to the event, what decisions were made throughout the process, etc.), cognitively process those experiences, and ultimately work to develop an account or explanation for the failure, thereby enabling learning (Shepherd et al. 2011; Weick, Sutcliffe, and Obstfeld 2005). In offering an important caveat to this understanding, our findings (Shepherd et al. 2014) suggest that time provided during delayed-project termination explained learning (i.e., who learns more) as opposed to a traditional focus on providing time immediately after the project failure for learning. Specifically, our findings suggest that in R&D organizations that rapidly redeploy personnel following a project failure, team members learn more during a delayed termination (i.e., while the project is failing but has not yet terminated) than those who experience a surprising and rapid project termination. Our findings suggest that this occurs because under conditions of rapid redeployment after project termination, a delay in project termination provides both time and motivation for individual team members to learn as it facilitates (1) reflection on the failure, (2) articulation of what went well and what did not, and (3) codification of these learning points for subsequent reference or use.

DISCUSSION

In this chapter (and its underlying study [Shepherd et al. 2014]), we contributed to the scholarly conversation on project-termination timing and learning from failure by analyzing and exploring contextual factors that potentially explain the connection between learning from failure and whether a project is terminated rapidly or has a delayed termination. Prior research has explored cognitions associated with the decision to terminate a project (Ross and Staw 1993; Staw and Ross 1987) and their implication on organizational learning. In particular, this past research has specifically focused on those who own the option – that is, the primary project decision maker (McGrath et al. 2004). However, extant research has not explored (as it was not its purpose) the contextual factors linking termination timing and reactions to failure by those who are the option (i.e., project team members) (McGrath et al. 2004).We have begun to take a step toward addressing these unexplored areas of research, contributing both to the literature on business failure (and learning from failure) as well as project termination.

Learning from failure: The role of negative emotions

We provided three primary insights into the relationship between negative emotions and learning from failure. First, we found that members of R&D teams prioritized working on complex engineering challenges over being on specific projects. Given these priorities, project failure (i.e., actual termination) generated very few negative emotions among team members. Rather, R&D team members had negative emotional reactions when the failure process was delayed; their inability to move forward to the next engineering challenge was the primary source of frustration and anxiety. In explaining negative emotional reactions to project termination in this way, we broaden our understanding of what organizational team members value (at least those in R&D-intensive environments as the one explored here) and how those values are challenged during a failure event. This understanding can have implications in managing termination decisions as well as learning expectations from a failed project.

Second, when team members experienced negative emotions during the delayed termination of a project (as they were blocked from working on interesting project work), they were motivated to focus on solving other problems – namely, making sense of the failed project. Therefore, while typically assumed to generate adverse consequences, negative emotions in this context could provide a positive outcome in that they motivate team members to engage in the challenge of learning from the failure event. In contrast, teams that rapidly terminated projects and redeployed team members experienced very little negative emotions and were thus not motivated to reflect on what went wrong, articulate those reflections to fellow team members, or codify lessons learned for future use. Thus, these teams experienced lower overall negative emotions but also experienced lower levels of learning from the failed project.

Finally, beyond the learning motivation generated by negative emotions, delayed-project termination gave team members time to organize team discussions. These discussions provided a venue for project reflection (e.g., what went poorly, etc.); articulation and discussion of what could have been done differently; and, importantly, codification of this knowledge for future use. The counterintuitive insight from this finding specifically relates to the timing of learning from failure. Typically, learning from failure has been conceptualized as a process that occurs over time (Cardon and McGrath 1999; Cope 2011), specifically as a process that happens only after a project is terminated (Shepherd 2003; Shepherd et al. 2011; Ucbasaran, Shepherd, Lockett, and Lyon 2013). However, as mentioned throughout this chapter, in contexts in which team members are immediately redeployed to new and complex projects following the termination of an existing assignment, learning from failure must occur primarily before the termination. Therefore, a delay in termination extends the window of opportunity for learning despite the negative emotions it generates.

Overall, higher levels of learning occur for project team members who experience high negative emotions due to project-termination delay, or creeping death (and the inability to move forward to a new engineering challenge); however, this delay and the resulting desire to work on new challenges provide individuals the time and motivation to reflect on, articulate, and codify key learnings from a failing project before team members are redeployed to new R&D assignments.

Team members' perspective on the timing of project termination

We also generated insights that have implications for managing entrepreneurial firms, specifically in terms of understanding the perspective of team members working on projects. First, team members were able to reduce the negative emotions associated with a failed project by engaging in an engineering mindset. The engineering mindset (i.e., focusing attention on a challenge that was interesting and stimulating) guided team members' attention during and after project failures, which meant that a failed project resulted in very few negative emotions and presented very few obstacles in rapid redeployment to the next project assignment. However, when the transition to a new project was delayed (due to management's inability to decide to terminate a project), team members experienced intense negative emotions. What is interesting here is that negative emotions were generated when a failing project was not terminated as opposed to when it ultimately concluded. Therefore, the engineering mindset provided individuals not only with a cognitive script that guided problem-solving activities but also with an attentional focus on specific tasks that superseded their commitment to a project. Therefore, those managing entrepreneurial teams in a similar environment might have more flexibility (in terms of team members' emotional reactions) in rapidly terminating projects, yet this could come at a cost (i.e., lack of learning). Therefore, team managers might balance the importance of learning from a failure event, the need for redeployment, and other needs when making project-termination decisions, all while considering how these type of team members primarily attend to engineering challenges.

Second, during a delayed termination, team members might be uncomfortable with the ambiguity of the situation; however, the delay does provide time for them to learn from the failure. In the time provided by a delay, team members remain together, and can reflect individually and as a team on personal mistakes (i.e., missteps in a particular process, miscalculations, etc.); issues that occurred at the organizational level (i.e., management decisions that led to failure, interdepartment coordination problems, etc.); specific technical challenges, miscalculations, or issues (i.e., technical problems from an engineering perspective); and industry-specific or market issues (i.e., institutional or governmental influence in product development, customer participation, etc.). Such reflections captured in the context of the team environment within the ongoing project provide team members the opportunity to discuss, articulate, and codify lessons learned – critical steps for organizational-level learning (see Zollo and Winter 2002). The key insight is that when team members are rapidly redeployed, learning largely does not occur for them after the project concludes given the loss of team structure and loss of time for learning outcomes to transpire.

Finally, negative emotions from creeping death motivate team members to learn from failure events. From a managerial perspective, negative emotions can be an effective tool for learning as they signal to team members that something went wrong with the project and that what was occurring on the project is no longer valued by the organization. Although negative emotions can be destructive, managers can redirect team members' frustration with having to wait for a new engineering challenge to engagement in the challenge of working out what went wrong. In this way, negative emotions generated by the delay facilitate rather than obstruct learning from failure.

In sum, by taking team members' perspective (i.e., those who are the option), we highlighted individual team members' reactions to how managers time the termination of projects and how they are able to learn from failure. Specifically, in the context of a delayed termination, project team members should (1) mitigate and reduce negative emotions associated with project failure by highlighting the importance of working on any – as opposed to a specific (project-related) – engineering challenge; (2) supply an adequate period of time to reflect on, articulate, and codify lessons learned; and (3) redirect negative emotions away from the creeping death associated with the delay to the challenge of understanding and fully learning from the failure event. In the following chapter, we more closely examine how individual emotional intelligence as well as organizational emotional capabilities can play an important role in both grief recovery and sensemaking.

Implications for portfolio management and corporate entrepreneurship

Extant theories of corporate entrepreneurship and project portfolio management are central to understanding the linkages between when and how projects are terminated and learning from a failed project. We generated insights that contribute to both streams of research. First, we provided a deeper understanding of the interrelationships among portfolio management's primary components. We reaffirmed the importance of projects functioning as probes (Brown and Eisenhardt 1997) or options (McGrath 1999) that assist in managing the uncertainty associated with (potentially) risky R&D endeavors. Under these conditions, corporate R&D decision makers can improve the overall performance of the broader organization by rapidly terminating failing or failed projects so that critical resources (e.g., human, technological, etc.) can be redeployed to other activities that show more promise

(Brown and Eisenhardt 1997; McGrath 1999). However, another "resource" to consider in the termination process is the learning that can occur as a result of a failure. Insights from this study suggest that learning occurs primarily before a project is terminated, a factor that should be reflected in decisions regarding termination speed. While failure should capture team members' attention and motivate learning (after the failure event) (Chuang and Baum 2003; Sitkin 1992), our data did not support this conventional wisdom. Rather, our findings suggest that a more powerful motivator than failure driving attention and sensemaking was the desire to work on a new engineering challenge. Because of this motivation and their rapid redeployment to new projects, individuals lacked both the time and cognitive capacity to engage in learning activities after a project was officially terminated.

This finding has implications for the real-options reasoning and portfolio-management perspectives for managing innovation projects. A relevant and implied mechanism associated with managing uncertainty in a corporate environment using R&D projects as probes or options is that they generate new information, which can contribute to organizational knowledge and capabilities, including learning (McGrath 1999). A real-options approach to managing projects advocates for (1) the rapid termination of projects that are failing to meet specified standards, (2) the rapid redeployment of project team members (i.e., human resources) after the termination decision, and (3) learning from the failures that led to the demise of the project (Brown and Eisenhardt 1997; McGrath 1999; McGrath and Cardon 1997). However, based on the findings reported in this chapter, we propose that organizations can have two but not necessarily all three of these attributes. Specifically, organizations can rapidly terminate failing projects and subsequently redeploy human resources, but doing so will limit or even eliminate opportunities for individuals to learn from the failure. Similarly, learning from R&D project failures occurred for team members when the termination decision was delayed. This delay, consistent with real-options reasoning (McGrath 1999), was considered costly by corporate management; subsidiary management; and, specifically, those directly involved in project operations. Furthermore, delay in human-resource redeployment was deplored by all those involved in the projects.

However, the novelty of our findings is that termination delay can provide certain benefits as it provides time for (and motivates) reflection on, articulation of, and codification of lessons learned from project experiences. While the data in our study did not include variation in the speed of redeployment (i.e., all individuals were immediately redeployed to new assignments), we suspect – and hope future research investigates – that delay in human-resource redeployment following a failed project termination could positively influence learning. Given how important learning is to R&D-intensive organizations both in reducing future costs and identifying innovative new products (Hoang and Rothaermel 2005; McGrath 1999), our findings highlight the importance of focusing on the immediate financial impact of project-termination decisions in the broader context of individual and organizational learning outcomes that may have a more long-term impact.

Second, our findings contribute to the literature on corporate entrepreneurship, specifically theories related to cognition. While we reiterated the importance of timing when making project-termination decisions, we took the perspective of those directly influenced by the decision and ultimately those responsible for generating firm-level learning. Prior research has primarily focused on who makes the decision to terminate a project and how those decisions influence both those decision makers and their organizations (McGrath 1999; Royer 2003; Sitkin 1992). For example, Corbett and colleagues (2007) explored how corporate entrepreneurs (i.e., decision makers over corporate projects) use various cognitive scripts in their approach to project failure. They found that learning can be limited if decision makers fail to develop an understanding of market and organizational factors when terminating projects (i.e., "undisciplined termination") or when maintaining projects beyond their useful lifespan without connecting the persistence with any strategic goals (i.e., "innovation drift"). In contrast, Corbett and colleagues found that corporate entrepreneurs who make project-termination decisions based on considerations of market and strategic goals (i.e., "strategic termination") are better positioned to learn about the key organizational and market factors needed to succeed (2007: 838). Corbett and colleagues' (2007) insights have enhanced our understanding of the cognitions and "termination scripts" of decision makers in terms of whether and when projects should be terminated, particularly in relation to how learning can benefit a firm's capabilities (Corbett et al. 2007). These findings are consistent with a real-options reasoning approach that, as mentioned earlier, has traditionally focused on owners of the option as opposed to those who are the option (e.g., McGrath 1999; McGrath et al. 2004). However, those who are the option are likely to have a very different reaction to a failure event given their embeddedness in the project. In exploring the perspective of project team members who are not project-termination decision makers, we contributed to research on the implications of decision makers' termination scripts by understanding emotional implications for the team. Our findings suggest that R&D project team members and decision makers may differ in termination timing, and these differences impact learning. The key takeaway is that if team members perceive that a subsidiary manager is taking too long to terminate a project, they generally have negative emotional reactions but also take the opportunity to learn from their experience.

Finally, the literature on loss has found that a majority of individuals experience negative emotional reactions when they lose something important to them (Archer 1999). Examples of loss include valued relationships associated with divorce (Kitson, Babri, Roach, and Placidi 1989); loss of a family member, friend, or loved one through death (Archer 1999); and bankruptcy (Shepherd 2003). Similarly, and as discussed extensively in Chapter 3, Shepherd and colleagues (2011) found that research scientists value their research projects to such an extent that they can experience negative emotional reactions when these projects fail. However, despite these findings in extant literature, we did not observe this in our data. Specifically, all team members in all teams (both those terminated rapidly and those with delayed termination) had minimal negative emotional reactions specifically as they applied to the loss of a particular project. One potential explanation for this lack of emotional reaction is that team members had become overly accustomed to these types of failure either through extensive personal experience with failure or due to their membership in a broader environment (i.e., the R&D group) that normalizes failure (Ashforth and Kreiner 2002). However, our data suggest an alternative explanation. Consistent with prior literature on loss, our findings suggest that team members did experience negative emotions with something they "lost," but the loss was not the project; rather, it was the inability to work on engineering challenges. While failure was not considered to be normal for individuals in our sample, rapidly moving on to a new project was very much the norm and was a general expectation each team member expressed. Therefore, when moving on to a new project is considered normal, a delay in this transition could be considered non-normal or non-routine, which is likely to lead to negative emotional reactions among team members. This reasoning is consistent with what we found in our data: team members' engineering mindset motivated them to quickly move on. Thus, when team members did move on quickly, they experienced very few negative emotions, which appeared to have little to do with project failure being normalized at the organizational level.

Advantages of the engineering mindset include an ability to quickly re-engage human resources on new assignments, a lower likelihood of persisting unnecessarily in poorly performing projects (i.e., escalation of commitment), and a reduced need for intervention due to low levels of negative emotion. However, these "wins" might not outweigh the losses associated with team members not adequately learning from the failings of a project, which is consistent with criticisms that small wins may not be large enough to capture sufficient attention (Sitkin 1992).

CONCLUSION

In this chapter (and its underlying study [Shepherd et al. 2014]), we explored the relationship between failed projects in an R&D-intensive organization and team member level learning and how that learning was influenced by project-termination style (i.e., rapid or delayed) and negative emotions. As we were given unusual access to a large multinational firm (i.e., four subsidiaries and eight teams within those subsidiaries), we were able to deeply explore our research questions on this important topic. While research has acknowledged the connection between project-termination timing and organizational outcomes (e.g., learning from failure), these studies have focused almost exclusively on the role of decision makers' cognitions. Here, we took an alternative perspective – that of those who are the option, or the project team members – providing a number of counterintuitive and theory-generating insights. Rather than maintaining a commitment to failing or poorly performing projects, project team members viewed a delay in the decision to terminate these projects as creeping death. Also, the failed projects (and their ultimate termination) did not generate negative emotions for project team members. Rather, it was the inability to move on to the next engineering challenge (during the delayed termination) that generated negative emotions. Finally, rather than obstructing learning, negative emotions associated with a delay in termination motivated team members to learn from the experience by making sense of the failing project. Therefore, R&D team members' cognitive and emotional reactions to project-termination timing decisions are likely to play a more substantial role in future research seeking to understand learning from failure.

In conclusion, it appears that under different circumstances, delayed termination can be of benefit. When the business (or project) is one of prime importance to the individual, some delay in termination allows for emotional preparation so that less grief is generated by the failure. With less grief, emotional obstacles to learning from the experience are eliminated. However, when the engineering challenge is of primary importance, delay generates a greater negative emotional reaction, but these emotions motivate learning from the experience before failure occurs, and delay provides the time to reflect, articulate, and codify (i.e., steps necessary for organizational learning [Zollo and Winter 2002]) that is not available after the failure event.

REFERENCES

Allen, N. J. and Meyer, J. P. 1990. The measurement and antecedents of affective, continuance and normative commitment to the organization. *Journal of Occupational Psychology*, 63(1): 1–18.

Anderson, C. J. 2003. The psychology of doing nothing: Forms of decision avoidance result from reason and emotion. *Psychological Bulletin*, 129(1): 139–167.

Ansic, D. and Pugh, G. 1999. An experimental test of trade hysteresis: Market exit and entry decisions in the presence of sunk costs and exchange rate uncertainty. *Applied Economics*, 31(4): 427–436.

Archer, J. 1999. *The Nature of Grief: The Evolution and Psychology of Reactions to Loss*. New York: Routledge.

Arkes, H. R. and Blumer, C. 1985. The psychology of sunk costs. *Organizational Behavior & Human Decision Processes*, 35(1): 124–140.

Ashforth, B. E. and Kreiner, G. E. 2002. Normalizing emotion in organizations: Making the extraordinary seem ordinary. *Human Resource Management Review*, 12(2): 215–235.

Bower, G. H. 1992. How might emotions affect learning?. In S. Christianson (ed.), *The Handbook of Emotion and Memory: Research and Theory*: 3–31. Hillsdale, NJ: Lawrence Erlbaum.

Brockner, J. 1992. The escalation of commitment to a failing course of action: Toward theoretical progress. *Academy of Management Review*, 17(1): 39–61.

Brown, S. L. and Eisenhardt, K. M. 1997. The art of continuous change: linking complexity theory and time-paced evolution in relentlessly shifting organizations. *Administrative Science Quarterly*, 42(1): 1–34.

Cannon, M. D. and Edmondson, A. C. 2005. Failing to learn and learning to fail (intelligently): How great organizations put failure to work to innovate and improve. *Long Range Planning*, 38(3): 299–319.

Cardon, M. and McGrath, R. G. 1999. *When the going gets tough: Toward a psychology of entrepreneurial failure and re-motivation*. Paper presented at the Babson College Entrepreneurship Research Conference, University of South Carolina.

Chuang, Y.-T. and Baum, J. A. C. 2003. It's all in the name: Failure-induced learning by multiunit chains. *Administrative Science Quarterly*, 48(1): 33–59.

Cooper, R. G. 2008. Perspective: The stage-gate (R) idea-to-launch process-update, what's new, and NexGen systems. *Journal of Product Innovation Management*, 25(3): 213–232.

Cope, J. 2011. Entrepreneurial learning from failure: An interpretative phenomenological analysis. *Journal of Business Venturing*, 26(6): 604–623.

Corbett, A. C., Neck, H. M., and DeTienne, D. R. 2007. How corporate entrepreneurs learn from fledgling innovation initiatives: Cognition and the development of a termination script. *Entrepreneurship Theory and Practice*, 31(6): 829–852.

Cyert, R. and March, J. 1963. *A Behavioral Theory of the Firm*. Upper Saddle River, N.J.: Prentice Hall/Pearson Education.

Dixit, R. K. and Pindyck, R. S. 2008. *Investment under Uncertainty*. Princeton, NJ: Princeton University Press.

Estrada, C. A., Isen, A. M., and Young, M. J. 1997. Positive affect facilitates integration of information and decreases anchoring in reasoning among physicians. *Organizational Behavior and Human Decision Processes*, 72(1): 117–135.

Fiol, C. M. and Lyles, M. A. 1985. Organizational learning. *Academy of Management Review*, 10(4): 803–813.

Frank, M. G. and Gilovich, T. 1989. Effect of memory perspective on retrospective causal attributions. *Journal of Personality and Social Psychology*, 57(3): 399–403.

Fredrickson, B. L. 2001. The role of positive emotions in positive psychology: The broaden-and-build theory of positive emotions. *American Psychologist*, 56(3): 218.

Fredrickson, B. L. and Branigan, C. 2005. Positive emotions broaden the scope of attention and thought-action repertoires. *Cognition & Emotion*, 19(3): 313–332.

Garland, H., Sandefur, C., and Rogers, A. 1990. De-escalation of commitment in oil exploration: When sunk losses and negative feedback coincide. *Journal of Applied Psychology*, 75: 721–727.

Ginsberg, A. 1988. Measuring and modeling changes in strategy: Theoretical foundations and empirical directions. *Strategic Management Journal*, 9(6): 559–575.

Gong, Y., Law, K. S., Chang, S., and Xin, K. R. 2009. Human resources management and firm performance: The differential role of managerial affective and continuance commitment. *Journal of Applied Psychology*, 94(1): 263.

Green, S. G. and Welsh, M. A. 2003. Advocacy, performance, and threshold influences on decisions to terminate new product development. *Academy of Management Journal*, 46(4): 419–434.

Green, S. G., Welsh, M. A., and Dehler, G. E. 2003. Advocacy, performance, and threshold influences on decisions to terminate new product development. *Academy of Management Journal*, 46(4): 419–434.

Guler, I. 2007. Throwing good money after bad? Political and institutional influences on sequential decision making in the venture capital industry. *Administrative Science Quarterly*, 52(2): 248–285.

Hoang, H. and Rothaermel, F. T. 2005. The effect of general and partner-specific alliance experience on joint R&D project performance. *Academy of Management Journal*, 48(2): 332–345.

Isen, A. M., Daubman, K. A., and Nowicki, G. P. 1987. Positive affect facilitates creative problem solving. *Journal of Personality and Social Psychology*, 52(6): 1122.

Kiesler, S. and Sproull, L. 1982. Managerial responses to changing environments: Perspectives on problem sensing from social cognition. *Administrative Science Quarterly*, 27(4): 548–570.

Kitson, G. C., Babri, K. B., Roach, M. J., and Placidi, K. S. 1989. Adjustment to widowhood and divorce: A review. *Journal of Family Issues*, 10(1): 5–32.

Masters, J. C., Barden, R. C., and Ford, M. E. 1979. Affective states, expressive behavior, and learning in children. *Journal of Personality and Social Psychology*, 37(3): 380.

McGrath, R. 1999. Falling forward: Real options reasoning and entrepreneurial failure. *Academy of Management Review*, 24: 13–30.

McGrath, R. G. and Cardon, M. S. 1997. *Entrepreneurship and the functionality of failure*. Seventh Annual Global Entrepreneurship Research Conference. Montreal, Canada.

McGrath, R. G. 2001. Exploratory learning, innovative capacity, and managerial oversight. *Academy of Management Journal*, 44(1): 118–131.

McGrath, R. G., Ferrier, W. J., and Mendelow, A. L. 2004. Real options as engines of choice and heterogeneity. *Academy of Management Review*, 29(1): 86–101.

McMullen, J. S. and Shepherd, D. A. 2006. Entrepreneurial action and the role of uncertainty in the theory of the entrepreneur. *Academy of Management Review*, 31(1): 132–152.

Meyer, M. and Zucker, L. 1989. *Permanently Failing Organizations*. Newbury Park, CA: Sage.

Morrison, E. W. 2002. Newcomers' relationships: The role of social network ties during socialization. *Academy of Management Journal*, 45(6): 1149–1160.

O'Reilly, C. A. and Chatman, J. 1986. Organizational commitment and psychological attachment: The effects of compliance, identification, and internalization on prosocial behavior. *Journal of Applied Psychology*, 71(3): 492.

Ohlson, J. A. 1980. Financial ratios and the probabilistic prediction of bankruptcy. *Journal of Accounting Research*, 18(1): 109–131.

Petroski, H. 1985. *To Engineer is Human: The Role of Failure in Successful Design.* New York: St. Martin's Press.

Pinto, J. K. and Prescott, J. E. 1988. Variations in critical success factors over the stages in the project life-cycle. *Journal of Management*, 14(1): 5–18.

Pinto, J. K. and Prescott, J. E. 1990. Planning and tactical factors in the project implementation process. *Journal of Management Studies*, 27(3): 305–327.

Popper, K. R. 1959. *The Logic of Scientific Discovery.* London: Hutchinson.

Prencipe, A. and Tell, F. 2001. Inter-project learning: Processes and outcomes of knowledge codification in project-based firms. *Research Policy*, 30(9): 1373–1394.

Pronin, E. and Ross, L. 2006. Temporal differences in trait self-ascription: When the self is seen as an other. *Journal of Personality and Social Psychology*, 90(2): 197.

Reich, W. 1949. *Character Analysis.* New York: Oregon Institute Press.

Ross, J. and Staw, B. M. 1993. Organizational escalation and exit: Lessons from the Shoreham Nuclear Power Plan. *Academy of Management Journal*, 36(4): 701–732.

Royer, I. 2003. Why bad projects are so hard to kill. *Harvard Business Review*, 81: 48–56.

Schmidt, J. B. and Calantone, R. J. 1998. Are really new product development projects harder to shut down? *Journal of Product Innovation Management*, 15(2): 111–123.

Shepherd, D. A. 2003. Learning from business failure: Propositions of grief recovery for the self-employed. *Academy of Management Review*, 28(2): 318–328.

Shepherd, D. A. and Cardon, M. S. 2009. Negative emotional reactions to project failure and the self-compassion to learn from the experience. *Journal of Management Studies*, 46(6): 923–949.

Shepherd, D. A., Covin, J. G., and Kuratko, D. F. 2009. Project failure from corporate entrepreneurship: Managing the grief process. *Journal of Business Venturing*, 24(6): 588–600.

Shepherd, D. A., Patzelt, H., and Wolfe, M. 2011. Moving forward from project failure: Negative emotions, affective commitment, and learning from the experience. *Academy of Management Journal*, 54(6): 1229–1259.

Shepherd, D. A., Patzelt, H., Williams, T. A., and Warnecke, D. 2014. How does project termination impact project team members? Rapid termination, 'creeping death', and learning from failure. *Journal of Management Studies*, 51(4): 513–546.

Sitkin, S. B. 1992. Learning through failure: The strategy of small losses. In B. M. Staw and L. L. Cummings (eds.), *Research in Organizational Behavior*, Vol. 14: 231–266. Greenwich, CT: JAI Press.

Staw, B. M. and Ross, J. 1987. Behavior in escalation situations: Antecedents, prototypes, and solutions. *Research in Organizational Behavior*, 9: 39–78.

Staw, B. M., Barsade, S. G., and Koput, K. W. 1997. Escalation at the credit window: A longitudinal study of bank executives' recognition and write-off of problem loans. *Journal of Applied Psychology*, 82(1): 130–142.

Ucbasaran, D., Shepherd, D. A., Lockett, A., and Lyon, S. J. 2013. Life after business failure the process and consequences of business failure for entrepreneurs. *Journal of Management*, 39(1): 163–202.

Van Eerde, W. 2000. Procrastination: Self-regulation in initiating aversive goals. *Applied Psychology-an International Review-Psychologie Appliquee-Revue Internationale*, 49(3): 372–389.

van Witteloostuijn, A. 1998. Bridging behavioral and economic theories of decline: Organizational inertia, strategic competition, and chronic failure. *Management Science*, 44(4): 501–519.

Wagner, J. A. and Gooding, R. Z. 1997. Equivocal information and attribution: An investigation of patterns of managerial sensemaking. *Strategic Management Journal*, 18(4): 275–286.

Weick, K. E. 1990. The vulnerable system: An analysis of the Tenerife air disaster. *Journal of Management*, 16(3): 571–593.

Weick, K. E., Sutcliffe, K. M., and Obstfeld, D. 2005. Organizing and the process of sensemaking. *Organization Science*, 16(4): 409–421.

Weick, K. E. and Sutcliffe, K. M. 2007. *Managing the Unexpected: Resilient Performance in an Age of Uncertainty*. San Francisco, CA: Jossey-Bass.

Zollo, M. and Winter, S. G. 2002. Deliberate learning and the evolution of dynamic capabilities. *Organization Science*, 13(3): 339–351.

6 Emotional intelligence, emotional capability, and both grief recovery and sensemaking

In Chapter 5, we discussed in detail the potential "creeping death" experienced with project failure in an organizational context. We now turn our attention to how certain individual characteristics (i.e., emotional intelligence) as well as organizational routines (i.e., emotional capabilities) can assist in both the grief recovery and the sensemaking process. Emotions are generated and exhibited in organizations. That is, emotions are both important input and outcome of organizational processes (Gooty, Gavin, and Ashkanasy 2009). Emotions are an important input to organizational processes at several levels, including between individuals (e.g., emotional intelligence, organizational commitment, satisfaction) (Fisher and Ashkanasy 2000; Mayer and Salovey 1997; Meyer and Allen 1997); within groups and teams (e.g., group affective tone and emotional contagion) (George 1990; Kelly and Barsade 2001); and organization wide, such as the overarching emotional climate (see for review, Ashkanasy and Humphrey 2011). Emotions are also often generated by organizational events. For example, members' emotions can be triggered in reaction to the implementation of change (Kiefer 2005), such as with the introduction of a radical project change (Huy 1999, 2002; Seo, Barrett, and Bartunek 2004).

Over and above the emotions associated with change, some initiatives, particularly those that are entrepreneurial in nature, will result in failure sometimes. These failures are often considered to be highly negative events (by individuals [Shepherd and Cardon 2009; Shepherd et al. 2011] and at the organizational level [Cannon and Edmondson 2001]) and frequently trigger negative emotional responses. As discussed throughout this book, the generation of these negative emotions can obstruct learning and diminish individuals' motivation to try again in the pursuit of entrepreneurial projects.

With obstructed learning and diminished motivation to further engage in entrepreneurial action, the organization suffers from employees who are now less committed to the organization (Ng, Butts, Vandenberg, DeJoy, and Wilson 2006), so there is likely to be less knowledge transfer between organizational members and a reduction in the creation of new organizational knowledge (Egan, Yang, and Bartlett 2004). Therefore, even though failure offers an opportunity for individuals to learn, emotional responses to failure have the potential to obstruct such learning. Furthermore, there could be limited time to learn following a failure (Shepherd, Patzelt, Williams, and Warnecke 2014), or learning that does occur could fail to transfer from the individual at hand to organizational performance because the individual is less motivated to try again (i.e., act on his or her new knowledge) and less likely to share what he or she has learned with others. Given that employee commitment and knowledge transfer are critical for organizational performance, there is a need to understand the role of emotion and learning from failure events, which have the potential to provide unique information and knowledge that can benefit individuals and their organizations.

Recent research on the "management" of emotions, particularly research on the management of negative emotions over loss associated with failure, has focused on one of two approaches. One approach has focused on gaining a deeper understanding of how some organizations are able to reduce or eliminate the generation of negative emotions from failure events (Härtel, Hsu, and Boyle 2002; Kelly and Barsade 2001). This can be achieved by organizations that normalize failure. Normalization captures "institutionalized processes by which extraordinary situations are rendered seemingly ordinary" (Ashforth and Kreiner, 2002). Specifically, in the entrepreneurial context, organizations have processes (perhaps also norms and routines) that communicate to their organizational members that failure is simply a normal part of the entrepreneurial process. The idea is that to the extent organizational members internalize the organization's normalization processes, when they do experience failure, it is likely to generate less (or under extreme conditions of normalization, no) negative emotional reactions to project failure.

The other approach has focused on regulating emotions with the underlying perspective that organizations can develop an emotional capability – namely, processes, norms, and procedures for managing emotions generated in the organizational context (Huy 1999). An emotionally capable organization does not try to eliminate the generation of negative emotions (as is the case in organizations that normalize failure) but helps organizational members regulate emotions so that they can more quickly eliminate grief and, in doing so, remove the obstacles to learning from the failure experience, communicate lessons learned to others in the organization, and maintain the motivation to try again.

In this chapter, we investigate each of these processes in greater detail, as highlighted in Figure 6.1, in which we offer a multilevel model of responses to negative emotion and learning from failure. We proceed as follows. First, we discuss the normalization of failure and

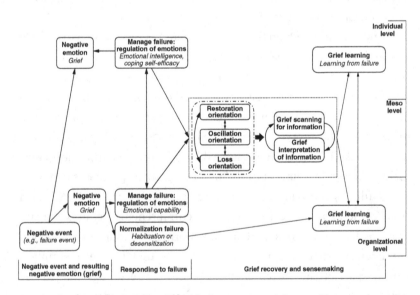

FIGURE 6.1: Multilevel model of responses to failure and learning from the experience

the implications for both individuals and organizations. Second, we integrate our discussions on failure normalization and management by analyzing how individuals manage grief and make sense of failure and how this influences learning and subsequent entrepreneurial action. Third, we explore how individuals and organizations manage failure, discussing emotional intelligence and capability. Finally, we discuss implications for scholars and practitioners and offer suggestions for future research.

RESPONDING TO FAILURE – NORMALIZATION OR EMOTIONAL REGULATION

As indicated in Figure 6.1, individuals and organizations respond to failure by either normalizing that failure or managing it through emotional regulation. These responses have consequences in how negative emotions influence subsequent action, including making sense of the failure event and learning. Similarly, responses to the negative emotions generated by a failure event can vary at the individual and organizational level (Ashkanasy and Humphrey 2011), so individual and organizational responses are likely to interact. We now turn to normalizing failure, the first potential response to negative emotional reactions to failure.

Normalizing failure

Generally, normalization in the organizational context refers to processes that contribute to organizational members interpreting an event as being normal that had previously been considered unusual. Specific to failure, normalization refers to organizational processes that render failure a normal occurrence. That is, to the extent the organization is entrepreneurial in its orientation, its members realize that (1) in the pursuit of opportunities, there is considerable uncertainty, and (2) this high uncertainty means that beliefs about any one focal opportunity could be wrong and could lead to failure. In this context, at the organizational level, failure is a natural and even essential part of the entrepreneurial process (Ashforth and Kreiner 2002; Shepherd, Covin, and Kuratko 2009).

An advantage of normalizing failure is that it helps minimize or eliminate negative emotional reactions to failure events, which has a number of important implications. Negative emotions have been found to undermine members' commitment to their organization (Belschak and Hartog 2009). In contrast, positive emotions increase creativity and cognitive flexibility (Fredrickson 2001; Isen 2000), positively influencing organizational processes at the employee (e.g., individual tasks, activities, etc.) and organizational (e.g., innovation, new product development, etc.) levels (Amabile, Barsade, Mueller, and Staw 2005; Rank and Frese 2008). To the extent that there is a reduction in members' commitment to the organization as a result of negative emotions, there is likely a corresponding decrease in employee performance (Meyer, Paunonen, Gellatly, Goffin, and Jackson 1989) and organizational advantages, such as innovation and product development (Amabile et al. 2005). Habituation and desensitization are two mechanisms by which failure can become normalized for organizational members of entrepreneurial firms.

Habituation: Habituation occurs when people face continued exposure to a stimuli (e.g., failure). The more they face this stimuli, the weaker their reaction to it becomes (Ashforth and Kreiner 2002). For example, Shepherd and colleagues (Shepherd et al. 2014) highlighted how entrepreneurial research and development (R&D) teams in a large corporation experienced frequent project failures as they explored innovative new products. They found that the habitual occurrence of failure resulted in reduced negative emotional reactions to project termination for individuals involved in the failed projects. The more an organizational member experiences project failure, the weaker the aversive nature of the project failure becomes over time, thereby generating less (or no) negative emotional reactions.

Habituation is not only something that an individual develops through his or her own experiences; it can also result from social processes that build toward a collective level of habituation (Ashforth and Kreiner 2002). That is, broader collectives (in this case, an entrepreneurial organization) facilitate the creation and maintenance of classifications for organizational events, including failure (Zerubavel 1991), which influences habituation. Specifically, these classifications are value laden and distinguish between good, bad, helpful, and/or destructive events for an organization (Zerubavel 1991). For example, an individual might be part of an organization that stigmatizes individuals who take large risks and come up short on ambitious projects. In contrast, another organization might celebrate risk taking and innovativeness even if an early idea fails to materialize as planned (cf., Shepherd and Haynie 2011). Therefore, in the failure context, this means that organizations normalize responses to failure, providing organizational members with cues regarding the organization's or profession's ideology (Ashforth and Kreiner 2002; Zerubavel 1991). In turn, these ideologies influence individual emotional responses to failure events, including perceptions of failure as "habitual."

Desensitization: The second mechanism that can contribute to normalization is desensitization. It refers to the process by which experiencing negative stimuli of increasing magnitude reduces the mismatch between what is experienced and what is expected such that negative emotional reactions to these aversive stimuli are reduced (St Onge 1995). Desensitization has been explored in a number of the social sciences, where the extraordinary seems acceptable, justified, and even commonplace. For example, politicians frequently downplay crises or disturbances, attributing them to "normal" variance in political life in order to calm voters' potential concerns and return to the status quo (Ritter and Kirk 1995). Similarly, law enforcement officers often offer "reasonable explanations" to the accused when conducting interrogations as an attempt to diminish the negative outcomes of crimes (i.e., framing them as justified or accidental) to solicit confessions (Simon 1991).

    In the failure context, desensitization can occur when an individual faces failures of increasing magnitude such that they experience less of a mismatch between what they expect and what they achieve. When this occurs, there is reduced negative emotional reactions despite an increasing magnitude of failure. In normalizing failure, organizations provide experiences, practices, and procedures that make project failure an ordinary event – and they can do this by orchestrating desensitization. In doing so, project failure is less likely to generate negative emotions and therefore less likely to create emotional obstacles to learning from the failure experience (Shepherd et al. 2009).

Indeed, people do become accustomed to aversive tasks so that over time, the tasks appear less aversive (Reed 1989). In a culture that normalizes failure (including those with failure-tolerant leaders [Farson and Keyes 2002]), it appears possible that project failure no longer generates grief (at least to the same extent). That is, when organizational members begin to consider project failures simply as normal events (facilitated by organizational culture and top management), they are likely to have less severe negative emotional reactions (i.e., grief) to them (Ashforth and Kreiner 1999; Gusterson 1996; Palmer 1978).

For instance, in a study of 257 research scientists, we (Shepherd et al. 2011) found that organizational members who perceived project failure as being highly normalized in their organizations experienced fewer negative emotional reactions to project failure than those in organizations in which project failure was perceived as being less normalized. However, we did not find statistically significant support for the relationship between normalization and learning from failure. Therefore, although normalization may remove obstacles to learning, it may not necessarily facilitate learning from failure. Indeed, as we now propose, it may influence an outcome that is consistent with the failure to learn: increased likelihood of subsequent projects failing.

First, when failure becomes "normal" for individuals and negative emotions are reduced, these events (that would have previously generated emotional responses) may cease to capture individuals' attention for the purposes of scanning and processing, which are necessary for learning (see Ellis and Chase 1971; Schwarz and Clore 1988;

Wood, Saltzberg, Neale, Stone, and Rachmiel 1990). Negative emotions, while painful, can also serve as critical signals that something has gone wrong, driving individuals to identify and remove the cause of this "pain" through learning (Shepherd et al. 2014). In terms of making failure more likely, there is the possibility that by eliminating emotion as an outcome of project failure, individuals will invest less emotion in the project. Emotional investments, such as commitment, are important inputs to creativity (Amabile et al. 2005), and with less creativity, project performance is likely to deteriorate (Amabile 1997; Amabile et al. 2005). Thus, project failure becomes more likely.

Interestingly, in a study of oncology doctors, those who became desensitized to patient death became more callous and indifferent to their patients, resulting in less effective patient care (Peeters and Le Blanc 2001). While the negative emotions associated with death were removed, so too were the emotion-driven concerns that had previously motivated the doctors' pursuit of high-quality patient care. As learned from this example, individuals must balance the normalization (and to an extreme, elimination) of negative emotions with the need to recognize negative emotions as signals of something being important, needing attention, or requiring ongoing investment (despite a loss). If not balanced appropriately, failure could cease to function as a catalyst for renewed commitment or learning following a failure event (Shepherd et al. 2009).

REGULATING GRIEF TO LEARN FROM THE FAILURE EXPERIENCE

Failure events can result in negative emotions, which, if left unchecked, can result in a number of negative outcomes for both individuals and organizations (Prigerson et al. 1997; Shepherd 2009). Reducing negative emotions (e.g., grief) facilitates one's ability to make sense of the failure (Huy 1999), and making sense of the failure reduces grief (Shepherd 2009). To gain a deeper understanding of learning from failure, we need to explore the interrelationship between grief-recovery modes (i.e., the mechanisms of a loss orientation, a restoration orientation, and an oscillation orientation that moves between the two) and sensemaking activities (i.e., the mechanisms of scanning, interpreting, and acting). We first discuss these modes and then return to a discussion of how individual and organizational grief-regulation factors influence both recovery and learning from failure.

Grief-recovery modes and sensemaking activities

The primary grief-recovery modes we explore in the model illustrated in Figure 6.1 are a loss orientation, a restoration orientation, and an oscillation orientation. As stated earlier (e.g., in Chapter 1), an individual with a loss orientation confronts the loss by revisiting the events leading up to project failure and works through his or her negative emotional reactions to the lost project; a person with a restoration orientation distracts from the loss event and attempts to address secondary causes of stress; and an individual with an oscillation orientation transitions back and forth between a loss and a restoration orientation (Shepherd 2003; Stroebe and Schut 1999: see also Chapter 1).

Specifically, we propose that in enacting *a loss orientation*, actors (i.e., individuals and organizations) improve their ability to learn from a failure experience through enhanced scanning of information, which is critical for understanding the causes of project failure. In enacting *a restoration orientation*, actors enhance their ability to learn from a failure experience by "freeing up" their information-processing capacity to process information about the potential causes of project failure. Finally, in enacting *an oscillation orientation*, actors are able to benefit from both the scanning of a loss orientation and the freeing up of information processing of a restoration orientation while minimizing the costs of maintaining each of these orientations for an extended period of time. The cost associated with an extended loss orientation is a focus on the negative emotions of project failure, thus escalating grief (e.g., ruminations) and obstructing sensemaking. The cost of an extended restoration orientation is that the individual cannot allocate sufficient attention to noticing and interpreting signals of possible causes for the failure. Sensemaking itself is an interpretive process whereby individuals assign meaning to the events they experience (Gioia and Chittipeddi 1991: 442). It is an ongoing process of interpretation that informs and is informed by action (Morrison 2002; Thomas, Clark, and Gioia 1993). Therefore, to understand recovery from project failure, we need to investigate the ongoing interrelationship between sense making and grief-recovery modes.

The primary sensemaking activities we explore in this model are scanning, interpreting, and learning (Gioia and Chittipeddi 1991; Thomas et al. 1993; Weick 1979), all of which help explain the extent to which actors can capitalize on their failure experiences. *Scanning* refers to a process whereby individuals attend to and collect information that may be relevant to the sensemaking process (Gioia and Chittipeddi 1991). That is, individuals allocate attention to notice signals of possible causes for project failure. *Interpreting* refers to the categorization, organization, or codification of information into structures that facilitate the individual's understanding of the various signals noticed during scanning (Gioia 1986; Taylor and Crocker 1981). It involves ways of comprehending the signals of what might have led to the failure event, including themes, recurring issues, and categories of issues (e.g., the market, management, and so forth). In the sensemaking perspective, *learning* refers to changes in ongoing beliefs and practices (Ginsberg 1988; Thomas et al. 1993) reflected in subsequent actions (Daft and Weick 1984), including applying knowledge toward the development of a new venture (Ucbasaran, Westhead, Wright, and Flores 2010). Although scanning, interpreting, and learning are different elements of sense making, they are highly related. For example, learning (i.e., changed actions) reveals new information that is captured through scanning and understood through interpreting (Daft and Weick 1984; Dutton and Duncan 1987; Hambrick 1982). In turn, this interpreting informs action (Bartunek 1984; Dutton, Fahey, and Narayanan 1983; Gioia and Chittipeddi 1991), and this action enables the scanning of new terrain, which reveals new information to be interpreted (Daft and Weick 1984). We now discuss the relationship between grief-recovery modes and scanning as a sensemaking activity.

Grief-recovery modes and scanning for information about project failure

In a loss orientation, actors are motivated to remove the mismatch between expected performance and the failure outcome – namely, the source of the negative emotional reaction – and to do so by allocating attention (Clore 1992; Schwarz and Clore 1996; Weick 1990) and resources (Pieters and Van Raaij 1988) to this task. The relationship between emotion and sensemaking is reflected in research demonstrating that individuals prioritize emotional events when scanning and interpreting information over emotionally neutral events (cf. Ellis and Ashbrook 1988; Ellis and Ashbrook 1989; Ellis and Chase 1971). In contrast to a loss orientation that directs attention to scanning for information to remove the mismatch between expected (desired) outcomes and the outcome experienced, a restoration orientation largely distracts attention away from the mismatch in an attempt to avoid the negative emotions associated with this analysis and also directs attention to addressing secondary causes of stress. Given that individuals and organizations have limited attentional capacity, the more attention is allocated to addressing secondary causes of stress, the less attention there is available to scan for information about the possible causes of project failure. That is, there are competing demands that reduce attention for the purposes of scanning.

Although a loss orientation can enhance information scanning that can inform individuals' understanding of why a project failed, extended use of a loss orientation can result in a shift of attention from the events leading up to the project failure to the emotions surrounding the failure (at the time of the failure and/or current emotions) (Stroebe and Schut 2001). Attention is no longer focused on scanning for signals as opportunities to make sense of the failure.

Focusing on the emotions surrounding the loss can escalate negative emotions through ruminations (Lyubomirsky and Nolen-Hoeksema 1995; Nolen-Hoeksema, Parker, and Larson 1994). Ruminations are passive and repetitive thoughts that direct attention to the symptoms of one's adverse situation (e.g., the negative emotions associated with a failure event) rather than the cause of the adverse situation, which often leads to negative emotions being escalated and maintained for an extended period (Lyubomirsky and Nolen-Hoeksema 1995; Nolen-Hoeksema and Morrow 1991; Nolen-Hoeksema et al. 1994). As such, ruminations can increase feelings of grief (Lyubomirsky and Nolen-Hoeksema 1995; Nolen-Hoeksema et al. 1994). Therefore, not only is attention redirected to emotions (rather than signals of the potential causes of the failure), but increased negative emotions also further narrow attention (Gladstein and Reilly 1985; Staw, Sandelands, and Dutton 1981; Sutton and D'Aunno 1989) and even obstruct (Mogg, Mathews, Bird, and Macgregor-Morris 1990) one's ability to scan for information about the underlying causes of venture failure.

This is where the oscillation orientation – in this case, moving from a loss orientation to a restoration orientation – can be very helpful in that it helps individuals distract thoughts from the failure (and the emotions surrounding the failure) to stop the further escalation of grief that occurs through ruminations. Although, as aforementioned, a restoration orientation provides little opportunity for individuals to scan for information underlying project failure, it does provide a respite and an opportunity to recharge one's "emotional batteries" for a subsequent switch back to a loss orientation. A switch back to a loss orientation once again enables the individual to scan for information about the causes of the failure to develop an account for why the event occurred and perhaps, how it can be avoided in the future. That is, as the loss orientation starts to detract from one's ability to scan for information about the failure, an oscillation orientation provides an opportunity for the individual to pause before once again engaging in scanning activities.

Grief-recovery modes and interpreting information about project failure

As discussed earlier, although a restoration orientation directs attention to aspects of one's life not directly associated with the failure (and
thus reduces attention available for scanning), it has the positive
effect of reducing the negative emotions associated with the loss
event (Cuisner, Janssen, Graauw, Bakker, and Hoogduin 1996; Shuchter 1986). Just as this respite can help individuals scan for information,
it can also help them process previously scanned information. That is,
as a restoration orientation can be used to reduce negative emotions,
it helps remove the emotional obstacles to processing information
about the failure event because negative emotions obstruct information processing. However, it is unlikely that repressing negative emotions to facilitate information processing is an effective strategy in the
long run. Indeed, it appears that it is very difficult to suppress emotions for an extended period. Rather, these suppressed emotions tend
to reappear at inopportune times (Wegner and Erber 1993) and can
further obstruct information processing. Indeed, in a restoration orientation, attention is allocated to processing information on the dis-
tractor task (which may be addressing secondary causes of stress).
Therefore, given individuals' limited attention (Ocasio 2011), there
is less attention "available" for processing information related to
understanding the causes of failure.

Transitioning to a loss orientation redirects an individual's
attention so he or she is able to process information about the events
leading up to the failure. By returning to thinking about and processing information obtained through scanning but with fewer negative
emotions that would have otherwise obstructed information processing (De Sousa 1987; cf. Fineman 1996; Frank 1993; Hirshleifer 1993;
Weick 1990), individuals are able to continue to build an account for
why the failure occurred. This increased information processing
(through the reduction of negative emotions) can take a number of
forms, including finding analogies (Gentner and Holyoak 1997;

Markman and Gentner 2001) that can be used to gain a deeper understanding of the failure event.

However, again, a loss orientation can become less effective over time as one's thoughts begin to shift focus from the events leading up to the failure to the negative emotions felt during and after the failure event. These negative emotions (including ruminations) obstruct information processing and therefore obstruct the individual's opportunity to learn from the failure event.

Grief-recovery modes and learning about project failure

Learning through changes in belief and actions typically reflects an individual's ability to scan and process information that helps him or her build an account of business failure. Immediately after a failure (and, for that matter, during and immediately prior to a failure), the negative emotions surrounding the event are likely to be high (and higher for some than others; see Chapter 2). As detailed earlier, these negative emotions are likely to obstruct both scanning and information processing and, as a result, learning from the experience. That is, it is likely to be particularly tough for an entrepreneur to immediately scan, interpret, and learn the causes of a failure early in the grieving process. Rather, the individual needs to engage in a recovery process, and learning is part of that process – recovery enhances learning, and learning enhances recovery.

Given the high negative emotions immediately following project failure, a restoration orientation helps the individual begin to lessen some of those negative emotions by reducing thoughts about the failure event. A restoration orientation directs thoughts and actions toward the reduction of secondary causes of stress. Secondary causes of stress after a business failure may include selling a house, finding new accommodations, changing children's school (if the new housing is in another district), applying for jobs, and so on. By reducing secondary sources of stress, the primary stressor (i.e., the business failure) no longer looms as large. Furthermore, some studies have reported psychological and health problems from attempting to suppress thoughts and emotions over an extended period of time (Archer 1999), which can interfere with the learning.

Moreover, while restoration activities can indirectly reveal potentially important information for understanding the causes of failure, individuals exhaust these information sources relatively quickly, and processing this information is still largely obstructed because attention and processing capacity are allocated to competing tasks. Again, however, a loss orientation can become less effective over time. Individuals become emotionally exhausted from engaging in "grief work," and they often begin to engage in ruminations. When ruminating, an entrepreneur of a failed business tends to focus thoughts on answering questions like "Will I ever feel happy again," "Why am I such a basket case," and "Why can't I just get on with my life?" Focusing on these questions provides little benefit in revealing information necessary for making sense of the failure; rather, they have the effect of shifting attention to the symptoms of the failure event, further escalating negative emotions (Nolen-Hoeksema et al. 1994).

When in a loss orientation (especially with rumination), individuals often experience failure events as threats, such as a threat to their self-identity and other related identities. Research on threats has indicated that those who feel threatened are likely to cling to (i.e., rely heavily on) well-rehearsed routines and practices despite the ineffectiveness of those actions (Cameron, Kim, and Whetten 1987; Cameron, Whetten, and Kim 1987; Nystrom and Starbuck 1984). Therefore, when a loss orientation leads to ruminations and/or high feelings of threat, little is learned, and little is changed in terms of action. Breaking this cycle requires transitioning to a restoration orientation.

Therefore, throughout the sensemaking process, a loss orientation and a restoration orientation have pros and cons. A loss orientation can be focused on the failure event for the purposes of collecting and processing information to build an account for why the business failed and inform subsequent action. However, it is also emotionally exhausting, and if maintained for an extended period, it can lead to ruminations and escalated negative emotions, thereby obstructing the sensemaking process. A restoration orientation can help alleviate some of the negative emotions and, in addressing some of the secondary sources of stress, can help alleviate some of the overall stress and perhaps also some of the stress associated with the main stressor – the business failure. However, in focusing on restoration activities, an individual with this orientation undertakes little scanning and information processing, which is necessary for learning from the failure experience. It is the combination of these mechanisms in an oscillation orientation through which the individual transitions between the two phases, that maximizes grief recovery and learning from the experience (Shepherd 2003; Stroebe and Schut 1999).

Grief recovery, sensemaking, and learning at the organizational level

Grief, sensemaking, and learning can take place at multiple levels, including the group and organizational levels (Kogut and Zander 1996; Shepherd et al. 2009). Organizations can either facilitate or discourage activities that affect the thoughts, feelings, and actions in a workplace in response to a failure event (Brief and Weiss 2002; Huy 2011). The social psychology literature highlights the organizational influences on how individuals cope with grief (e.g., restoration or loss orientation) (Archer 1999), which can in turn influence learning outcomes. Similarly, individual learning from failure can also influence organizational learning to the extent that the lessons are articulated and codified (Huy 2011; Zollo and Winter 2002).

As discussed previously, some organizations normalize failure, which may influence both individual and organizational learning. In contrast, other organizations manage failure and its negative emotional outcomes through their emotional capability, or the ability to regulate emotional responses (Huy 1999, 2011). As we now discuss, emotional capability likely influences individuals' grief-response modes, providing a social context that either facilitates or obstructs grief responses, sensemaking, and – ultimately – learning from a failure event. Furthermore, emotional capability and its influence on recovery and learning are influenced by individuals' emotional intelligence, to which we now turn.

EMOTIONAL INTELLIGENCE, CAPABILITY, AND THE EFFECTIVENESS OF GRIEF-RECOVERY MODES TO ENHANCE LEARNING FROM FAILURE

Why are some individuals and organizations more effective at undertaking the sensemaking process described earlier? The answer, as shown in Figure 6.1, lies in both individual and organizational emotional responses to failure events. Specifically, individual-level emotional intelligence and organization-level emotional capability likely influence grief processes, which in turn influence sensemaking activities and thus learning from failure. In this section, we define and discuss emotional intelligence and capability, and see how these influence both one another and the process influencing recovery from failure.

Emotional intelligence

One way to explain the selection and effectiveness of grief-recovery modes is through understanding emotional intelligence. An emotionally intelligent person is one who is aware of and understands his or her emotions (e.g., grief) and can regulate those emotions (through grief dynamics). An emotionally intelligent individual will also recognize and understand when his or her emotions start to escalate (from an extended period of loss orientation) and realize that it is time to transition to a restoration orientation. For example, if an individual recognizes the need to engage in a loss orientation to work through a loss and start to build an account for a failure experience, he or she will know the person with the right sort of emotional makeup and skills to help with the activities of this orientation – that is, someone comfortable talking about emotions and/or someone knowledgeable of the failure who also has sufficient sensitivity to discuss some of the causes of the business failure.

Similarly, an emotionally intelligent individual likely knows which people feel more comfortable and able to engage in restoration-orientation activities, such as addressing secondary causes of stress or going to a football game. Selecting these individuals and having social interactions with them provides an opportunity to be distracted from the business failure in order to recharge one's emotional batteries for a subsequent round of loss orientation. Therefore, an emotionally intelligent person knows how and with whom to successfully engage in a loss orientation; knows how and with whom to successfully engage in a restoration orientation; and, importantly, knows when to switch between the two.

In the context of project failure and our previous work on managing grief, emotional intelligence represents an individual ability that facilitates oscillation between a loss orientation and a restoration orientation, which is critical to reduce grief over project failure (Shepherd et al. 2011). That is, the more emotionally intelligent individuals are, the more they are able to recognize and understand their emotional reactions to failure and to manage these emotions in an effective manner to more quickly reduce the emotional obstacles to learning from failure and increase their motivation to try again.

Emotional intelligence and interaction with the broader social context

The aforementioned descriptions of the grief process and emotional intelligence largely focus on how an individual's thoughts and actions contribute to recovery from grief (Archer 1999; Shepherd 2003; Stroebe and Schut 1999). However, such an approach underestimates the powerful role that social interactions can have in the grief-recovery process. Indeed, individuals' social interactions are important in explaining why some people quickly recover and learn from their failure experiences while others languish in grief without a positive action path forward. Indeed, we know from research on the loss of a loved one that when an individual faces such a loss, he or she wants to talk about the loss and his or her emotions about the loss with another person (Lepore and Brown 1997; Lepore, Silver, Wortman, and Wayment 1996; Pennebaker 1989, 1995). This type of social interaction forms an important part of an effective loss-orientation approach: it helps people work through the loss to make sense of their experiences (for reviews, see Pennebaker 1989, 1993). Emotional intelligence is likely to influence how individuals interact socially, but the social environment also likely influences individuals' emotional intelligence.

However, social interaction is not a panacea: not all social interactions help recovery or sensemaking (Herbert and Dunkel-Schetter 1992; House 1981; Rook 1984). For example, someone could say something to "hurt the feelings" of a grieving individual as people facing loss often feel particularly vulnerable and sensitive, which could escalate negative emotions (rather than reduce them) and set back grief recovery (House 1981; Lehman, Ellard, and Wortman 1986; Thoits 1982). Similarly, in some social environments, people may respond negatively to grieving individuals (e.g., disinterest, stigma, etc.), which could potentially exacerbate negative events for grieving individuals. Finally, those in a grieving individual's social environment might feel the need to provide an ear and comforting words but find themselves nervous that they may say the "wrong" thing. As a result, they deliver a message in an awkward way or simply fail to say anything at all (Nolen-Hoeksema and Davis 1999).

Therefore, not everyone might be the right person to help someone deal with a loss (e.g., the failure of a business). We do know that many people facing a major loss seek out family members with whom they can discuss the situation (Rimé 1995), but in some instances, these other family members may also be dealing with grief. Take the example of the loss of a family member, a situation in which all the family members may be feeling grief. This could mean that dyads of family members might be highly effective at helping each other with a loss orientation, but it could also make it more difficult. For example, a family member might be less likely to ask for help from a close other when he or she knows that that person is also suffering; the person does not want his or her own problems to exacerbate the grief the other individual is feeling (Vachon and Stylianos 1988). It seems that the variance of outcomes in such situations is likely to be large. Take, for instance, cofounders of a failed business. Perhaps they could socially interact to grieve. This social interaction could lead to a very positive outcome if the cofounders share their emotions, recognize that these feelings of grief are normal, and acknowledge that they are not alone, and it could help in constructing a story of the business failure from someone who understands the conditions surrounding the failure event well. However, it could also work out as a very negative outcome. For example, interacting with the cofounder of the business may lead to attributions of blame, with both escalating negative emotions and further obstructing the generation of a plausible story for the failure.

In exploring the social influence on grief recovery, we now investigate the concept of organization-level emotional capability; its interaction with individual-level emotional intelligence; and its influence on the grief-recovery process, sensemaking, and learning from a failure event.

Emotional capability of organizations

At the organizational level, rather than creating processes for normalizing failure to reduce or eliminate negative emotional reactions to failure, some organizations develop an emotional capability that can help "manage" the emotions involved in the entrepreneurial process. Building on the notion of emotional intelligence at the individual level, Huy (1999: 325–326) developed a model of *emotional capability*, which he defined as follows:

> [The] organization's ability to acknowledge, recognize, monitor, discriminate, and attend to its members' emotions and it is manifested in the organization's norms and routines related to feeling (Schein 1992). These routines reflect organizational

behaviors that either express or evoke certain specific emotional states, and these behaviors [are termed] emotional dynamics.

Similar to emotionally intelligent individuals, emotionally capable organizations are better able to help members recognize, understand, and regulate their emotions. That is, these organizations have created norms and routines to help their members deal with grief by facilitating the expression of negative emotions over project failure and helping employees develop accounts for project failure. In turn, organizational members are distracted from thoughts about the failure and can recharge their emotional batteries, address secondary causes of stress, and begin to recognize when and how to switch between the two. This emotional capability is likely to influence individuals' grief responses (i.e., restoration, loss, or oscillation orientation), which in turn influences learning.

Emotional capability provides a number of specific positive outcomes. For example, emotional capability appears to influence organizational members' emotional reactions to change, with the collective emotional response either helping or hurting during the change process (Sanchez-Burks and Huy 2009). When capabilities are developed broadly, the organization is more capable of understanding and adapting to required changes. Similarly, groups within organizations (i.e., newcomers versus long-timers, etc.) vary in their emotional capability and their emotional responses to change initiatives, and these responses can influence decisions to either support or covertly dismiss broader organizational changes (Huy 2011). The collective emotional capability of these groups has been shown to be more influential than individual emotions alone, providing validation and external support for an emotional response from other group members (Smith, Seger, and Mackie 2007).

It is important to note that unlike normalization, emotional capability does not attempt to eliminate the generation of negative emotions after failure. Rather, it enhances the organization's ability to manage these emotions to maximize their benefits while more quickly reducing their negative effect on employees' ability to learn from failure and their motivation to try again. Indeed, as members of a highly emotionally capable organization, individuals may "allow" themselves to experience negative emotions over project failure knowing that the organization can help them manage these emotions to reduce their negative consequences more quickly. Similarly, and in contrast to more emotionless organizations (as a result of the normalization of failure), some organizations choose to acknowledge grief over project failure. In doing so with practices and procedures for regulating emotions, these organizations can help their members more effectively regulate grief, understand the underlying causes that need to be addressed, and more quickly resolve them (Shepherd et al. 2009).

Emotional capability and coping through social support

The organizational practices and procedures associated with emotional capability can help build individual-level coping self-efficacy. *Coping self-efficacy* refers to "beliefs in one's capabilities to mobilize the motivation, cognitive resources, and courses of action needed to recover from setbacks arising from the organization's entrepreneurial activities" (Shepherd et al. 2009: 593). With higher coping self-efficacy, individuals are more proactive toward changing their situation to make it less threatening. That is, they respond to the causes of their negative emotions by making appropriate and relevant changes (Shepherd et al. 2009) and enduring in this response (Bandura 1986). Furthermore, coping self-efficacy has been linked to less grief. For example, Benight and colleagues (2001) studied a sample of recent widows and found that those with higher coping self-efficacy had higher psychological and physical well-being. Therefore, it appears that coping self-efficacy "is accompanied by benign appraisals of potential threats, weaker stress reactions to them, less ruminative preoccupation with them, better behavioral management of threats, and faster recovery of well-being from any experienced distress over them" (Benight and Bandura 2003: 1133).

There may be a number of factors that contribute to coping self-efficacy, but one way for an organization to facilitate coping self-efficacy in its members is by creating support groups. Support groups are used to help individuals regulate their emotions, and they are implemented in a variety of organizations for a variety of reasons. For the purpose of dealing with grief, Balk and colleagues (1993: 432) described the goal of a support group in this way, "The goal of the social support group [is] to facilitate coping with grief and to assist in resolving the difficulties associated with mourning through education regarding adaptive tasks and coping skills pertinent to life crises and through opening channels of communication between groups".

As for the specific structure and activities of these groups, social support groups that facilitate coping with grief over project failure can follow the form of other successful support groups (see Caserta and Lund 1996). That is, social support groups that help individuals cope with grief over project failure (and thus help build coping self-efficacy) are likely to be led by an individual who has experience with the failure of projects that he or she highly valued, provide a climate for open information sharing (about emotions and coping mechanisms), and be structured in such a way that participants perceive a low-threat environment. These support groups (depending on their purpose) could in turn influence grief responses, including helping individuals discuss the grief they experienced (i.e., loss orientation), plan for next steps and action (i.e., restoration orientation), or oscillate between the two depending on the needs exhibited by the group.

In addition, these groups can be helpful in avoiding desensitization, lack of learning, and lower performance. Previously, we discussed how oncology care providers who had become desensitized to patient deaths became more callous and detached from their patients, which had negative implications for the patients' health. In contrast, the doctors who avoided desensitization relied on the social support of colleagues to cope with the negative emotional reactions to their patients dying, resulting in better coping self-efficacy and ultimately better patient care (Peeters and Le Blanc 2001). Whether formally constructed by the organization in terms of social support teams or more informally in terms of one colleague helping another, it appears that social support provides a basis for individuals to recover from grief over project failure more quickly without a "drop off" in their emotional investment in subsequent projects. This investment is critical to project success yet absent or substantially reduced for those desensitized to failure (or for those who otherwise normalize project failure).

As an illustration of what we have discussed till now, in the case of the loss of a family member, grief is likely to be generated in each family member and to also exist at the group (i.e., the family) level. Some families are better able to deal with this grief: they have the emotional capability to express grief (Davies, Spinetta, Martinson, McClowry, and Kulenkamp 1986; Kissane et al. 1996a) – as is consistent with a loss orientation – and to avoid grief (Kissane 1994) – as is consistent with a restoration orientation – and they likely have the emotional capability to know when and how to switch orientations. These differences in capability across families help explain why some families recover more quickly from losses than others (Edwards and Clarke 2004; Kissane et al. 1996a; Kissane, Bloch, Onghena, and McKenzie 1996c; Kissane, Bloch, McKenzie, Mcdowall, and Nitzan 1998). However, it is one thing to recognize the importance of a capability and another thing to understand how to acquire it. Emotional capability can emerge in a group of individuals who each have high emotional intelligence. However, while this is possible, it does not always occur. It could be that the organization's norms and routines are such that they do not capture and utilize the emotional intelligence of its members, leading to poor grief recovery at the group level. The opposite is also the case: members of the group may not have high emotional intelligence on their own, but the organization may have such high emotional capability that the group can "manage" and recover from grief.

Overall, an emotionally intelligent individual is better able to detect, understand, and regulate his or her emotions to more quickly recover from grief and make sense of a failure experience. Similarly, an emotionally capable organization has the norms and routines to effectively manage grief to more quickly recover and maximize organizational learning from the failure experience.

Emotional capability and coping through rituals

An extension of this notion of social support at the dyad or group level is an organizational ritual that we have found in some innovative firms. In a study of parting ceremonies by employees of organizations that have died, Harris and Sutton (1986) found that parting ceremonies, or "wakes," allow employees to exchange emotional support as well as facilitate self-reflection and "editing" of the social system and the event itself. These parting ceremonies for work-related losses serve a similar purpose as funerals (i.e., Irish wakes) for humans and have taken on a number of different titles, such as "the last supper," "the last hurrah," and "the final party" (Harris and Sutton 1986: 13). They provide opportunities to realize that a loss has actually occurred and represent a time to reminisce, connect with those involved (perhaps for the last time), and say goodbye (Trice and Beyer 1984).

These events tend to vary in timing, invitees, and location. For example, one organization (a hospital) held a "last supper" party funded by one of the doctors, at which employees and those already laid off were able to get together to share emotions (Harris and Sutton 1986). In contrast, another party, the "last hurrah," was sponsored by a union for an auto plant that was closing. The objective was to deplete the remaining budget but also give an earful to management (who was also invited). The party served as a defiant act to both management and the national union (which was asking for any remaining funds), and also provided an outlet for shared emotion and experience (Harris and Sutton 1986: 13).

Emotional capability – cross-level effects

As indicated in the aforementioned arguments and examples, firms with high emotional capability provide social opportunities for individuals to manage emotions. Some of these (e.g., support groups, etc.) can be more productive, whereas others (e.g., the "last hurrah" example) may serve as a mechanism to allow individuals to release emotional pressure. The effectiveness of such events, programs, or activities is likely dependent on individuals' emotional intelligence or at least on the interaction between individual-level intelligence and organization-level emotional capability.

EMOTIONAL INTELLIGENCE, EMOTIONAL CAPABILITY, AND LEARNING FROM FAILURE

An emotionally intelligent individual can use his or her skills to personally recover from grief even though these actions may come at the expense of others in the organization. Such actions can generate feelings of distrust and a lack of harmony at the group level, thus undermining the organization's emotional capability. In contrast, an emotionally intelligent individual might provide leadership in constructing norms and routines for managing grief over the loss of entrepreneurial projects that is useful for helping organizational members recover from grief and for enabling the organization as a whole to make sense of failure experiences.

Furthermore, the group level could also influence the individual level. An emotionally capable organization can provide norms and routines that create a context in which individuals can learn to recognize, understand, and regulate their own emotions. That is, an emotionally capable organization can help build emotionally intelligent members. However, the group level might contain disharmony over emotion regulation, thus obstructing sensemaking. Indeed, research has suggested that tension can arise from disharmony in coping styles, such as middle managers having different goals from upper management or groups of organizational members feeling alienated from other non-group members (Huy 2011).

Heterogeneity in coping styles and the type and intensity of emotion over project failure do not necessarily create disharmony. In some instances, this diversity could be an emotional capability.

For example, we know that grief may lead to obstructed sensemaking when a loss orientation is maintained for too long. This is particularly problematic in an organization that is homogenous with members whose natural, or default, approach is a loss orientation. Problems may also arise in organizations that are homogenous with a restoration orientation. Heterogeneity in grief orientation likely provides a deeper understanding of when an orientation switch is needed and the mechanisms for enacting the switch. That is, diversity can be used to harmonize grief recovery and enhance sensemaking. This diversity as a harmonizing force is more likely to occur when there are emotionally intelligent individuals, an emotionally capably organization, and an interaction between the two.

Given the interaction of emotionally intelligent individuals with group dynamics, an individual being deeply immersed in his or her own thoughts and emotions does not necessarily result in positive outcomes; rather, learning from negative events can and does involve interactions with others. While we normally think of cognitions and emotions at the individual level of analysis, there is a considerable body of research on cognition at the group level (e.g., of the top management team [Harrison and Klein 2007; Huber and Lewis 2010; Kerr and Tindale 2004]) and a small but important stream of research about emotions at the group level (Barsade 2002; Huy 1999, 2011). As an emotion, grief is typically considered and dealt with at the individual level of analysis, but grief can exist at the group level. For example, a negative event can result in a lower valuation of a group identity (e.g., membership in a failed organization), which can arouse group-level negative emotions, including anger and fear (Mackie, Devos, and Smith 2000). Similarly, group members who feel they are collectively at a disadvantage can experience community-wide negative emotions or grief due to their situation (Huy 2011).

An emotionally capable organization has norms and routines for dealing with emotions surrounding an event that directly impact the organization (Huy 1999). Although in the case of business failure, the organization itself is likely dissolved (or remains in a substantially weakened form), this is not the case when the failure is an entrepreneurial project within an organization. In such an instance, a project fails, but the organization remains. In these situations, an emotionally capable organization has the norms and routines for effectively managing grief to more quickly recover and thereby make sense of the failure experience. Thus, we anticipate that individuals with higher levels of emotional intelligence *and* access to an emotionally capable organization will undertake more effective activities for coping with their negative emotions and will have higher levels of learning.

DISCUSSION

In this chapter, we developed a multilevel model for individuals' responses to negative emotions and the implications for learning from failure. We highlighted divergent paths organizations follow in responding to failure (i.e., normalizing it versus managing it) and the implications this has on negative emotions and learning. Beyond the organization alone, we took a systems perspective on negative emotions, responses to negative emotions, grieving processes, and learning, providing a basis for understanding members nested within an organization and the interaction between the two levels of analysis. There are a number of implications of this research from a systems perspective. First, an organization cannot be understood solely through its constituent parts. That is, an organization cannot be fully understood through an understanding of its members. Second, an organization is made up of subsystems at different levels nested within it, such as individuals, dyads, and teams, and interactions occur across these levels (up and down). Third, the organization can adapt to changes in its environment through coordinated actions in its subsystems – the different levels of analysis within the organization – while simultaneously maintaining its boundaries. Therefore, to gain a deeper understanding of organizations' adaptive responses to project failure, we need to understand changes at one level of analysis (i.e., the individual) and those changes' influence on changes at another level (i.e., the organization) and vice versa. This approach provides a more comprehensive understanding of emotions within organizations (Huy 1999) and thus serves as a basis for a deeper understanding of why some organizations (and their members) are better able to process emotions to learn from failure experiences and thus make progress in entrepreneurial action.

The cross-level components of the model (i.e., the mesolevel as shown in Figure 6.1) demonstrate the *contingent relationships* between levels at multiple stages of addressing negative events. This includes the organizational and individual levels' (1) negative emotions, (2) approaches to managing negative emotions (i.e., emotional capability, emotional intelligence), (3) grief dynamics, and (4) learning from failure. In the next three subsections, we briefly discuss the implications of this dependency. In the following chapter, we turn our attention to the stigma associated with project failure and how impression management can be used to minimize or eliminate stigmatization from failure.

Implications for research on the regulation of emotions

Organizational effectiveness at managing challenging negative emotions is likely dependent on individual factors, including emotional intelligence. Awareness of these influences is critically important in developing programs, processes, and routines that assist in managing negative emotions associated with failure. Individuals can vary considerably in their emotional self-awareness as well as in their ability to regulate (and manage) negative emotions, especially when responding to surprising negative events like project failure (Grandey, Fisk, Mattila, Jansen, and Sideman 2005; Williams 2003). Therefore, awareness of different individuals' grief dynamics and processes to facilitate recovery are likely to only partially address negative outcomes associated with grief as individuals will vary in their transition from grieving to learning. Organizations should therefore develop systems and processes that include the development of individual-level emotional intelligence, thus capturing the benefits of managing negative emotions across levels and developing both emotional capability and intelligence.

Specifically, entrepreneurs or members of organizations that launch entrepreneurial projects have opportunities to enhance emotional intelligence. These enhancements could potentially be incorporated in an organization's broader system of emotional capability. First, while debate continues regarding the precise definition of emotional intelligence (Ashkanasy and Daus 2005), a general consensus is that there is adequate research on the topic to identify approaches to cultivate and enhance emotional intelligence in individuals, specifically with regard to attending to others' emotional state and drawing upon that information when making decisions (Mayer and Salovey 1997). These practices have led to positive results in contexts like leadership and negation courses (Ashkanasy and Dasborough 2003; Ogilvie and Carsky 2002), thus supporting research that emotional self-regulation can be taught.

Second, while there is very little research on how organization-level emotional capability is developed, that promising research on emotional intelligence (discussed earlier) suggests that there could be promise in this area. As additional research emerges on collective emotions (cf., Huy 2011), we anticipate additional opportunities to better understand how to develop organizational systems that facilitate an oscillation grief process and learning from failure.

Third, general education (at the individual level) may help entrepreneurs, members of entrepreneurial organizations, and team/group members understand how to regulate negative emotions to achieve better outcomes. For example, we (Shepherd, 2004) offered suggestions for how this topic might be better introduced and incorporated in a classroom setting, which could have positive outcomes for individual-level emotional intelligence. Building off this, there may be opportunities to incorporate education on the development of emotional capability in organizations.

Implications for scholars of project failure

In connection to the previous implications, this chapter offers several important implications for understanding how to manage project failure. First, we discussed the implications of different responses to a failure, suggesting that regulation is likely to be more effective in generating positive learning outcomes. However, regulation is not always possible, especially when an organization lacks the individual resources (i.e., individuals with high emotional intelligence or coping self-efficacy). Organizations should align their goals with the types of resources needed to manage failure. If the organization's primary functions involve regular experimentation, risk taking, and iteration, then the normalization and celebration of failure might be most appropriate. However, organizations will likely need structures and systems in place to ensure members are learning from failures as opposed to becoming desensitized.

Second, and related to the previous point, organizations should be mindful of the message they send regarding project or organizational failures as this message is central to determining a need for normalization or regulation approaches to grief management. If learning from failure is essential in an organization, systems should be established, such as support groups that either (1) communicate the "normal" nature of failure or (2) emphasize the essential process of grieving over and learning from a failure experience. The organization should then focus on other elements of its structure and routines, including culture, reward system, and so forth, to support its focus. Organizations should be fully aware of the sacrifices they make in selecting a normalization strategy as well as the challenges of a regulation strategy (e.g., identifying employees with coping self-efficacy, developing these skills, etc.). As with other major organizational decisions, there are tradeoffs associated with how organizations view failure, recover from failure, and capture resulting knowledge.

Finally, beyond support groups, organizations could consider additional activities (e.g., parting ceremonies, etc.) to better facilitate group grieving processes. The importance of the group in grieving has only recently been developed in the bereavement literature (Shepherd 2009), and there are considerable opportunities to draw upon lessons learned in the management literature of group behavior that can be applied to loss situations.

CONCLUSION

Organizations experience failure, and these events generate negative emotions at both the individual and organizational levels. Feelings of loss and grief in these situations follow similar patterns of loss in other settings as do potential options to overcome the grief. How individuals and organizations manage this grief has important implications for subsequent action, including the desire to pursue new entrepreneurial opportunities, desensitization, individual performance within an organization, and so forth. By developing both individual abilities to manage grief (i.e., emotional intelligence) and organization-level processes and routines to cultivate healthy responses to failure (i.e., emotional capability), organizations are better equipped to make sense of failure events, learn from those events, and improve subsequent activities.

REFERENCES

Amabile, T. M. 1997. Entrepreneurial creativity through motivational synergy. *The Journal of Creative Behavior*, 31(1): 18–26.

Amabile, T. M., Barsade, S. G., Mueller, J. S., and Staw, B. M. 2005. Affect and creativity at work. *Administrative Science Quarterly*, 50(3): 367–403.

Archer, J. 1999. *The Nature of Grief: The Evolution and Psychology of Reactions to Loss*. New York: Routledge.

Ashforth, B. E. and Kreiner, G. E. 1999. 'How can you do it?': Dirty work and the challenge of constructing a positive identity. *Academy of Management Review*, 24(3): 413–434.

Ashforth, B. E. and Kreiner, G. E. 2002. Normalizing emotion in organizations: Making the extraordinary seem ordinary. *Human Resource Management Review*, 12(2): 215–235.

Ashkanasy, N. M. and Dasborough, M. T. 2003. Emotional awareness and emotional intelligence in leadership teaching. *Journal of Education for Business*, 79(1): 18–22.

Ashkanasy, N. M. and Daus, C. S. 2005. Rumors of the death of emotional intelligence in organizational behavior are vastly exaggerated. *Journal of Organizational Behavior*, 26(4): 441–452.

Ashkanasy, N. M. and Humphrey, R. H. 2011. Current emotion research in organizational behavior. *Emotion Review*, 3(2): 214–224.

Balk, D. E., Tyson-Rawson, K., and Colletti-Wetzel, J. 1993. Social support as an intervention with bereaved college students. *Death Studies*, 17(5): 427–450.

Bandura, A. 1986. *Social Foundations of Thought and Action: A Social Cognitive Theory*. Englewood Cliffs, NJ: Prentice-Hall.

Barsade, S. G. 2002. The ripple effect: Emotional contagion and its influence on group behavior. *Administrative Science Quarterly*, 47(4): 644–675.

Bartunek, J. M. 1984. Changing interpretive schemes and organizational restructuring: The example of a religious order. *Administrative Science Quarterly*, 29(3): 355–372.

Belschak, F. D. and Hartog, D. N. D. 2009. Consequences of positive and negative feedback: The impact on emotions and extra-role behaviors. *Applied Psychology*, 58(2): 274–303.

Benight, C. C. and Bandura, A. 2003. Social cognitive theory of traumatic recovery: The role of perceived self-efficacy. *Behaviour Research and Therapy*, 42: 1129–1148.

Brief, A. P. and Weiss, H. M. 2002. Organizational behavior: Affect in the workplace. *Annual Review of Psychology*, 53(1): 279–307.

Benight, J. F., Ty Tashiro, C. 2001. Bereavement coping self-efficacy in cancer widows. *Death Studies*, 25(2): 97–125.

Cameron, K. S., Kim, M. U., and Whetten, D. A. 1987. Organizational effects of decline and turbulence. *Administrative Science Quarterly*, 32(2): 222–240.

Cameron, K. S., Whetten, D. A., and Kim, M. U. 1987. Organizational dysfunctions of decline. *Academy of Management Journal*, 30(1): 126–138.

Cannon, M. D. and Edmondson, A. C. 2001. Confronting failure: Antecedents and consequences of shared beliefs about failure in organizational work groups. *Journal of Organizational Behavior*, 22(2): 161–177.

Caserta, M. S. and Lund, D. A. 1996. Beyond bereavement support group meetings: Exploring outside social contacts among the members. *Death Studies*, 20(6): 537–556.

Clore, G. L. 1992. Cognitive phenomenology: Feelings and the construction of judgment. In L. L. Martin and A. Tesser (eds.), *The Construction of Social Judgments*, Vol. 10: 133–163. Hillsdale, NJ: Erlbaum.

Cuisner, M., Janssen, H., Graauw, C., Bakker, S., and Hoogduin, C. 1996. Pregnancy following miscarriage: Curse of grief and some determining factors. *Journal of Psychometric Obstetrics and Gynecology*, 17: 168–174.

Daft, R. and Weick, K. E. 1984. Toward a model of organizations and interpretation systems. *Academy of Management Review*, 9(2): 284–296.

Davies, B., Spinetta, J., Martinson, I., McClowry, S., and Kulenkamp, E. 1986. Manifestations of levels of functioning in grieving families. *Journal of Family Issues*, 7(3): 297–313.

De Sousa, R. 1987. *The Rationality of Emotion*. Cambridge, MA/London: MIT Press.

Deigh, J. 1994. Cognitivism in the theory of emotions. *Ethics*, 104: 824–854.

Dutton, J. E., Fahey, L., and Narayanan, V. K. 1983. Toward understanding strategic issue diagnosis. *Strategic Management Journal*, 4(4): 307–323.

Dutton, J. E. and Duncan, R. B. 1987. The creation of momentum for change through the process of strategic issue diagnosis. *Strategic Management Journal*, 8(3): 279–295.

Edwards, B. and Clarke, V. 2004. The psychological impact of a cancer diagnosis on families: the influence of family functioning and patients' illness characteristics on depression and anxiety. *Psycho-Oncology*, 13(8): 562–576.

Egan, T. M., Yang, B., and Bartlett, K. R. 2004. The effects of organizational learning culture and job satisfaction on motivation to transfer learning and turnover intention. *Human Resource Development Quarterly*, 15(3): 279–301.

Ellis, H. C. and Ashbrook, P. W. 1988. Resource allocation model of the effects of depressed mood states on memory. In K. Fiedler and J. Forgas (eds.), *Affect, Cognition and Social Behavior*: 25–43. Toronto, Canada: Hogreff.

Ellis, H. C. and Ashbrook, P. W. 1989. The" state" of mood and memory research: A selective review. *Journal of Social Behavior & Personality*, 4(2): 1–22.

Ellis, S. H. and Chase, W. G. 1971. Parallel processing in item recognition. *Perception & Psychophysics*, 10(5): 379–384.

Farson, R. and Keyes, R. 2002. The failure-tolerant leader. *Harvard Business Review*, 80: 64–71.

Fineman, S. 1996. Emotion and organizing. In S. R. Clegg, C. Hardy, and W. R. Nord (eds.), *Handbook of Organization Studies*: 543–564. London: Sage.

Fisher, C. D. and Ashkanasy, N. M. 2000. The emerging role of emotions in work life: An introduction. *Journal of Organizational Behavior*, 21(2): 123–129.

Frank, R. H. 1993. The strategic role of the emotions reconciling over- and under-socialized accounts of behavior. *Rationality and Society*, 5(2): 160–184.

Fredrickson, B. L. 2001. The role of positive emotions in positive psychology: The broaden-and-build theory of positive emotions. *American Psychologist*, 56(3): 218.

Gentner, D. and Holyoak, K. J. 1997. Reasoning and learning by analogy. *American Psychologist*, 52(1): 32.

George, G. M. 1990. Personality, affect, and behavior in groups. *Journal of Applied Psychology*, 76: 299–307.

Ginsberg, A. 1988. Measuring and modeling changes in strategy: Theoretical foundations and empirical directions. *Strategic Management Journal*, 9(6): 559–575.

Gioia, D. A. 1986. Symbols, scripts, and sensemaking: Creating meaning in the organizational experience. In H. P. Sims and D. A. Gioia (eds.), *The Thinking Organization*: 49–74. San Francisco, CA: Jossey-Bass.

Gioia, D. A. and Chittipeddi, K. 1991. Sensemaking and sensegiving in strategic change initiation. *Strategic Management Journal*, 12(6): 433–448.

Gladstein, D. L. and Reilly, N. P. 1985. Group decision making under threat: The tycoon game. *Academy of Management Journal*, 28(3): 613–627.

Gooty, J., Gavin, M., and Ashkanasy, N. M. 2009. Emotions research in OB: The challenges that lie ahead. *Journal of Organizational Behavior*, 30(6): 833–838.

Grandey, A. A., Fisk, G. M., Mattila, A. S., Jansen, K. J., and Sideman, L. A. 2005. Is "service with a smile" enough? Authenticity of positive displays during service encounters. *Organizational Behavior and Human Decision Processes*, 96(1): 38–55.

Gusterson, H. 1996. *Nuclear Rites: A Weapons Laboratory at the End of the Cold War*. Los Angeles, CA: University of California Press.

Hambrick, D. C. 1982. Environmental scanning and organizational strategy. *Strategic Management Journal*, 3(2): 159–174.

Harris, S. G. and Sutton, R. I. 1986. Functions of parting ceremonies in dying organizations. *Academy of Management Journal*, 29(1): 5–30.

Harrison, D. A. and Klein, K. J. 2007. What's the difference? Diversity constructs as separation, variety, or disparity in organizations. *Academy of Management Review*, 32(4): 1199–1228.

Härtel, C. E., Hsu, A. C., and Boyle, M. V. 2002. A conceptual examination of the causal sequences of emotional labor, emotional dissonance, and emotional exhaustion: The argument for the role of contextual and provider characteristics. In N. M. Ashkanasy, W. J. Zerbe, and C. E. Härtel (eds.), *Managing Emotions in the Workplace*: 251. London, UK: M.E. Sharpe.

Herbert, T. B. and Dunkel-Schetter, C. 1992. Negative social reactions to victims: An overview of responses and their determinants. In L. Montada (ed.), *Life Crises and Experiences of Loss in Adulthood*: 497–518. Hillsdale, NJ: Erlbaum.

Hirshleifer, J. 1993. The affections and the passions: their economic logic. *Rationality and Society*, 5(2): 185–202.

House, J. S. 1981. *Work Stress and Social Support*. Reading, MA: Addison-Wesley.

Huber, G. P. and Lewis, K. 2010. Cross-understanding: Implications for group cognition and performance. *Academy of Management Review*, 35(1): 6–26.

Huy, Q. N. 1999. Emotional capability, emotional intelligence, and radical change. *Academy of Management Review*, 24(2): 325–345.

Huy, Q. N. 2002. Emotional balancing of organizational continuity and radical change: The contribution of middle managers. *Administrative Science Quarterly*, 47(1): 31–69.

Huy, Q. N. 2011. How middle managers' group-focus emotions and social identities influence strategy implementation. *Strategic Management Journal*, 32(13): 1387–1410.

Isen, A. M. 2000. Positive affect and decision making. *Handbook of Emotions*, 2: 417–435.

Kelly, J. R. and Barsade, S. G. 2001. Mood and emotions in small groups and work teams. *Organizational Behavior and Human Decision Processes*, 86(1): 99–130.

Kerr, N. L. and Tindale, R. S. 2004. Group performance and decision making. *Annual Review of Psychology*, 55: 623–655.

Kiefer, T. 2005. Feeling bad: Antecedents and consequences of negative emotions in ongoing change. *Journal of Organizational Behavior*, 26(8): 875–897.

Kissane, D. 1994. Grief and the family. In S. Block, J. Hafner, E. Harari, and G. I. Szmukler (eds.), *The Family in Clinical Psychiatry*: 71–91. Oxford, England: Oxford University Press.

Kissane, D. W., Bloch, S., Dowe, D. L., Snyder, R. D., Onghena, P., McKenzie, D. P., and Wallace, C. S. 1996a. The Melbourne family grief study, I: Perceptions of family functioning in bereavement. *American Journal of Psychiatry*, 153(5): 650–658.

Kissane, D. W., Bloch, S., Onghena, P., and McKenzie, D. P. 1996c. The Melbourne family grief study, II: Psychosocial morbidity and grief in bereaved families. *American Journal of Psychiatry*, 153: 659–666.

Kissane, D. W., Bloch, S., McKenzie, M., Mcdowall, A. C., and Nitzan, R. 1998. Family grief therapy: A preliminary account of a new model to promote healthy family functioning during palliative care and bereavement. *Psycho-Oncology*, 7(1): 14–25.

Kogut, B. and Zander, U. 1996. What firms do? Coordination, identity, and learning. *Organization Science*, 7(5): 502–518.

Lehman, D. R., Ellard, J. H., and Wortman, C. B. 1986. Social support for the bereaved: Recipients' and providers' perspectives on what is helpful. *Journal of Consulting and Clinical Psychology*, 54(4): 438–446.

Lepore, L. and Brown, R. 1997. Category and stereotype activation: Is prejudice inevitable? *Journal of Personality and Social Psychology*, 72(2): 275–287.

Lepore, S. J., Silver, R. C., Wortman, C. B., and Wayment, H. A. 1996. Social constraints, intrusive thoughts, and depressive symptoms among bereaved mothers. *Journal of Personality and Social Psychology*, 70(2): 271–282.

Lyubomirsky, S. and Nolen-Hoeksema, S. 1995. Effects of self-focused rumination on negative thinking and interpersonal problem solving. *Journal of Personality and Social Psychology*, 69(1): 176–190.

Mackie, D. M., Devos, T., and Smith, E. R. 2000. Intergroup emotions: Explaining offensive action tendencies in an intergroup context. *Journal of Personality and Social Psychology*, 79(4): 602–616.

Markman, A. B. and Gentner, D. 2001. Thinking. *Annual Review of Psychology*, 52(1): 223–247.

Mayer, J. D. and Salovey, P. 1997. What is emotional intelligence? In P. Salovey and D. Sluyter (eds.), *Emotional Development and Emotional Intelligence: Implications for Educators*: 3–31. New York: Basic Books.

Meyer, J. P., Paunonen, S. V., Gellatly, I. R., Goffin, R. D., and Jackson, D. N. 1989. Organizational commitment and job performance: It's the nature of the commitment that counts. *Journal of Applied Psychology*, 74(1): 152–156.

Meyer, J. P. and Allen, N. J. 1997. *Commitment in the Workplace: Theory, Research, and Application*. Thousand Oaks, CA: Sage.

Mogg, K., Mathews, A., Bird, C., and Macgregor-Morris, R. 1990. Effects of stress and anxiety on the processing of threat stimuli. *Journal of Personality and Social Psychology*, 59(6): 1230.

Morrison, J. B. 2002. *The right shock to initiate change: A sense making perspective*. Paper presented at the Academy of Management Proceedings Denver, CO.

Ng, T. W. H., Butts, M. M., Vandenberg, R. J., DeJoy, D. M., and Wilson, M. G. 2006. Effects of management communication, opportunity for learning, and work schedule flexibility on organizational commitment. *Journal of Vocational Behavior*, 68(3): 474–489.

Nolen-Hoeksema, S. and Morrow, J. 1991. A prospective study of depression and posttraumatic stress symptoms after a natural disaster: The 1989 Loma Prieta Earthquake. *Journal of Personality and Social Psychology*, 61(1): 115–121.

Nolen-Hoeksema, S., Parker, L. E., and Larson, J. 1994. Ruminative coping with depressed mood following loss. *Journal of Personality and Social Psychology*, 67(1): 92–104.

Nolen-Hoeksema, S. and Davis, C. G. 1999. "Thanks for sharing that": Ruminators and their social support networks. *Journal of Personality and Social Psychology*, 77(4): 801–814.

Nystrom, P. C. and Starbuck, W. H. 1984. To avoid organizational crises, unlearn. *Organizational Dynamics*, 12(4): 53–65.

Ocasio, W. 2011. Attention to attention. *Organization Science*, 22(5): 1286–1296.

Ogilvie, J. R. and Carsky, M. L. 2002. Building emotional intelligence in negotiations. *International Journal of Conflict Management*, 13(4): 381–400.

Palmer, S. 1978. Fundamental aspects of cognitive representation. In E. Rosch and B. B. Lloyds (eds.), *Cognition and Categorization*: 259–303. Hillsdale, NJ: Erlbaum.

Peeters, M. C. and Le Blanc, P. M. 2001. Towards a match between job demands and sources of social support: A study among oncology care providers. *European Journal of Work and Organizational Psychology*, 10(1): 53–72.

Pennebaker, J. W. 1989. Confession, inhibition, and disease. In L. Berkowitz (ed.), *Advances in Experimental Social Psychology*, Vol. 22: 211–244. New York: Academic Press.

Pennebaker, J. W. 1993. Putting stress into words: Health, linguistic, and therapeutic implications. *Behaviour Research and Therapy*, 31(6): 539–548.

Pennebaker, J. W. 1995. *Emotion, Disclosure, and Health*. Washington, DC: American Psychological Association.

Pieters, R. G. and Van Raaij, W. F. 1988. Functions and management of affect: Applications to economic behavior. *Journal of Economic Psychology*, 9(2): 251–282.

Prigerson, H., Bierhals, A., Kasl, S., Reynolds, C., 3rd, Shear, M., Day, N., Beery, L., Newsom, J., and Jacobs, S. 1997. Traumatic grief as a risk factor for mental and physical morbidity. *American Journal of Psychiatry*, 154(5): 616–623.

Rank, J. and Frese, M. 2008. The impact of emotions, moods, and other affect-related variables on creativity, innovation and initiative in organizations. In N. M. Ashkanasy and C. L. Cooper (eds.), *Research Companion to Emotion in Organizations*: 103–119. Northhampton, Maine: Edward Elgar Publishing.

Reed, D. A. 1989. *An orderly world: The social construction of reality within an occupation*. Unpublished doctoral dissertation, Indiana University, Bloomington, IN.

Rimé, B. 1995. Mental rumination, social sharing, and the recovery from emotional exposure. In J. W. Pennebaker (ed.), *Emotion, Disclosure, and Health*: 271–292. Washington, DC: American Psychological Association.

Ritter, A. R. and Kirk, J. M. 1995. *Cuba in the International System: Normalization and Integration*. New York: St. Martin's Press.

Rook, K. S. 1984. Research on social support, loneliness, and social isolation: Toward an integration. *Review of Personality & Social Psychology*, 5: 239–264.

Sanchez-Burks, J. and Huy, Q. N. 2009. Emotional aperture and strategic change: The accurate recognition of collective emotions. *Organization Science*, 20(1): 22–34.

Schein, E. H. 1992. *Organizational Culture and Leadership*. San Francisco: Jossey-Bass.

Schwarz, N. and Clore, G. L. 1988. How do I feel about it? The informative function of affective states. *Affect, Cognition, and Social Behavior*: 44–62.

Schwarz, N. and Clore, G. L. 1996. Feelings and phenomenal experiences. In E. T. Higgins and A. W. Kruglanski (eds.), *Social Psychology: Handbook of Basic Principles*: 433–465. New York: Guilford Press.

Seo, M.-G., Barrett, L. F., and Bartunek, J. M. 2004. The role of affective experience in work motivation. *Academy of Management Review*, 29(3): 423–439.

Shepherd, D. A. 2003. Learning from business failure: Propositions of grief recovery for the self-employed. *Academy of Management Review*, 28(2): 318–328.

Shepherd, D. A. 2004. Educating entrepreneurship students about emotion and learning from failure. *Academy of Management Learning & Education*, 3(3): 274–287.

Shepherd, D. A. 2009. Grief recovery from the loss of a family business: A multi- and meso-level theory. *Journal of Business Venturing*, 24(1): 81–97.

Shepherd, D. A. and Cardon, M. S. 2009. Negative emotional reactions to project failure and the self-compassion to learn from the experience. *Journal of Management Studies*, 46(6): 923–949.

Shepherd, D. A., Covin, J. G., and Kuratko, D. F. 2009. Project failure from corporate entrepreneurship: Managing the grief process. *Journal of Business Venturing*, 24(6): 588–600.

Shepherd, D. A. and Haynie, J. M. 2011. Venture failure, stigma, and impression management: A self-verification, self-determination view. *Strategic Entrepreneurship Journal*, 5(2): 178–197.

Shepherd, D. A., Patzelt, H., and Wolfe, M. 2011. Moving forward from project failure: Negative emotions, affective commitment, and learning from the experience. *Academy of Management Journal*, 54(6): 1229–1259.

Shepherd, D. A., Patzelt, H., Williams, T. A., and Warnecke, D. 2014. How does project termination impact project team members? Rapid termination,'creeping death', and learning from failure. *Journal of Management Studies*, 51(4): 513–546.

Shuchter, S. R. 1986. *Dimensions of Grief: Adjusting to the Death of a Spouse*. New York: Jossey-Bass.

Simon, D. 1991. *Homicide: A Year on the Killing Streets*. Boston, MA: Houghton Mifflin.

Smith, E. R., Seger, C. R., and Mackie, D. M. 2007. Can emotions be truly group level? Evidence regarding four conceptual criteria. *Journal of Personality and Social Psychology*, 93(3): 431–446.

St Onge, S. 1995. Systematic desensitization. In M. Ballou (ed.), *Psychological Interventions: A Guide to Strategies*: 95–115. Westport, CT: Greenwood Publishing Group.

Staw, B. M., Sandelands, L. E., and Dutton, J. E. 1981. Threat-rigidity effects in organizational behavior: A multilevel analysis. *Administrative Science Quarterly*, 26(4): 501–524.

Stroebe, M. and Schut, H. 1999. The dual process model of coping with bereavement: Rationale and description. *Death Studies*, 23(3): 197–224.

Stroebe, M. S. and Schut, H. 2001. Models of coping with bereavement: A review. In M. S. Stroebe, R. O. Hansson, W. Stroebe, and H. Schut (eds.), *Handbook of Bereavement Research: Consequences, Coping, and Care*, Vol. XV: 375–403. Washington, DC: American Psychological Association.

Sutton, R. I. and D'Aunno, T. 1989. Decreasing organizational size: Untangling the effects of money and people. *Academy of management Review*, 14(2): 194–212.

Taylor, S. E. and Crocker, J. 1981. Schematic bases of social information processing. In E. T. Higgins, C. P. Herman, and M. P. Zanna (eds.), *Social Cognition*, Vol. 1: 89–134. Hillsdale, NJ: LEA.

Thoits, P. A. 1982. Life stress, social support, and psychological vulnerability: Epidemiological considerations. *Journal of Community Psychology*, 10(4): 341–362.

Thomas, J. B., Clark, S. M., and Gioia, D. A. 1993. Strategic sensemaking and organizational performance: Linkages among scanning, interpretation, action, and outcomes. *Academy of Management Journal*, 36: 239–270.

Trice, H. M. and Beyer, J. M. 1984. Studying organizational cultures through rites and ceremonials. *Academy of Management Review*, 9(4): 653–669.

Ucbasaran, D., Westhead, P., Wright, M., and Flores, M. 2010. The nature of entrepreneurial experience, business failure and comparative optimism. *Journal of Business Venturing*, 25(6): 541–555.

Vachon, M. L. and Stylianos, S. K. 1988. The role of social support in bereavement. *Journal of Social Issues*, 44(3): 175–190.

Wegner, D. M. and Erber, R. 1993. Social foundations of mental control. In D. M. Wegner and J. W. Pennebaker (eds.), *Handbook of Mental Control*: 36–56. Englewood Cliffs, NJ: Prentice–Hall.

Weick, K. 1979. *The Social Psychology of Organizing*. Reading, MA: Addison-Wesley.

Weick, K. E. 1990. The vulnerable system: An analysis of the Tenerife air disaster. *Journal of Management*, 16(3): 571–593.

Williams, C. 2003. Sky service: The demands of emotional labour in the airline industry. *Gender, Work & Organization*, 10(5): 513–550.

Wood, J. V., Saltzberg, J. A., Neale, J. M., Stone, A. A., and Rachmiel, T. B. 1990. Self-focused attention, coping responses, and distressed mood in everyday life. *Journal of Personality and Social Psychology*, 58(6): 1027.

Zerubavel, E. 1991. *The Fine Line: Making Distinctions in Everyday Life*. New York: Free Press.

Zollo, M. and Winter, S. G. 2002. Deliberate learning and the evolution of dynamic capabilities. *Organization Science*, 13(3): 339–351.

7 Stigma over failure and impression management

In Chapter 6, we discussed how specific individual characteristics (i.e., emotional intelligence) and organizational routines (i.e., emotional capabilities) can help mitigate the negative consequences of failure, thereby enhancing the processes of learning and sensemaking. While these characteristics and processes can prove to be beneficial in helping individuals and organizations cope internally with project failure, they do not address potential external sources that could be responsible for negative emotions arising as a result of failure. One specific threat from failure has to do with how others see the person whose business (or project) has failed. At the turn of the century, individuals who became bankrupt were treated with disdain; they were often humiliated in public, such as sitting in the public square with baskets on their heads, engaging in humiliating tasks, or wearing disgusting clothes (Efrat 2006). This stigma – "some attribute or characteristic that conveys a social identity that is devalued in a particular context" (Crocker, Major, and Steele 1998: 505) – in most places of the world seems to still exist. For example, in a study of executives of failing banks, Semadeni, Cannella, Fraser, and Lee (2008) found that those who "jumped ship" early were able to avoid some of the stigma of bankruptcy, but those who were stigmatized suffered negative labor market consequences (e.g., found it hard to find another job). Notably, not all environments stigmatize failure. For example, for Silicon Valley, it has been argued that a failed start-up can be seen as a badge of honor (Landier 2005). However, as we will outline here, Silicon Valley is a rare exception, and more often than not, failed entrepreneurs face considerable stigmatization from various others.

Not surprisingly, the negative consequences of stigma from failure diminish individuals' psychological well-being. Indeed, stigma from failure (e.g., business failure and perhaps also project failure) represents a threat to entrepreneurs' social identity because their role expectation (held by stakeholders and the entrepreneurs themselves) is to create a business that adds value, and a minimum threshold for achieving this is business survival. Therefore, Chapter 11 bankruptcy (in the United States Bankruptcy Code) indicates that a business is failing, and other forms of bankruptcy (e.g., Chapter 7 in the United States Bankruptcy Code) mean that the business has failed. Bankruptcy represents a public signal that directly contradicts what is at the core of an entrepreneurial identity. Thus, failure can mark entrepreneurs, which in turn creates a number of difficulties for them. For example, failed entrepreneurs are likely to find it more difficult to raise capital and/or find it more costly to do so (with the possible exception of in Silicon Valley). Even when entrepreneurs did not cause the failure themselves (e.g., by misinterpreting market data or making faulty strategic decisions), they may well be stigmatized by others in the environment (Kulik, Bainbridge, and Cregan 2008; Neuberg, Smith, Hoffman, and Russell 1994).

However, are all entrepreneurs and project team members likely to experience the same level of stigmatization from failure, and are all observers in the social environment likely to stigmatize failed entrepreneurs and project team members to a similar extent? How can regional and national differences explain the levels of stigmatization, and importantly, what can those who failed do to minimize the level of stigmatization and/or cope with the stigma experienced? This chapter addresses these questions by exploring the antecedents and consequences of stigmatization for failed entrepreneurs and project team members. Figure 7.1 summarizes the chapter's structure. First, we explore the conditions under which the failure of businesses or entrepreneurial projects leads to stigmatization (characteristics of those who failed and those who evaluate regional characteristics). Second, we explore stigma's negative consequences. Finally, we explore how entrepreneurs and managers use impression-management strategies to mitigate potential negative consequences from stigmatizing failure. We start this chapter by illustrating that stigma is indeed a problem for those whose businesses and entrepreneurial projects fail.

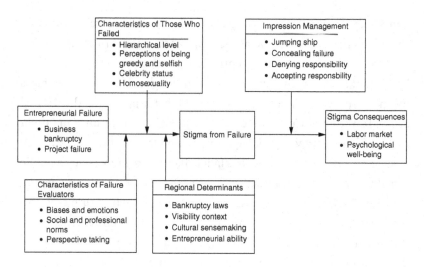

FIGURE 7.1: Antecedents and consequences of stigma from entrepreneurial failure

BUSINESS FAILURE AND THE STIGMATIZATION OF ENTREPRENEURS

Acquiring the resources necessary to start and run a business requires that entrepreneurs build up and maintain legitimacy by adhering to expectations that prevail in business environments (DiMaggio and Powell 1983). Perhaps the strongest expectation is that entrepreneurs are successful in what they are doing – that is, that they are able to successfully run and grow their business. Not adhering to these expectations by failing with their business can create stigma, which can negatively impact future business foundations (Efrat 2006; Landier 2005). There is ample anecdotal evidence that business failure leads to stigmatization of entrepreneurs and managers. For example, Landier (2005: 9) quoted a communication by the European Commission from 1998 as follows:

> In Europe, a serious social stigma is attached to bankruptcy. In the USA bankruptcy laws THEY allow entrepreneurs who fail to start again relatively quickly and failure is considered part of a learning process. In Europe those who go bankrupt tend to be considered as "losers." They face great difficulty to finance a new venture.

Two years later, Erkki Liikanen, the Commissioner for Enterprise and Information Society at the European Commission, was quoted as follows (Landier 2005: 9):

> An important factor underlying Europe's poor record on entrepreneurship is the stigma of failure. Many would-be entrepreneurs and good ideas are put-off by the fear that if you fail once, you will lose everything. This must change. Failure can be regarded as part of the learning curve. We must change mentalities. Failure is not accepted in Europe. An entrepreneur must have a second chance. Changing business cultures is the toughest challenge.

Similarly, Chong Lit Cheong, the Managing Director of Singapore's National Science and Technology Board, said the following in May 2000 (Landier 2005: 9):

> To embrace the spirit of risk-taking, we need to accept failure as a possible outcome of technopreneurship. A sustainable technopreneurial environment is not one that promises no failures to continue to pursue their dreams.

In addition to these quotes from politicians and political reports, entrepreneurs themselves often report about the stigma they associate with failure. For example, German entrepreneur Bent A. Jensen, the founder of the fashion label Herr von Eden, went bankrupt after fourteen years and was left with more than 500,000 euros debt. Reflecting on the time after the failure, he reported the following in a newspaper interview (Mühlauer and Radomski 2005):

> The first time [I had] negative press, this hurt me a lot. I had to fight to keep face and retain my composure—and nevertheless leave the house. This was often not easy, for example to continue visiting the Café Paris in Hamburg. There was no champagne anymore, just one or two beers. I did have to swallow and retain composure.

Another article published in a leading German newspaper (Zappe 2011) described that in nine German and one Austrian cities, self-help groups called Anonymous Bankruptcies have been founded.

These self-help groups, which are organized under a nationwide association, were initiated in 2007 by Attila von Unruh, who had experienced the hardship of business failure himself. In the article, he described himself as having been "left alone" when he had filed for insolvency and explained that nobody would have understood that he had not acted carelessly but had just trusted the wrong people. Therefore, he had kept the failure a secret, not showing up at meetings with business partners anymore and facing the threat of social isolation. He was quoted as follows:

> [If you have failed as an entrepreneur] you do not get a bank account, no new lease for offices, no credibility for loans, no contract with a telephone operating company. In this situation it is hard to get a foot on the ground again.

The article goes on to describe Stephan Schramm, another failed entrepreneur, who had run a learning academy for health occupations for ten years. Schramm reported that after his business went bankrupt, "many friends disappeared. Well, those, of which I thought they would be friends." Indeed, he had lost many social relationships and just like von Unruh, the stigma of failure drove him into social isolation. Even several months after the bankruptcy, Schramm had not yet found a salaried job. As the article quotes him,

> "I have written 20 to 30 application letters to positions targeting my qualification profile. But if you are applying as a former entrepreneur and your CV shows an insolvency, you are not even invited for a job talk... This social isolation following stigma makes von Unruh's organization of self-help groups for anonymous failed entrepreneurs so valuable."

Finally, the stigmatization of failed entrepreneurs can be found in all parts of the world, even in the United States, which is often lauded for its entrepreneurial spirit and culture of tolerating failures. For example, Sutton and Callahan (1987) quoted two executives of failed computer ventures as follows: "I feel as if I committed some kind of sin" and "I think that it is the equivalent of having accidently killed your spouse and then having to live with it the rest of your life."

In sum, what the aforementioned examples show is that stigma seems to be a widespread consequence of business failure for entrepreneurs in most business and societal environments.

PROJECT FAILURE AND THE STIGMATIZATION OF PROJECT TEAM MEMBERS

While entrepreneurs who failed with their businesses experience stigmatization from the external environment, failure of entrepreneurial projects can also lead to stigmatization within the organization. Indeed, some studies have explored stigmatization within organizations. For example, Kulik et al. (2008) developed a model of stigma formation by association in the workplace. They proposed that co-workers' initial impressions of an organizational member are formed when co-workers connect the member with a stigma source (e.g., mental illness, drug use, previous imprisonment, obesity, homosexuality, etc.) in their minds. The extent of stigmatization, however, depends on the characteristics of the co-workers and their relationship with the stigmatized person. Further, according to Kulik et al. (2008), stigmatization is less likely if the organizational members' association with the sources of stigma is voluntary and the stigmatizing attribute is not contagious. Clair, Beatty, and Maclean (2005) and Ragins (2008) developed theoretical models on when employees decide to disclose or hide "invisible" stigmas (e.g., homosexuality). Both models emphasize the role of individual differences (e.g., risk-taking propensity, motives, self-verification processes) and contextual factors (e.g., organizational diversity climate, professional norms, supportive relationships) as important contingencies that determine the costs and benefits of revealing (potentially) stigmatizing characteristics in an organizational context. Although these studies did not (explicitly) focus on stigma emerging from project failures, the models are to some extent also applicable to this context. This is particularly important since in our interviews with managers and members of failed projects, some participants reported feeling stigmatized from both the environment within their firm and the external environment.

For example, in our study on project terminations within a large German technology company (Shepherd, Patzelt, Williams, and Warnecke 2014), one manager described the reactions of his colleagues:

> Probably the worst time was when you were basically talking to people within manufacturing or production because they obviously would not have heard about the failure. And then you had to explain to them and you just felt ... you know, the way that they react: "You got it wrong, didn't you?"

One of his colleagues working on a different failed project feared that he might lose standing in and connection with the scientific community not only within but also outside the organization. He reported, "I mean, let's be clear about it: a year ago, we were the pioneers, and everyone in the community around the world knew it.... The fact is we have not gotten that far.... That hurt me personally."

Similarly, in a newspaper interview, Joana Breidenbach, the founder of the Think-and-Do-Tank of the philanthropic donation platform betterplace.org, commented on the entrepreneurial climate in Germany, "And finally the societal climate is a hurdle to innovation. In the USA there is a completely different attitude towards risk. Failure is no flaw there. In Germany you are immediately stigmatized once a project has failed."

It becomes apparent that the stigmatization associated with entrepreneurial failure is not only a consequence of business bankruptcy, but it can also appear in organizations where team members and leaders might be stigmatized once their project has failed.

ATTRIBUTES OF THOSE WHO FAILED AND STIGMATIZATION

While the earlier examples support the notion that there is considerable stigmatization of those who failed with both independent businesses and corporate entrepreneurial projects, there is also variance in the level of stigmatization across individuals. One example for which this variance becomes manifest is the labor market for failed entrepreneurs and managers. For example, Cannella, Fraser, and Lee (1995) explored the labor market consequences for managers of failed banks. Specifically, the study compared the 1993 employment status of 1,002 managers (whether they were employed or not) who were working for 417 Texas banks that became insolvent in the period from 1985 to 1990 to the employment status of a matched sample of 1,063 managers of non-bankrupt Texas banks. An interesting finding from the analysis was that only high-level executives (e.g., chairmen, CEOs, presidents) had a lower probability of employment when they came from bankrupt versus solvent banks, but this difference was insignificant for middle and lower-level managers, indicating that accountability plays a key role in stigmatization. However, in case of very prominent and extraordinary big failures, such as Enron, Wiesenfeld, Wurthmann, and Hambrick (2008) argued that stigmatization involves all levels of employees and that "merely having the name Enron on their resumes may stir up negative associations in potential employers, clients, and headhunters" (2008: 237). Finally, Hermalin and Weisbach (1998) found that CEOs of poorly performing firms are more likely to be fired when they are monitored by boards with high levels of independency.

The work by Wiesenfeld et al. (2008) offered further insights when managers and entrepreneurs might be stigmatized most for firm failures. First, the authors described the process of "singling out" – that is, the extent to which one specific person is held culpable and warranting denigration, leading to higher levels of stigmatization. The singling out effect is particularly strong when a failed manager "is indicted by a legal arbiter for an alleged misdeed, is accused by a large shareholder of ineptitude, or is highlighted by a journalist for general dereliction" (2008: 238). Typically, CEOs are most likely to be singled out from the management team as lead entrepreneurs might be in an entrepreneurial team setting because they symbolically represent the failed endeavor and had the most influence on its development. Further, singling out (and thus stigmatization) seems particularly likely when the individual has enjoyed "celebrity status," has been attributed a willful misdirection of effort, and/or is perceived as selfish or greedy by the media and other observers (Wiesenfeld et al. 2008).

In a study with 212 public observers of hypothetical failure scenarios of entrepreneurs (Shepherd and Patzelt, forthcoming), we found further explanations for why some entrepreneurs are more harshly evaluated for their business failures by the public than other entrepreneurs of failed businesses. In this study, we argued from an attribution theory perspective (Weiner 1985) to suggest that the extent to which observers attribute the cause of failure to the individual entrepreneur partly determines the harshness of evaluation. More specifically, we propose that the sexual orientation of the entrepreneurs of the failed businesses and the failed businesses' use of environmentally friendly technology can bias observers' evaluations.

First, we argued that a negative evaluation bias can emerge from failed entrepreneurs' sexual orientation. Attribution theory suggests that negative biases are formed when observers attribute the reasons for failure more to causes internal to the entrepreneur rather to causes outside the entrepreneur's control. Sexual prejudice (i.e., negative attitudes toward an individual because of his or her sexual orientation [Herek 2000: 19]) against homosexuals represents a general negative belief observers might hold against those who are homosexual, and this belief can lead them to interpret information related to the failed entrepreneur in an overly negative belief-reinforcing way. That is, our theory predicts that due to prevailing sexual prejudice in the public, observers are likely to evaluate failed entrepreneurs more harshly when they are homosexual than when they are heterosexual. In addition, our theorizing suggests that to the extent observers perceive homosexuality as not being based on genetic predisposition but rather as a choice, defect, or immoral behavior (Herek 1994, 2000; Herman 1997), observers may attribute a lack of self-control and discipline to failed entrepreneurs.

In contrast, we argued that a positive bias emerges if entrepreneurs have good intentions when founding and running their business as indicated by the use of environmentally friendly technology (Shepherd and Patzelt 2015). In this case, we suggest that in attributing the causes of failure, observers will acknowledge entrepreneurs' good intentions and thus give them credit in their evaluations. For example, "observers might consider the general difficulty of developing new technologies, the lack of governmental support for environmental initiatives, and/or the general complexity of nature and ecosystems as external causes of failure, thus evaluating the entrepreneur less harshly" (Shepherd and Patzelt 2015: 260). For failed entrepreneurs of ventures without environmentally friendly technologies, evaluators are more likely to attribute the causes of failure to entrepreneurs' lack of effort, errors they made, or a lack of entrepreneurial ability, leading to harsher evaluations than for those who were developing environmentally friendly technologies.

Our data were supportive of these two hypotheses. Specifically, when testing the hypotheses with a scenario-based conjoint approach on a sample of 212 public observers from two German cities (Munich and Leipzig), we found that failed entrepreneurs who were homosexual were evaluated more harshly by observers than those who were heterosexual, while entrepreneurs whose ventures used environmentally friendly technologies were evaluated less harshly than those who did not use such technologies (coefficient = –0.686, $p < 0.001$). While we also expected that both effects might interact because observers' prejudices about homosexuals might diminish the amount of credit given for the use of environmentally friendly technologies and thus reduce the positive bias from using such technologies, we did not find evidence of such an effect in our data.

To conclude, existing work indicates considerable variance in the stigmatization of failed entrepreneurs. The level of stigmatization appears to partly depend on the characteristics of the failed entrepreneur (e.g., sexual orientation, position within the firm/entrepreneurial team, media prominence) and his or her firm (e.g., use of environmentally friendly technology).

ATTRIBUTES OF THOSE WHO EVALUATE FAILURES AND STIGMATIZATION

Existing studies suggest that the characteristics of those who evaluate entrepreneurs who recently experienced a failure help explain the extent of stigmatization. For example, Wiesenfeld et al. (2008) proposed that members of failed organizations (including those which went bankrupt) are observed by social, legal, and economic arbiters. Social arbiters "possess prominent and legitimate platforms for rendering assessments of firms and the individuals associated with them. These include members of the press (Chen and Meindl 1991; Hayward, Rindova, and Pollock 2004), governance watchdog groups, and academics" (Wiesenfeld et al. 224). In contrast, legal arbiters include state attorneys general, regulatory officials, stock exchange officials, judges, and juries – namely, individuals who contribute to making legal violations public. Finally, economic arbiters impact the extent to which others make economic transactions (e.g., hiring and payment decisions) with the entrepreneur. This group of evaluators includes members of the business elite, board members, members of professional networks, executive and personnel search firms, and so on. As Wiesenfeld et al. (2008) noted, arbiters' evaluations can be based on rational analyses, but they are also influenced by idiosyncratic biases. For example, the evaluators may be biased toward using more recent information but neglect older information (Tversky and Kahneman 1974), or emotions may bias their judgment (Slovic, Finucane, Peters, and MacGregor 2007). Specifically, Wiesenfeld et al. (2008) suggested that attribution errors may lead observers to "look for simple, stable, internal attributions for outcomes that may have complex causes, thus raising the likelihood that corporate failure will lead to negative judgments about the firm's leaders" (2008: 236).

In addition to biases, the study also suggests that observers' social context, including norms specific for the arbiters' profession (Chen and Meindl 1991), impact the level of stigmatization. As examples, Wiesenfeld et al. (2008) mentioned speed as a social norm for journalists when reporting about a failure and reporters' and prosecutors' role in serving and protecting the public might lead to the harsh punishment of those who violated social norms before or during the failure process. For example, the authors suggest that when journalists' "audience is 'out for blood,' they may render particularly negative evaluations, but when they expect the audience to resist negative judgments, perhaps because of the goodwill they harbor for elites with high social capital (Adler and Kwon 2002), their evaluations may be less negative" (2002: 236).

Our own work provides further evidence on the impact of observer characteristics on failure evaluations for entrepreneurs. Specifically, our study on how harshly 212 observers from the public judged failed entrepreneurs (Shepherd and Patzelt, forthcoming) provided a number of insights. As outlined earlier, an important finding of this study is that the harshness of business failure evaluations is higher for those failed entrepreneurs who are homosexual and lower for those failed entrepreneurs who adopted environmentally friendly technologies potentially because they are "given credit for good intentions." However, as we argued, these effects are likely to be influenced by observers' perspective taking – that is, "actively contemplating others' psychological experiences" (Todd, Galinsky, and Bodenhausen 2012: 95). Research has found that individuals who are better able to take others' perspective are better at resolving conflict (Sessa 1996) and cooperating with others (Johnson 1975), while those who lack the ability to take others' perspectives tend to be more aggressive and arrogant (Richardson, Hammock, Smith, Gardner, and Signo 1994) and suffer from social dysfunction more often than those high in perspective taking (Baron-Cohen 1995). Importantly, research has also explored the role of perspective taking in stigmatizing others and has shown that it can actually reduce negative evaluation biases (Galinsky and Ku 2004; Todd, Bodenhausen, Richeson, and Galinsky 2011) and prejudice (Bodenhausen and Wyer 1985; Galinsky and Ku 2004; Todd et al. 2011). Based on these previous studies, in our article, we argued that observers high in perspective taking interpret information about entrepreneurs of failed businesses more favorably than those low in perspective taking, including information about the sexual orientation of these entrepreneurs and the environmental friendliness of the technology they used for their businesses. More specifically, this more favorable interpretation reduced how harshly individuals evaluated failed entrepreneurs who were homosexual as well as failed entrepreneurs who had used environmentally friendly technology. While our data did not show the proposed effect for failed entrepreneurs' sexual orientation, we found that evaluators high in perspective taking gave failed entrepreneurs who had used environmentally friendly technologies more credit for their good intentions and thus evaluated them less harshly than observers who were low in perspective taking. These findings suggest that perspective taking is an important characteristic of those who evaluate failure when it comes to the harshness of their evaluation and thus stigmatization.

REGIONAL DETERMINANTS OF STIGMATIZATION

Since stigma is a social phenomenon that occurs when individuals violate normative expectations prevailing in the environment in which they operate, much work on the stigmatization of failed entrepreneurs has focused on explaining regional differences. At the regional level, research has explored the different forms and extent to which people are stigmatized when their entrepreneurial endeavors fail. First, bankruptcy laws specify the extent to which entrepreneurs are legally punished for failure. These institutional norms can be seen as a reflection of the societal attitude toward failed entrepreneurs, with more punishing laws reflecting higher levels of stigmatization in the society (Simmons, Wiklund, and Levie 2014). Second, there is variance in the visibility of failure based on regional/national regulations for disclosure, which impact to what extent stigmatization can lead to barriers to re-entry for entrepreneurs who have previously experienced business failure. Third, regions differ in their cultural sensemaking of failure which is, for example, reflected in the description of failed entrepreneurs in the media. Finally, the entrepreneurial ability of individuals differs across failure, which can lead to the stigmatization of those who failed when they try to raise capital for re-entry. We will now describe each of these regional differences in more detail.

Bankruptcy laws

An important topic in entrepreneurship research has been to understand how bankruptcy laws can stigmatize entrepreneurs for failure and, in doing so, prevent future entrepreneurial entry. Bankruptcy laws create stigma when entrepreneurs are extensively punished for business failure, for example, when there is no (or only far delayed) possibility of discharge from personal liabilities or when these entrepreneurs suffer civic or economic disabilities (Armour and Cumming 2008). Indeed, the stigmatizing effect of strict bankruptcy laws has been recognized by policymakers in various countries, and legal changes have been made to provide a more forgiving personal bankruptcy law that makes it easier for entrepreneurs who have gone bankrupt to obtain a discharge from indebtedness. With easier discharge, individuals are expected to more readily become first-time entrepreneurs because the anticipated consequences of failure have been reduced, and after failure, there is a greater chance of being able to start anew. For example, at the beginning of the century, the European Commission (European Commission 2003) urged its member states to revise personal bankruptcy laws to facilitate new entry for entrepreneurs of failed businesses. These changes have subsequently been introduced by several European governments (e.g., those in the Netherlands, Germany, and the United Kingdom [Armour and Cumming 2008]).

In a study on the stigmatizing effects of bankruptcy laws, Armour and Cumming (2008) focused on self-employment data over sixteen years in North America and in fifteen European states. This study operationalized the extent to which bankrupt and indebted entrepreneurs are punished in different ways, including discharge from indebtedness (i.e., general availability and time to discharge), the level of personal items these entrepreneurs can retain from debtors, disabilities (i.e., loss of civic and economic rights for the period of bankruptcy), and composition (i.e., the difficulty a failed or indebted entrepreneur faces in reaching a discharge agreement with his or her creditors). The study found that the more stigmatizing (i.e., punishing) the national bankruptcy laws were for individual entrepreneurs, the lower the entry rates were in the respective country. These effects were both statistically significant and economically meaningful. The study also found that minimum capital requirements to found a limited liability company (a legal form of business that provides a shield for individual entrepreneurs' personal bankruptcy consequences) negatively impact entrepreneurial activity. Interestingly, the study also found an interaction effect: highly stigmatizing (i.e., punishing) bankruptcy laws had a less severe effect on entrepreneurship when there were less minimum capital requirement for founding a limited liability company. It appears that the availability of limited liability somewhat counteracts the negative consequences of stigma over personal bankruptcy. Armour and Cumming's (2008) results are consistent with other studies also finding that the nature of national bankruptcy laws explains a significant amount of variance in a region's entrepreneurial activity (Djankov, McLiesh, and Shleifer 2007; Fan and White 2003).

While institutional norms, such as bankruptcy laws, can reflect the stigmatization of entrepreneurs who fail in a region (or nation), some authors have emphasized that there is variance in the extent to which these norms indeed translate into stigma. For example, Lee, Peng, and Barney (2007) applied real-options logic to the societal level in order to theorize about when more or less punishing bankruptcy laws impact entrepreneurial activity. More specifically, their model suggests that bankruptcy laws are more "entrepreneur friendly" (i.e., less punishing) when (1) there is the option for reorganization bankruptcy, (2) the bankruptcy procedure is quicker, (3), there is an opportunity for a "fresh start" in bankruptcy, (4) assets can automatically stay within the bankrupt business, and (5) managers of the failed business are provided the opportunity to continue working on their job during bankruptcy. However, as the authors argued, bankruptcy laws that provide these options have a less negative impact on entrepreneurial activity in societies with high uncertainty-avoidance cultures – that is, cultures in which people fear the risk of business failure because it is associated with high levels of shame or is even considered a criminal act. Lee et al. (2007) referred to the example of Japan, where the stigma of failure is so substantial that some managers of failed businesses commit suicide, suggesting that stigma from cultural norms is so strong that the impact of an entrepreneur-friendly bankruptcy law would only have a minor effect on entrepreneurial activity. In contrast, in low uncertainty-avoidance cultures like the United States, people are more likely to base their decision to take the risk of entrepreneurial action based on institutional norms because cultural norms already entail a high tolerance for failure. As an example, the authors quote managers of West Airlines, who, after their firm had filed for reorganization bankruptcy, motivated employees by emphasizing that business failure is "nothing to be ashamed of."

Visibility context of business failures

In contrast to Lee and colleagues' (2007) focus on explaining how national bankruptcy and stigma from cultural norms interact in explaining regional entrepreneurial activity, the study by Simmons et al. (2014) proposed that the visibility of bankruptcy impacts how stigmatization influences entrepreneurship. In their view, the visibility of failure is reflected by the information repositories and information conveyed by the regulatory environment of a country. The authors argued that in a context in which societies strongly stigmatize entrepreneurs for business failure and information about these failures is easily available, there will be particularly low re-entry rates among these entrepreneurs. The authors also argued that when stigma is high but there is little visibility of information about their prior failures, entrepreneurs can regulate their stigma by delaying re-entry.

In the same context, the authors suggested that re-entering as part of a founding team allows entrepreneurs to conceal part of the stigma from their prior failure, thus discouraging solo ownership entries. Further, describing a scenario in which entrepreneurs of a failed business face little stigma in society but operate in a high-visibility context for failure, Simmons et al. (2014) suggested that these entrepreneurs of failed businesses are particularly encouraged to engage in corporate entrepreneurship. On the one hand, this form of re-entry allows such entrepreneurs to continue their entrepreneurial activity. On the other hand, the re-entry enables entrepreneurs to escape the negative consequences of information availability of prior failures, such as a lower chance to obtain a bank loan for an independent start-up (because banks will rely on the available information about prior failure in their lending decision). Finally, the authors argued that a low-stigma and low-visibility context provides the best setting for re-entry after failure.

Cultural sensemaking of entrepreneurial failure

Taking a cultural sensemaking perspective on business failure, Cardon, Stevens, and Potter (2011) analyzed regional variation in stigmatizing business failure based on reports in US newspapers. When making sense of an event, individuals seek relevant information in the environment, try to understand and interpret it, and then choose to act in a particular way based on this understanding and interpretation (Gioia and Chittipeddi 1991). Typically, sensemaking is contingent on the social context because understanding an event takes place while individuals interact with others in their environment (Weick 1979). Therefore, from a cultural sensemaking perspective, "communities of people may scan the environment for instances of business failures and then interpret those failures, ascribing meaning to them, allowing others in the culture to act upon those interpretations" (Cardon et al. 2011: 82). However, as Cardon et al. (2011) argued, there is likely heterogeneity across regions in terms of cultural sensemaking of business failure because formal and informal rules (e.g., laws and cultural values) vary. Specifically, the authors suggest that the population size of a region, its economic development, the general level of entrepreneurship, and the number of business bankruptcies might impact the cultural sensemaking of failures. Due to these differences in cultural sensemaking, media descriptions will differ across regions in their attributions of business failures as being either due to misfortune (i.e., reasons outside the control of the entrepreneur, including natural disasters or economic decline) or due to mistakes (i.e., reasons under the control of the entrepreneur, including errors, insufficient competency or motivation, or an unsuccessful business model). To test these propositions, Cardon et al. (2011) analyzed 281 articles that appeared in regional newspapers of six major US cities and reported on 389 business failures. Interestingly, the study found that in three regions (Chicago, New York, and Washington, DC), newspaper articles attributed failures substantially more to entrepreneurs' mistakes, whereas in the other three regions (Atlanta, Austin, and San Francisco) substantially more of the failures were attributed to misfortunes. Further, the authors found that the regions where newspapers most often attributed failures to mistakes were the same regions where entrepreneurs described themselves as being stigmatized. Cardon et al. (2011) concluded that regions vary in both their attributions of business failures and the impact these failures have on the entrepreneurs involved. These results suggest that cultural sensemaking can explain regional variance in the stigmatization of those individuals whose entrepreneurial endeavors fail.

Indeed, our own work (Shepherd and Patzelt, forthcoming) is consistent with a cultural sensemaking perspective of entrepreneurs being stigmatized for their failed ventures. As we outlined earlier, in that article, we argued that entrepreneurs who were homosexual were more harshly evaluated for their failures by others compared to those who were heterosexual because observers who stigmatized those who were homosexual were more likely to attribute the failure to causes under the entrepreneurs' control (as opposed to, for example, bad luck). However, in the statistical analysis, interesting regional differences emerged. While hierarchical linear modeling analysis showed a clearly statistically significant effect for the whole sample, the results became less clear once we split the sample by geographic region. Specifically, our data were collected from two major German cities – one in the state of Bavaria (Munich) and one in the state of Saxony (Leipzig) – and we found a significant effect only for the Munich subsample but not for the Leipzig subsample. While the cities are comparable in a number of characteristics (e.g., inhabitants, residence of universities), one major difference is that Munich is located in Western Germany, while Leipzig is located in Eastern Germany. Leipzig thus looks back to a forty-year history of communism after World War II when Germany was divided, and Leipzig was part of the German Democratic Republic (GDR). During GDR times, the communist regime counteracted religious tendencies in the population, which still today results in the diminished influence of the church and religion in general (Pollack 2002). Therefore, religious tendencies to stigmatize failed entrepreneurs who are homosexual are likely lower in Leipzig than in many parts of Western Germany, where religion plays a more dominant role in public life. Indeed, being the capital of the state of Bavaria, Munich's history is characterized by a strong Roman Catholic tradition, and religious influences are widely embedded in the local society. Given the Catholic Church's critical view on homosexuality (Gerhards 2010), it is not surprising that observers from Munich evaluate entrepreneurs more harshly for their failures when they are homosexual than when they are heterosexual. Thus, our findings indicate that religious cultures may explain regional differences in the level of stigmatization failed entrepreneurs face.

ENTREPRENEURIAL ABILITY

While most studies explaining the stigma of failure have focused on factors exogenous to entrepreneurial activity, such as cultural values and institutional norms, Landier (2005) developed a theoretical model that views stigma as an endogenous factor. The model assumes that first, entrepreneurs need to raise money to finance new ventures, and second, venture success depends on entrepreneurial ability and luck. Based on private information, entrepreneurs decide to continue the current venture or quit and start anew. This decision is influenced by the costs of capital for the new venture (i.e., after failure), which can be interpreted as a form of failure stigmatization. Landier's model reveals two types of equilibria. First, in regions with high levels of stigmatization (i.e., high costs of capital to start anew), entrepreneurs quit only ventures performing badly but persist with ventures performing moderately well even if the entrepreneurs possess high entrepreneurial ability. Since only the worst ventures are ended, the pool of failed entrepreneurs is of relatively low quality, which justifies the high costs of capital (i.e., higher stigmatization) for failed entrepreneurs. In this "conservative" equilibrium situation, there is an overall low level of high-quality entrepreneurial activity since ventures with moderate performance are continued. In contrast, in regions with low levels of stigma (i.e., low costs of capital), starting new ventures is relatively easy, leading entrepreneurs to more readily quit ventures with moderate performance in favor of starting more promising businesses. In this situation, the pool of entrepreneurs after failure has higher entrepreneurial abilities, thus justifying the low costs of capital. In this "experimental" equilibrium situation, there are more high-quality new ventures since those with moderate performance are abandoned. An important implication of Landier's model is that in regions where entrepreneurship operates at the technological frontier (e.g., Silicon Valley), the experimental equilibrium is socially more efficient, while in regions where entrepreneurship is more imitative (e.g., many European regions), the conservative equilibrium is more efficient. The model also outlines potential pitfalls when policymakers try to shift from one equilibrium to the other, as exemplified by the European Union's attempts to foster high-technology entrepreneurship. To illustrate these regional differences between Europe and the United States, Landier (2005: 27) quoted Eric Behamon, a French Silicon Valley entrepreneur:

Twenty years ago, as a student at Stanford, I realized how naïve I had been to believe I could start a business in France.... In France, you keep all your life the stigma of failure. Here [in Silicon Valley] it is the mark of your entrepreneurial spirit.... In France, it is common practice to give up on growth in order to limit risk. Here, when you start a venture, your goal is to become number one of your sector.

Landier (2005) also noted, however, that even within the United States there are considerable regional differences in the stigmatization of failed entrepreneurs. While in Silicon Valley entrepreneurial ability is high and failure is almost seen as a badge of honor, the opposite is true for other states. For example, he quoted W. Donaldson, President of Strategic Venture Planning, as follows: "The culture in Southeastern Virginia is that there is still a lot of stigma attached to failure. Business people in this area are very conservative."(Landier, 2005: 9)

In sum, existing studies have shown that regional differences explain considerable variance in the stigmatization from business failure. Explanations for these differences include national bankruptcy laws, the visibility of failures, cultural sensemaking, and the entrepreneurial ability of those living in a region.

IMPRESSION MANAGEMENT OF THOSE WHO FAILED AND STIGMATIZATION

Given the negative consequences of failure, research has investigated how to manage the situation in a way that minimizes damage. For example, Sutton and Callahan (1987) investigated four cases of bankrupt computer firms in Silicon Valley and explored how executives used impression-management strategies in an attempt to minimize stigma. In the best times, these companies had between 175 and 525 employees, and their unsecured debt ranged from $1.2 to $11.5 million at the time of bankruptcy. At that time, the firms were between 3.5 and 12 years old. Sutton and Callahan interviewed between four and seven people from each firm, including the CEOs, other former executives, creditors, and lawyers involved in the insolvencies. The study found that managers tried five different strategies to manage stigma: conceal-ing the problem, defining the failure situation in a positive light, deny-ing responsibility for the failure, accepting responsibility for the failure, and trying to withdraw from the situation. For example, Sutton and Callahan quoted the president and former president of a failed firm, both of whom refused to take responsibility (1987: 423–424):

> The marketplace went away and the Japanese competition came on board. (President)

> The negative financial situation was completely because of external reasons. (Founder and ex-president)

> The [former] president was unable or unwilling [to] do anything about it. (President)

In contrast, as an example of those who accepted responsibility, Sut-ton and Callahan quoted the president and former president of another venture (1987: 424):

> If I had been a little more experience, perhaps I may have been able to cope with it better. (President)

> Well, I guess I hold the board responsible of whom I was a member. . . . Yes, I admit that I was responsible for the problems we had with the [product]. . . . I am really sorry that it had happened. It didn't need to happen." (Founder and ex-president)

While Sutton and Callahan's study is important because it clearly highlights different ways failed executives cope with stigma, it was not the purpose of the study to understand how effective the five impression-management strategies were.

In another study on how executives cope with the stigma of failure, Semadeni et al. (2008) explored the consequences of "jumping ship" as a stigma-management strategy. According to the authors, jumping ship referred to executives distancing themselves before the failure event either by leaving the firm before the failure, which enabled them to deny responsibility, or by relocating to a geographically distant area, which allowed them to hide their association with the failure because information flow diminishes over large geographical distances. Specifically, the authors proposed that because "stigma cannot be assigned until *after* the event and so exit *prior* to the event should loosen or sever the individual's link to the stigmatizing event" (2008: 559), those who jump ship experience less stigma and thus suffer fewer employment consequences than those who remain with a firm until it files for bankruptcy. Further, the authors argued that because jumping ship might be an effective stigma-management strategy, more executives will leave declining firms prior to failure than non-failing firms. Drawing on a sample of 437 failing Texas banks and a matched sample of non-failing banks (a total of 1,155 executives from failed banks and 1,171 executives from matching banks), the authors found support for both hypotheses. Thus, jumping ship not only seems to be an effective stigma-management strategy, but also one that is frequently applied.

SELF-VERIFICATION OF THOSE WHO FAILED AND STIGMATIZATION

While Semadeni et al. (2008) explored how stigma and impression management impacts failed entrepreneurs in terms of labor market consequences, in Shepherd and Haynie (2011), we built on self-verification theory to understand how people with different self-views after failure engage in very different impression-management strategies and how these strategies can contribute to maintaining psychological well-being after failure. Although entrepreneurs are well known for holding a positive self-view (e.g., being overconfident in their abilities to perform the tasks necessary for success [Hayward, Shepherd, and Griffin 2006]), failure can certainly lead to a change in view. For example, in our article, we cited a journalist who interviewed a failed entrepreneur stating the following:

> As anyone who has suffered through a business failure can tell you, the aftermath isn't pretty. You're wallowing in debt (often money

that you've mooched from friends and relatives), your self-esteem has nose-dived into the depths, your future is in grave doubt and everyone around you is giving you that Elephant Man look—equal parts pity, revulsion, and fear. (see Shepherd and Patzelt 2015: 253)

In developing our theoretical model, we (Shepherd and Haynie, 2011) focused on self-view in terms of self-esteem – the belief that "one is an object of primary value in a world of meaningful action" (Becker, 1971: 71). This self-esteem is most vulnerable to "failures in domains in which their self-worth is contingent" (Niiya, Crocker, and Bartmess 2004: 801). This is often the case at work, where people's self-worth is highly dependent on how they perform at their work tasks (Kreiner and Ashforth 2004; Pierce, Gardner, Cummings, and Dunham 1989). For example, if the entrepreneur's identity is highly intertwined with that of the failing firm, his or her self-esteem is likely to take a bigger hit (Chreim 2002; Corley and Gioia 2004; Shepherd and Haynie 2011).

Although others might largely blame the entrepreneur for the failure, it is the amount of self-blame that impacts the drop in self-esteem. Indeed, some entrepreneurs are effective at using ego-protective strategies after failure, which can help them maintain (or at least reduce the impact on) self-esteem (Baumeister 1993; Blaine and Crocker 1993; Greenberg and Pyszczynski 1985). For example, by attributing blame for the failure to external causes, the entrepreneur can protect his or her self-esteem from the failure event (at least in his or her own mind). However, not all entrepreneurs deny responsibility, and to the extent that they accept responsibility for this negative outcome, their self-esteem will be lowered (Brewin and Furnham 1986; Crocker and Major 1994; Tennen and Herzberger 1987). Entrepreneurs are likely to accept greater responsibility for the failure when the environment for business is perceived to be favorable (e.g., infrequent failures, low uncertainty, low dynamism, low hostility) and when the firm is new and/or small (Shepherd and Haynie 2011). This discussion of self-esteem and self-view is important because the entrepreneur's self-view – ones strongly held beliefs and feelings about oneself (Swann 1983) – impacts the strategies he or she uses to maintain high psychological well-being. The impression-management strategies individuals use can impact their psychological well-being. However, as we will see, those entrepreneurs with low self-esteem pursue a completely different path to psychological well-being than those with high self-esteem (Shepherd and Haynie 2011).

Specifically, entrepreneurs of failed businesses who maintain high self-esteem are likely to pursue the strategies detailed by Sutton and Callahan (1987), which we described earlier, in order to maintain psychological well-being. Nevertheless, there is nothing really surprising about these impression-management strategies: they work to make sure people maintain a positive impression of themselves (or, if this does not work, they avoid people altogether). Although we may assume that people want others to have a high impression of them, there is ample evidence that this is not the case, at least for those who hold a negative view of themselves. We have already established that business failure can create a negative self-view, and these entrepreneurs are likely to use impression-management strategies in a different way to maintain or enhance their psychological well-being.

The basic tenets of self-verification theory is that "people are motivated and take actions that confirm their own feelings and beliefs with regards to self, and they also seek out and interact with others who share their self-view" (Shepherd and Haynie 2011; Swann 1983). That is, people take actions to stabilize their view that they hold of themselves (Secord and Backman 1964; Swann Jr 2005). As we argued in Haynie and Shepherd (2011), this includes taking actions (and having interactions with others) to confirm rather than change a negative self-view. This is opposite the view that individuals always use impression management to make themselves seem more positive in others' eyes; rather, they want to be authentic in that they want people to see them as they really are. Therefore, those who hold a negative self-view after business failure are likely to enhance psychological well-being using impression management to have others verify this negative self-view in a number of important ways.

First, people who hold a negative self-view often seek out and choose to interact with those who also have a negative impression of them. In one study of 84 university students, Swann (1992) found that those who had a negative self-view preferred to interact with evaluators who provided an unfavorable impression of them than evaluators who offered a more favorable impression. One individual in the study indicated that "I think #1 [the unfavorable evaluator as compared to a favorable evaluator] is a better choice because ...he sums up basically how I feel" (Swann 1992: 395). This demonstrates that in seeking feedback about the self, individuals tend to seek self-confirming social evaluations (McCall and Simmons 1966).

Second, when faced with those who hold an opposing positive view, individuals tend to actively try to change others' view to one that is consistent with their self-view (Swann and Ely 1984). They do this to try and correct the others' mistaken views of them to eventually gain self-confirming feedback (Curtis and Miller 1986). Therefore, they may avoid family and friends that hold an overly positive view of them and seek out those that recognize the seriousness of the consequences of their failure and their role in the failure. Alternatively, they may attempt to change the view of those who hold a positive view of them (including family) by using impression management to communicate the negative consequences of the failure and to take responsibility for the failure, which might require disavowing the notion that the failure was someone else's fault and/or that it was beyond their personal control.

Finally, when facing a disconfirming view (in this case, someone else holding a positive view of them), entrepreneurs might flee the situation. For example, in a study of college students, Swann Jr. and Pelham (2002) found that those with a negative self-view were more likely to terminate relationships with roommates who held a favorable impression of them. This indicated the use of withdrawal as a strategy to maintain a stable self-view (even when that self-view was negative). There is also anecdotal evidence that entrepreneurs become withdrawn, particularly with family, after a business failure. A possible explanation for this withdrawal, at least in part, is that they are avoiding non-self-confirming evidence. Although self-verification explains why entrepreneurs may use impression-management strategies to change or avoid others' favorable impressions of them, the question then becomes to what effect? What is the impact on the individual of successfully confirming one's negative self-view?

To address these questions, Shepherd and Haynie (2011) drew on the notion of psychological well-being and its associated needs for correspondence, relatedness, and autonomy. It appears that in the aftermath of failure, entrepreneurs with a negative self-view can enhance their psychological well-being through several impression-management strategies. First, although individuals have a need for competence, for those who hold a negative self-view, impression-management strategies aimed at enhancing others' view obstructs the process of learning from the experience and thus gaining mastery over the task (Covington 1984; Deci and Ryan 2000; Dweck 2000). Rather, the individual seeks "real" and "honest" feedback to enhance competence, and given a negative self-view, this is most likely to come from others who also hold an unfavorable impression. As long as this negative feedback is perceived as building competence (Deci and Ryan 1985), it can help build psychological well-being.

Second, although individuals often think they can satisfy the psychological need for relatedness by being liked by others, it is often more than simply being liked. The need for relatedness is satisfied by relationships that are "close, mutually caring, and supportive" (Crocker and Park 2004). Such relationships involve give-and-take interactions (Baumeister and Leary 1995; Collins and Feeney 2000; Deci and Ryan 2000), and these relationships develop at a deep level such that the individuals truly "see the person for who they are" – an authentic relationship. The problem of a positive impression-management strategy used by someone who holds a negative self-view is that it hides the authentic and therefore obstructs the opportunity to form deeper relationships that help satisfy the need for relatedness. Indeed, in such instances, positive impression-management strategies can lead to isolation (Deci and Ryan 1995; Pyszczynski, Greenberg, Solomon, Arndt, and Schimel 2004), thereby thwarting the need for relatedness and hindering (or delaying) a "bounce back" in psychological well-being. For entrepreneurs of a failed business who hold a negative self-view, psychological well-being is likely enhanced by interacting with those who also hold an unfavorable impression of them because these individuals see them as they really are, which is the basis for an authentic relationship.

Finally, and related to the previous point, needs for autonomy can be satisfied by the creation and maintenance of authentic relationships with others (Crocker and Park 2004; Hodgins, Koestner, and Duncan 1996). Furthermore, feeling obligated to implement positive impression-management strategies to maintain relationships with other people has the effect of thwarting the need for autonomy. That is, individuals may feel forced to engage in behaviors that they would otherwise choose not to engage in (Deci, Eghrari, Patrick, and Leone 1994). In contrast, for those with a negative self-view, by interacting with those who really see them as they are, entrepreneurs can take ownership of the failure and thereby maintain (or take back) control of their lives going forward (Haynie and Shepherd 2011). Therefore, recovering psychological well-being after a business failure may involve impression management, but rather than impression management always being used to create and maintain a favorable impression of the self among others, it appears to be more about using impression management to achieve a fit between the entrepreneur's self-view and others' view of the entrepreneur (consistent with Swann 1992). In the case of a negative self-view after business failure, impression-management strategies may be used to bring others' view of the entrepreneur into alignment (or to avoid interaction). Although changing others' impressions so they are less favorable may seem counterintuitive (and even destructive), it appears to help entrepreneurs enhance their psychological well-being.

Finally, as we argued in Haynie and Shepherd (2011), not only does impression management as self-verification enhance recovery by building psychological well-being, it can also help with learning from the failure. First, in forming a negative self-view after failure, the entrepreneur is accepting responsibility for the failure. Accepting responsibility indicates that the entrepreneur's actions have influence (i.e., he or she has control over his or her future) and that there is an opportunity to learn from the failure and exact that learning to achieve a different outcome next time. This learning can begin the process of reversing the effect of the failure event on the entrepreneur's self-view. In addition, in seeking others that blame the entrepreneur for the failure and avoiding those who do not, the entrepreneur is in a better position to form authentic relationships with people who are open and honest. When it comes to analyzing the events leading up to the failure, these relationships can be a source of valuable information to facilitate learning. That is, through his or her interactions with these authentic others, the entrepreneur is able to form and further develop a plausible account of the failure.

DISCUSSION

Implications for entrepreneurs and managers

Our review of the literature on stigma from entrepreneurial failure and its consequences entails a number of important implications for practicing entrepreneurs and managers of failing firms.

First, in order to avoid stigmatization from failure, it is insightful for entrepreneurs and managers to know how their personal characteristics and the characteristics of their firm impact others' evaluations of failure. To some extent, entrepreneurial failure is an "invisible" stigma (Clair et al. 2005; Ragins 2008) – that is, it is not visible for all observers immediately (unless they seek information on the person). Therefore, in many situations, entrepreneurs can decide whether their failure should be revealed or hidden to observers. It appears that those who hold higher positions in their failed firms, are more representative of their firm, enjoy "celebrity status," or are homosexual, are better off to hide their past failures when trying to avoid stigmatization. In contrast, those whose failed ventures signaled good intentions (e.g., pursued environmentally friendly technologies) seem to be given credit by observers and suffer less stigmatization when deciding to reveal their failure to others. In this case, it seems advisable to jointly communicate both the failure and the good intentions to observers.

Second, in addition to understanding whether to reveal a failure to others at all, it is insightful for entrepreneurs and managers to know that observers will react differently. It seems that revealing a failure to individuals who tend to simplify complex situations, who are subject to social norms that foster such simplification (e.g., speed for journalists or protecting the public for reporters and persecutors [Wiesenfeld et al. 2008]), and who have difficulties taking others' perspectives are particularly likely to come up with harsh failure evaluations. Failed entrepreneurs and managers might carefully consider revealing a failure openly to these groups of people.

Third, it is also insightful for practicing entrepreneurs and managers to know that different regional environments react differently to failures. Some entrepreneurs can choose where to start their ventures. In particular, when the business model includes high failure risk (e.g., in high-technology sectors), they might either consider starting their firms in regions where stigmatization is relatively low (e.g., those with "forgiving" bankruptcy laws and low public disclosure of failure, cultures that accept failure), or they might consider moving to such regions when moving on with their careers after failure.

Fourth, a particularly important factor for entrepreneurs and managers to consider across regions is entrepreneurial ability because in regions with higher entrepreneurial ability, stigmatization for failure seems considerably less (Landier 2005). Indeed, in regions like Silicon Valley, firm failure is seen as a normal part of trial-and-error learning. This finding highlights that moving to such regions is only advisable for those whose personality and attitude accept failure as something normal. Partly due to missing stigma, failure can occur frequently to even the same individual. As Max Levchin, cofounder of PayPal, noted (www.npr.org):

> The very first company I started failed with a great bang. The second one failed a little bit less, but still failed. The third one, you know, proper failed, but it was kind of okay. I recovered quickly. Number four almost didn't fail. It still didn't really feel great, but it did okay. Number five was PayPal.

Fifth, once failure becomes unavoidable or has already occurred, entrepreneurs and managers have a number of impression-management strategies they can use to minimize stigmatization. These strategies include concealing the problem, defining the failure situation in a positive light, denying responsibility for the failure, accepting responsibility for the failure, and trying to withdraw from the situation. However, it is important to note that a systematic study of how these strategies are effective in mitigating negative stigma consequences is still lacking. For example, Sutton and Callahan (1987) illustrated that withdrawing from the situation for too long may worsen it because it can sustainably damage relationships with stakeholders and thus harm one's future career. Thus, entrepreneurs and managers might be careful in using the impression-management strategies described earlier to escape stigmatization.

Sixth, one stigma-management strategy that seems to be both frequently applied and effective within the labor market is jumping ship – that is, leaving the firm once the failure seems unavoidable (Semadeni et al. 2008). Entrepreneurs and managers, however, should again be careful to apply this strategy because it remains unclear what other consequences it may entail, for example, for the psychological well-being of those who jumped ship (e.g., feelings of guilt) or for their personal relationships (e.g., with those who remained in the failed firm or supported it).

Finally, an important implication for entrepreneurs and managers is that the effectiveness of impression-management strategies for escaping stigma from failure depends on their self-view. While most work on impression-management strategies and their effectiveness have implicitly assumed a positive self-view, there is also the possibility that failing or failed entrepreneurs and managers hold a negative view of themselves. It seems helpful to be aware of one's own self-view when selecting the right strategies. Further, entrepreneurs and managers should also be aware of potential conflicts that can arise between using impression management to enhance personal well-being and moving a bankrupt firm forward (e.g., when restructuring after bankruptcy). If their negative self-views suggests impression-management strategies that conflict with the future recovery of a failed firm, exiting this firm might be the best option.

REFERENCES

Adler, P. S. and Kwon, S. W. 2002. Social capital: Prospects for a new concept. *Academy of Management Review*, 27(1): 17–40.

Armour, J. and Cumming, D. 2008. Bankruptcy law and entrepreneurship. *American Law and Economics Review*, 10(2): 303–350.

Baron-Cohen, S. 1995. *Mindblindness: An Essay on Autism and Theory of Mind.* Cambridge, MA: MIT Press.

Baumeister, R. F. 1993. *Self-esteem: The Puzzle of Low Self-regard:* Plenum Press, New York.

Baumeister, R. F. and Leary, M. R. 1995. The need to belong: Desire for interpersonal attachments as a fundamental human motivation. *Psychological Bulletin*, 117(3): 497.

Becker, E. 1971. *The Birth and Death of Meaning* (2 ed.). New York: Free Press.

Blaine, B. and Crocker, J. 1993. *Self-esteem and self-serving biases in reactions to positive and negative events: An integrative review, Self-esteem: The puzzle of low self-regard*: 55–85, New York: Plenum Press.

Bodenhausen, G. V. and Wyer, R. S. 1985. Effects of stereotypes in decision making and information-processing strategies. *Journal of Personality and Social Psychology*, 48(2): 267–282.

Brewin, C. R. and Furnham, A. 1986. Attributional versus preattributional variables in self-esteem and depression: A comparison and test of learned helplessness theory. *Journal of Personality and Social Psychology*, 50(5): 1013.

Cannella, A. A., Fraser, D. R., and Lee, D. S. 1995. Firm failure and managerial labor markets evidence from Texas banking. *Journal of Financial Economics*, 38(2): 185–210.

Cardon, M. S., Stevens, C. E., and Potter, D. R. 2011. Misfortunes or mistakes?: Cultural sensemaking of entrepreneurial failure. *Journal of Business Venturing*, 26(1): 79–92.

Chen, C. C. and Meindl, J. R. 1991. The construction of leadership images in the popular press: The case of Donald Burr and People Express. *Administrative Science Quarterly:* 521–551.

Chreim, S. 2002. Influencing organizational identification during major change: A communication-based perspective. *Human Relations*, 55(9): 1117–1137.

Clair, J. A., Beatty, J. E., and Maclean, T. L. 2005. Out of sight but not out of mind: Managing invisible social identities in the workplace. *Academy of Management Review*, 30(1): 78–96.

Collins, N. L. and Feeney, B. C. 2000. A safe haven: An attachment theory perspective on support seeking and caregiving in intimate relationships. *Journal of Personality and Social Psychology*, 78(6): 1053.

Corley, K. G. and Gioia, D. A. 2004. Identity ambiguity and change in the wake of a corporate spin-off. *Administrative Science Quarterly*, 49(2): 173–208.

Covington, M. V. 1984. The self-worth theory of achievement motivation: Findings and implications. *The Elementary School Journal:* 5–20.

Crocker, J. and Major, B. 1994. Reactions to stigma: The moderating role of justifications. Paper presented at The Psychology of Prejudice: The Ontario Symposium.

Crocker, J., Major, B., and Steele, C. 1998. Social stigma. In S. T. Fiske, D. Gilbert, and G. Lindzey (eds.), *Handbook of Social Psychology*, Vol. 2: 504–553. Boston, MA: McGraw-Hill.

Crocker, J. and Park, L. E. 2004. The costly pursuit of self-esteem. *Psychological Bulletin*, 130(3): 392.

Curtis, R. C. and Miller, K. 1986. Believing another likes or dislikes you: Behaviors making the beliefs come true. *Journal of Personality and Social Psychology*, 51(2): 284.

Deci, E. L. and Ryan, R. M. 1985. *Intrinsic Motivation and Self-Determination in Human Behavior*. New York, NY: Plenum.

Deci, E. L., Eghrari, H., Patrick, B. C., and Leone, D. R. 1994. Facilitating internalization: The self-determination theory perspective. *Journal of Personality*, 62(1): 119–142.

Deci, E. L., & Ryan, R. M. (1995). *Human autonomy: The basis for true self-esteem*. In M. Kemis (ed.), Efficacy, Agency, and Self-esteem: 31–49. New York: Plenum Press.

Deci, E. L. and Ryan, R. M. 2000. The" what" and" why" of goal pursuits: Human needs and the self-determination of behavior. *Psychological Inquiry*, 11(4): 227–268.

Dimaggio, P. J. and Powell, W. W. 1983. The iron cage revisited: Institutional isomorphism and collective rationality in organizational fields. *American Sociological Review*, 48(2): 147–160.

Djankov, S., McLiesh, C., and Shleifer, A. 2007. Private credit in 129 countries. *Journal of Financial Economics*, 84(2): 299–329.

Dweck, C. S. 2000. *Self-theories: Their Role in Motivation, Personality, and Development*. Philadelphia: Psychology Press.

Efrat, R. 2006. The evolution of bankruptcy stigma. *Theoretical Inquiries in Law*, 7(2): 365–393.

European Commission. 2003. *The New SME Definition-User Guide and Model Declaration*. Brussels, BE: Enterprise and Industry Declarations.

Fan, W. and White, M. J. 2003. Personal bankruptcy and the level of entrepreneurial activity. *Journal of Law & Economics*, 46: 543–567.

Galinsky, A. D. and Ku, G. 2004. The effects of perspective-taking on prejudice: The moderating role of self-evaluation. *Personality and Social Psychology Bulletin*, 30(5): 594–604.

Gerhards, J. 2010. Non-discrimination towards homosexuality: The European Union's policy and citizens' attitudes towards homosexuality in 27 European countries. *International Sociology*, 25(1): 5–28.

Gioia, D. A. and Chittipeddi, K. 1991. Sensemaking and sensegiving in strategic change initiation. *Strategic Management Journal*, 12(6): 433–448.

Greenberg, J. and Pyszczynski, T. 1985. Compensatory self-inflation: A response to the threat to self-regard of public failure. *Journal of Personality and Social Psychology*, 49(1): 273.

Haynie, J. M. and Shepherd, D. 2011. Toward a theory of discontinuous career transition: Investigating career transitions necessitated by traumatic life events. *Journal of Applied Psychology*, 96(3): 501–524.

Hayward, M. L., Rindova, V. P., and Pollock, T. G. 2004. Believing one's own press: The causes and consequences of CEO celebrity. *Strategic Management Journal*, 25(7): 637–653.

Hayward, M. L., Shepherd, D. A., and Griffin, D. 2006. A hubris theory of entrepreneurship. *Management Science*, 52(2): 160–172.

Herek, G. M. 1994. Assessing heterosexuals' attitudes toward lesbians and gay men: A review of empirical research with the ATLG scale. In B. Greene and G. M. Herek (eds.), *Lesbian and Gay Psychology: Theory, Research, and Clinical Application*: 206–228. Thousand Oaks, CA: Sage.

Herek, G. M. 2000. The psychology of sexual prejudice. *Current Directions in Psychological Science*, 9(1): 19–22.

Hermalin, B. E. and Weisbach, M. S. 1998. Endogenously chosen boards of directors and their monitoring of the CEO. *American Economic Review*, 88(1): 96–118.

Herman, D. 1997. *The Antigay Agenda: Orthodox Vision and the Christian Right*. Chicago: University of Chicago Press.

Hodgins, H. S., Koestner, R., and Duncan, N. 1996. On the compatibility of autonomy and relatedness. *Personality and Social Psychology Bulletin*, 22: 227–237.

Johnson, D. W. 1975. Cooperativeness and social perspective taking. *Journal of Personality and Social Psychology*, 31(2): 241–244.

Kreiner, G. E. and Ashforth, B. E. 2004. Evidence toward an expanded model of organizational identification. *Journal of Organizational Behavior*, 25(1): 1–27.

Kulik, C. T., Bainbridge, H. T. J., and Cregan, C. 2008. Known by the company we keep: Stigma-by-association effects in the workplace. *Academy of Management Review*, 33: 216–230.

Landier, A. 2005. Entrepreneurship and the Stigma of Failure. *Available at SSRN850446*. University of Chicago Graduate School of Business, Chicago.

Lee, S.-H., Peng, M. W., and Barney, J. B. 2007. Bankruptcy law and entrepreneurship development: A real options perspective. *Academy of Management Review*, 32(1): 257–272.

McCall, G. J. and Simmons, J. L. 1966. Identities and Interactions. New York: The Free Press.

Mühlauer, A. and Radomski, S. 2005. *Mein kleiner Kapitalist darf jetzt raus*, Süddeutsche Zeitung. www.sueddeutsche.de/geld/reden-wir-ueber-geld-mein-kleiner-kapitalist-darf-jetzt-raus-1.2287535

Neuberg, S. L., Smith, D. M., Hoffman, J. C., and Russell, F. J. 1994. When we observe stigmatized and "normal" individuals interacting: Stigma by association. *Personality and Social Psychology Bulletin*, 20(2): 196–209.

Niiya, Y., Crocker, J., and Bartmess, E. N. 2004. From vulnerability to resilience: Learning orientations buffer contingent self-esteem from failure. *Psychological Science*, 15(12): 801–805.

Pierce, J. L., Gardner, D. G., Cummings, L. L., and Dunham, R. B. 1989. Organization-based self-esteem: Construct definition, measurement, and validation. *Academy of Management Journal*, 32(3): 622–648.

Pollack, D. 2002. The change in religion and church in Eastern Germany after 1989: A research note. *Sociology of Religion*, 63(3): 373–387.

Pyszczynski, T., Greenberg, J., Solomon, S., Arndt, J., and Schimel, J. 2004. Why do people need self-esteem? A theoretical and empirical review. *Psychological Bulletin*, 130(3): 435.

Ragins, B. R. 2008. Disclosure disconnects: Antecedents and consequences of disclosing invisible stigmas across life domains. *Academy of Management Review*, 33(1): 194–215.

Richardson, D. R., Hammock, G. S., Smith, S. M., Gardner, W., and Signo, M. 1994. Empathy as a cognitive inhibitor of interpersonal aggression. *Aggressive Behavior*, 20(4): 275–289.

Secord, P. F. and Backman, C. W. 1964. An interpersonal approach to personality. *Progress in experimental personality research*, 2: 91–125.

Semadeni, M., Cannella, A. A., Fraser, D. R., and Lee, D. S. 2008. Fight or flight: Managing stigma in executive careers. *Strategic Management Journal*, 29(5): 557–567.

Sessa, V. I. 1996. Using perspective taking to manage conflict and affect in teams. *Journal of Applied Behavioral Science*, 32(1): 101–115.

Shepherd, D. A. and Haynie, J. M. 2011. Venture failure, stigma, and impression management: A self-verification, self-determination view. *Strategic Entrepreneurship Journal*, 5(2): 178–197.

Shepherd, D. A., Patzelt, H., Williams, T. A., and Warnecke, D. 2014. How does project termination impact project team members? Rapid termination, 'creeping death', and learning from failure. *Journal of Management Studies*, 51(4): 513–546.

Shepherd, D. A. and Patzelt, H. 2015. Harsh evaluations of entrepreneurs who fail: The role of sexual orientation, use of environmentally friendly technologies, and observers' perspective taking. *Journal of Management Studies*, 52: 253–284.

Simmons, S. A., Wiklund, J., and Levie, J. 2014. Stigma and business failure: implications for entrepreneurs' career choices. *Small Business Economics*, 42(3): 485–505.

Slovic, P., Finucane, M. L., Peters, E., and MacGregor, D. G. 2007. The affect heuristic. *European Journal of Operational Research*, 177(3): 1333–1352.

Sutton, R. I. and Callahan, A. L. 1987. The stigma of bankruptcy: Spoiled organizational image and its management. *Academy of Management Journal*, 30(3): 405–436.

Swann Jr, W. B. and Pelham, B. 2002. Who wants out when the going gets good? Psychological investment and preference for self-verifying college roommates. *Self and Identity*, 1(3): 219–233.

Swann Jr, W. B. 2005. The self and identity negotiation. *Interaction Studies*, 6(1): 69–83.

Swann, W. B. and Ely, R. J. 1984. A battle of wills: Self-verification versus behavioral confirmation. *Journal of Personality and Social Psychology*, 46(6): 1287.

Swann, W. B. 1992. Seeking "truth," finding despair: Some unhappy consequences of a negative self-concept. *Current Directions in Psychological Science*: 15–18.

Swann, W. B., Jr. 1983. Self-verification: Bringing social reality into harmony with the self. In J. Suls and A.G. Greenwald (ed.), *Psychological Perspectives on the Self*, Vol. 2: 33–66. Hillsdale, NJ: Erlbaum.

Tennen, H. and Herzberger, S. 1987. Depression, self-esteem, and the absence of self-protective attributional biases. *Journal of personality and social psychology*, 52(1): 72.

Todd, A. R., Bodenhausen, G. V., Richeson, J. A., and Galinsky, A. D. 2011. Perspective taking combats automatic expressions of racial bias. *Journal of Personality and Social Psychology*, 100(6): 1027–1042.

Todd, A. R., Galinsky, A. D., and Bodenhausen, G. V. 2012. Perspective taking undermines stereotype maintenance processes: Evidence from social memory, behavior explanation, and information solicitation. *Social Cognition*, 30(1): 94–108.

Tversky, A. and Kahneman, D. 1974. Judgment under uncertainty: Heuristics and biases. *Science*, 185(4157): 1124–1131.

Weick, K. 1979. *The Social Psychology of Organizing*. Reading, MA: Addison-Wesley.

Weiner, B. 1985. An attributional theory of achievement motivation and emotion. *Psychological Review*, 92(4): 548–573.

Wiesenfeld, B., Wurthmann, K., and Hambrick, D. 2008. The stigmatization and devaluation of elites associated with corporate failures: A process model. *Academy of Management Review*, 33(1): 231–251.

Zappe, C. 2011. Das Stigma des Scheiterns *Frankfurter Allgemeine Zeitung*. www.faz.net/aktuell/beruf-chance/arbeitswelt/wenn-unternehmer-pleite-gehen-das-stigma-des-scheiterns-1638565.html

8 Narratives of entrepreneurial failure

Whereas in earlier chapters we discussed the decision to terminate entrepreneurial projects and the learning associated with such failures, we now focus on the specific mechanisms underlying the sensemaking process. As we previously established, entrepreneurial projects are often characterized by greater levels of risk and uncertainty (Deeds, DeCarolis, and Coombs 2000), and because of this, they are at risk for higher rates of project failure (Corbett, Neck, and DeTienne 2007).

A particularly salient example of such projects and the failure rates associated with them can be found in new product development (NPD) efforts initiated by science-based organizations (Pisano 2010). Because such organizations operate in contexts in which the very feasibility of potential ideas is somewhat uncertain, innovative efforts result in failure more often than not (Pisano 2010). As a result of this high rate of failure, these organizations must develop systems to efficiently process, interpret, and understand failure so that they can utilize that knowledge on subsequent NPD activities. Therefore, project failures can prove to be beneficial as they often result in a more comprehensive understanding of the organization's situation (Popper and Lipshitz 2000). In addition, as we have seen from previous chapters, these failures can result in new knowledge being learned, which can lead to improved performance (McGrath 1999).

While failure can prove to be beneficial, it is not without its risks and can result in markedly negative effects (Shepherd, Wiklund, and Haynie 2009b). Experiencing high levels of failure can result in downward performance spirals (Lindsley, Brass, and Thomas 1995), which may ultimately force firms to reduce or even eliminate exploratory initiatives and instead focus on endeavors with less uncertainty

(March 1991). As touched upon previously, individuals who experience high levels of project failure can develop negative emotions (i.e., grief) as a result of such experiences (Shepherd, Patzelt, and Wolfe 2011b). These negative emotions can then be transmitted from the individual to other members of the organization through numerous mechanisms. Whether via emotional contagion (Hatfield, Cacioppo, and Rapson 1992), vicarious affect (Bandura 1986), or affective influence (Ashkanasy and Tse 2000), this transfer of emotions can result in the development of collective emotions and can ultimately impact team and firm performance (Barsade 2002; Dasborough, Ashkanasy, Tee, and Tse 2009; Hatfield, Cacioppo, and Rapson 1994). Taking into account the fact that failure produces both opportunities to learn as well as barriers to the learning process, it is imperative that we gain a deeper understanding of how organizations make sense of failure without impeding the learning associated with it in order to enhance the likelihood that future projects will be successful.

With regard to the sensemaking process, one of the most important elements involved in how both individuals and organizations make sense and understand failure events is communication (Weick 1995). Communication is important as a vehicle to transfer information, but it is also a vital mechanism through which that information can be organized and framed in order to convey a desired message (Boje 1994). Organizations that remain silent and refuse to actively engage in communication run the risk of developing the inability to change in order to address ever-shifting environments and, as a result, face the threat of obsolescence (Morrison and Milliken 2000). From an organizational perspective, one of the most prominent forms of communication that is utilized to convey key messages comes in the form of organizational narratives. Narratives have been shown to be vital parts of the sensemaking process (Brown, Stacey, and Nandhakumar 2008) and have been linked to important organizational outcomes, such as innovation (Bartel and Garud 2009), learning (Garud, Dunbar, and Bartel 2011), and change (Dunford and Jones 2000). As such, it is important for us to better understand how narratives and the messages they contain are employed by organizations in an attempt to communicate key messages as a component of the sensemaking process.

In this chapter, we first examine the role that narratives, more specifically narrative emotional content, play in the sensemaking process. By examining the role that narrative content plays in the sensemaking process, we draw attention to the fact that failures do influence organizational narratives. Specifically, we examine how organizational narratives might be altered with regard to their emotional content as a result of important events and how these alterations can serve as vital components of the sensemaking process. In doing so, we gain a deeper understanding of *the manner in which organizations alter their narratives as a result of either negative or positive performance events.* To provide richness to this discussion, we offer extensive examples of how large pharmaceutical firms have attempted to understand and make sense of failed drug projects. Indeed, project failure is a more likely occurrence than project success in the pharmaceutical industry (Pisano 2010), where the costs of project failures are usually remarkably high (DiMasi 2001; DiMasi, Hansen, and Grabowski 2003). Nevertheless, pharmaceutical firms cannot merely decide to forego undertaking research and development (R&D) initiatives in lieu of less risky activities since performance and viability are ultimately tied to R&D activities (Del Monte and Papagni 2003).

Second, we investigate the cognitive approaches reflected in narratives and how these can influence subsequent performance, particularly "bouncing back" from a failure event. Specifically, we build upon prior research regarding failure (Shepherd et al. 2011b), entrepreneurial orientation (Rauch, Wiklund, Lumpkin, and Frese 2009), and emotions (Shepherd 2009) in order to examine how specific narrative elements are communicated after failure and how those specific narrative elements are associated with subsequent performance. To add richness, we report on an analysis of the transcripts of head coaches of Division I college football programs (in the United States)

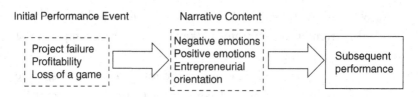

FIGURE 8.1: Conceptual model

immediately following their first loss of the season and performance in the next game (see Wolfe and Shepherd 2015k). Because college football programs can be viewed as more or less entrepreneurial organizations (Napier and Nilsson 2006; Sperber 2004), these narratives can be highly informative about the role and outcomes of different failure narratives. An illustration of the overall conceptual model detailed in this chapter can be seen in Figure 8.1.

The remainder of this chapter proceeds as follows. We first review the literature so as to establish the theoretical context for this chapter – narratives as sense making. Second, we answer each of the research questions, and finally, we explore the implications.

NARRATIVES AS PART OF THE SENSEMAKING PROCESS

Sensemaking relates to the process of continuously developing plausible retrospective accounts of past events that are used to inform current and future actions and activities (Weick, Sutcliffe, and Obstfeld 2005). It has been shown to be a critical process used by organizations to understand significant events, such as unexpected failure (Cannon 1999), restructuring (Balogun and Johnson 2004), and change (Luscher and Lewis 2008). Central to sensemaking is communication. Weick and colleagues stated that sensemaking "is embodied in written and spoken texts" (Weick et al. 2005: 409), and it has been stated that "reading, writing, conversing, and editing are crucial actions that serve as the media through which the invisible hand of institutions shapes conduct" (Gioia, Thomas, Clark, and Chittipeddi 1994). Therefore, it is vital to understand how communication is utilized in the sensemaking process. However, in doing so, it is important to establish that narratives are more than a mere collections of facts; rather, they are used to link causes and outcomes within various organizational contexts (Brown et al. 2008). Indeed, the main goal of sensemaking is not necessarily to provide an accurate explanation but to determine the plausibility of these interpretations and explore their influence on subsequent actions (Mills 2003). Plausibility refers to the likelihood that a given account of past events is credible and therefore believable to the target audience (Weick, Sutcliffe, and Obstfeld 1999). In this way, sensemaking assists organizations in noticing, arranging, labeling, and acting upon previous experiences (Weick et al. 2005).

Importantly, narratives are used to provide plausible explanations for organizational events as well as to create plausible accounts of past, present, and future actions (Quinn and Worline 2008). Narratives refer to the thematic sequenced accounts of interrelated events or actions that are undertaken by the characters who tell them or about whom they are told and convey meaning from the author to the reader (Barry and Elmes 1997; Czarniawska 1998). Although narratives vary widely in terms of content, they all share three key components: (1) a subject, (2) a desired object or goal, and (3) a set of factors that either assist or constrain the character from the desired object or goal (Fiol 1989). Narratives also contain a temporal element (either implicit or explicit), which generates a plot – the primary scheme or storyline being portrayed throughout the narrative (Barry and Elmes 1997; Gabriel 2000).

Project failure and narratives' negative emotional content

Organizational performance is often dependent upon the organization engaging in entrepreneurial action (Covin and Miles 1999; Rauch et al. 2009). In larger firms, these actions largely begin from R&D activities (Khandawalla 1977). It is customary for individuals involved in such projects to develop a sense of psychological ownership toward these projects (Pierce, Kostova, and Dirks 2001). This feeling of ownership can be seen as a positive psychological resource (Avey, Avolio, Crossley, and Luthans 2009), which can in turn result in increases in positive emotions as well as benefits for organizational change (Avey, Wernsing, and Luthans 2008). Furthermore, positive emotions experienced at the group level have been shown to enhance cooperation, reduce conflict, and positively influence perceived performance (Barsade 2002).

However, these benefits of entrepreneurial projects do not come without potential risks. While entrepreneurial projects can amplify individuals' motivation for success, they can also result in negative emotional consequences if the projects fail (which, given the high uncertainty surrounding these projects, is a likely outcome) (Shepherd, Covin, and Kuratko 2009a; Wiklund and Shepherd 2011). It is possible that if such negative emotions are felt acutely enough at the individual level, they can in turn produce similar emotions within the group as well, essentially forming "collective emotions" (Cannon and Edmondson 2001). Collective emotions are emotions that are experienced by a group of individuals within a shared society (Stephan and Stephan 2000). Just as individual emotions can influence the group, collectively held emotions can also serve to influence the emotions of the individuals within the group. These group-based emotions "can play a pivotal role in shaping individual and societal responses to conflicting events and in contributing to the evolvement of a social context that maintains the emotional climate and collective emotional orientation that have developed" (Bar-Tal, Halperin, and De Rivera 2007). Even though individuals within the group might experience varying personal emotions, it is possible that these commonly held collective emotions can lead group members to common actions that might not necessarily align with their individual emotions but are nonetheless in line with the group perspective.

As they relate to organizational narratives, collective emotions are often evident in the public dialogues organizations develop (Bar-Tal 2001). Excerpts from the annual reports we analyzed (Wolfe and Shepherd, 2015a) provide evidence of the generation of negative emotions resulting from project failure. An example of this can be seen from an annual report describing the organization's outlook on a failed drug application to the European Medicines Agency (EMA):

> In December 2006, the European Patent Office (EPO) ruled that one of the European substance patents for Nexium would be rejected following an appeal from the German generic manufacturer, ratiopharm GmbH. The original expiry date for this patent was 2014. Although disappointed with the EPO decision, we continue to have full confidence in the intellectual property portfolio protecting Nexium (AstraZeneca 2007).

This acknowledgment of emotions is important because, as we detail in the following text, these collective negative emotions can have substantial effects on work outcomes and performance (George and Brief 1992).

As a result of the collective negative emotions generated from project failure, organizations often alter the content of the narratives they construct about failure events (Dutton, Worline, Frost, and Lilius 2006). Over time, as these collective emotions become more common, they can potentially evolve into organizational routines and norms (Huy 1999) as they become ever more ingrained in the organization's systematic response to addressing negative emotions. Furthermore, it is possible that these routines and norms can impact the development of the organizational narrative and result in narratives regarding failure events containing greater levels of negative emotional content. Moreover, these failure narratives could be employed by organizations as a means of justifying or legitimating the activities that produced failed results (Vaara 2002). An example of the use of failure narratives to justify and lend credibility to negative events can be seen in the following passage:

> In 2007 (Glaxo Smith Kline's) share price fell by 5 percent compared to an increase in the FTSE 100 index of 4 percent. That was disappointing for our investors, a significant number of whom are

also our employees. We started 2007 strongly and achieved several important milestones including the launches of Tykerb and the FDA approval of alli. In the first quarter, we beat expectations and delivered EPS growth of 14 percent. As the market received this positive news our share price outperformed most of our peers. Then, in May 2007, an article in the New England Journal of Medicine (NEJM) suggested that there may be cardiovascular risk associated with Avandia, our second largest product. This was followed by intense media coverage and despite our efforts to explain the entirety of the data, which did not confirm this risk, doctors were reluctant to prescribe Avandia for new patients without further FDA guidance. Sales of Avandia dropped significantly and this had a negative impact on our share price. Following clarification from the FDA in October 2007, we now have a new approved label and can move ahead with more clarity (GlaxoSmithKline 2007).

While narratives consist of recounting previous events that are given meaning by the narrative plot, we note that the plot is not intrinsic to the events but rather is a construct used by the authors in an attempt to make sense of these occurrences (Vaara 2002). As a result, there is the potential to alter a particular narrative of project failure in the hopes of painting the experience in a more favorable, less disappointing manner.

More negative emotional content of a narrative about project failure could signal to key shareholders that even though these project efforts resulted in failure, the projects were important and that the firm remained optimistic about eventual future success regarding these projects. In addition, these messages about the importance of failure could communicate continued organizational commitment to R&D activities, which, as previously stated, are the key to future performance of many firms in knowledge-intensive industries. The following is an excerpt showing how an organization utilizes a narrative regarding a failure event as a mechanism to communicate future commitment to

R&D activity as well as optimism for the eventual success of the failed research initiatives:

> Myozyme was our greatest challenge and biggest disappointment in 2008. After our most successful global launch ever, manufacturing and regulatory issues did not allow us to treat all patients who could benefit from this breakthrough therapy for Pompe disease. In the United States, approval and production hurdles remain, but we are confident we can manage through these challenges and secure regulatory approvals for products manufactured at both the 2,000- and 4,000-liter bioreactor scale this year. In Europe, Myozyme manufactured at the 4,000-liter scale was approved in February 2009, ahead of projected timelines. With two 4,000-liter reactors in Europe and the anticipated U.S. approvals, we will soon be able to ensure adequate supply for patients and begin to realize Myozyme's tremendous potential worldwide (Genzyme 2008).

Even though we have begun to explore the importance of negative emotional content in narratives (here and earlier in the book), such a discussion is incomplete without also exploring the role of positive emotions, to which we now turn.

Narratives' positive and negative emotional content

Although positive and negative emotions are often regarded as related concepts, they remain distinctly separate and unique constructs. Substantial research has been done in this area and shows strong evidence that positive and negative emotions are largely independent of each other (Diener and Emmons 1984). Positive and negative emotions can be examined more closely based on their two underlying dimensions – frequency and intensity – and when this is done, the distinction between the two becomes clearer (Diener, Larsen, Levine, and Emmons 1985). Of course, time spent experiencing one emotion impacts the amount of time individuals can experience other emotions, and because of this, research has shown that in regard to the frequency dimension, the two forms of emotions are highly *negatively* correlated (Diener et al. 1985). Conversely, a predilection to experience one type of emotion more intensely can result in the tendency to experience another type of emotion more intensely as well. This results in the intensity dimension of both types of emotions being highly *positively* correlated (Diener et al. 1985). Therefore, because the average levels of affect one experiences are a result of both frequency (for which positive and negative emotions are negatively correlated) and intensity (for which positive and negative emotions are positively correlated), the overall correlations of positive and negative emotions are low. The independent nature of these two emotional constructs allows us to explore when and how they are related and what differential effects they have.

Positive emotions appear to be able to decrease the consequences of negative emotions via an "undoing" mechanism (Fredrickson, Mancuso, Branigan, and Tugade 2000). The undoing role of positive emotions refers to the ability that positive emotions have to reduce and/or eliminate the detrimental consequences experienced as a result of negative emotions (Fredrickson et al. 2000). As evidence of this undoing effect of positive emotions, Fredrickson and colleagues conducted a study of individuals' resilience following the terrorist attacks on 9/11 and found that positive emotions substantially benefited individuals by enhancing their overall resilience following negative experiences (Fredrickson, Tugade, Waugh, and Larkin 2003).

Over and above undoing negative emotions, it appears that positive emotions can "broaden one's thought–action repertoire, expanding the range of cognitions and behaviors that come to mind" (Tugade and Fredrickson 2004). By undoing negative emotions and broadening thought–action resources, positive emotions might prove to be helpful in regulating the negative emotions that can develop as a result of failure (Tugade and Fredrickson 2004). For example, positive emotions have been shown to increase individual resilience (Tugade and Fredrickson 2004), enhance the likelihood that failed entrepreneurs will put forth the effort to attempt new ventures (Hayward, Forster, Sarasvathy, and Fredrickson 2009), and assist organizations in accomplishing organizational transformation (Sekerka and Fredrickson 2008).

Some passages demonstrating positive emotional content from our sample include the following statement regarding an organization's hopeful perspective in terms of its developmental pipeline:

> We're pleased to have a robust group of potential medications in our pipeline. Behind our newest medications are promising late-stage compounds that include dasatinib, for chronic myelogenous leukemia, which is now under review by the FDA. Other compounds in Phase III development include ixabepilone, ipilimumab and vinflunine, for cancer; belatacept, for the prevention of solid organ transplantation rejection; and saxagliptin, for type 2 diabetes (Bristol Meyrs Squibb 2005).

This passage regarding one firm's positive outlook about their projected future growth also demonstrates this positive emotional content:

> Barring unforeseen events, Roche anticipates further positive growth in 2007. We expect the Group's and the Pharmaceuticals Division's sales to continue to grow at double-digit rates in local currencies. In both the Pharmaceuticals Division and the Diagnostics Division, Roche anticipates continued above-market sales growth in local currencies. Roche's target is for Core EPS to grow in line with Group sales, despite significant investments in research, development, production and marketing (Roche 2006).

Positive emotions and their effects (i.e., undoing and broadening) have been shown to exist at the organizational level (Fredrickson 2003). At the organizational level, positive emotions can stimulate "useful cognitive and social capabilities" (Sekerka and Fredrickson 2008), enhance cooperation as a result of building and reinforcing relational strength (Sekerka and Fredrickson 2008), and amplify the potential for organizational change (Avey et al. 2008). Specifically, emotions evolve in social settings, and as such, they can perform social functions (Fischer and Manstead 2008). For example, it has been suggested that positive emotions can serve as a form of "social glue," enhancing group members' affiliation with each other (Fischer and Manstead 2008), and studies have shown that positive emotional expressions by leaders or managers are predictive of overall group performance (George 1995). Nevertheless, how do these emotions and their effects play out in the use of organizational narratives for sensemaking purposes? We now turn to addressing this question.

Positive feedback and narratives' negative emotions

Although project failure is often perceived as a negative event (Iacovoc and Dexter 2005; Shepherd et al. 2011b), the failure of one or more projects does not necessarily reflect the overall performance of the firm. Indeed, it has been argued that performance is enhanced when organizations are more entrepreneurial, which involves experimenting more, probing the future, and quickly terminating projects that do not show promise (McGrath 1999). In essence, a higher frequency of project failure is common in firms that engage in greater levels of proactiveness and innovation (McGrath 1999), both of which comprise the fundamental building blocks of an overall entrepreneurial orientation (Covin, Green, and Slevin 2006). Furthermore, and as reinforced consistently throughout this book, failures represent an opportunity for individual and organizational learning (Chuang and Baum 2003), which are important antecedents to organizational success (Minniti and Bygrave 2001). Learning as a result of failure affords firms the opportunity to make sense and understand the underlying causes of those failures, thereby motivating future action and hopefully reducing the probability that similar mistakes will be repeated.

Because profitability has been shown to be such an important indicator of firm performance (Anderson, Fornell, and Lehmann 1994), increases in profitability are typically considered to be a positive event – namely, positive feedback indicative of improved firm performance. Positive feedback can produce a number of advantages, including increased group pride, involvement, and esteem (Nadler 1979), which can in turn facilitate member cooperation and collaboration (Druskat and Wolff 2001), reduce negative emotions, and enhance positive well-being (Salanova, Llorens, Cifre, Martínez, and Schaufeli 2003). As a result, in organizations where failure is likely to occur, it will be important for the organization to focus its attention on other sources of positive feedback, such as firm profitability, to counteract the potentially negative consequences that high project failure rates can have at both the individual and organizational levels.

Most often, organizations determine whether or not they are performing at an acceptable level by comparing their current performance with previously established thresholds (Greve 2002). The results of this evaluation often impact important organizational processes, such as innovation (Bolton 1993), strategic perspective (Grinyer and McKiernan 1990), and corporate re-orientation (Lant, Milliken, and Batra 1992). When analyzing performance from a threshold standpoint, organizations typically adopt the view that if current performance is above that of prior years, it is deemed acceptable and successful. However, if performance dips below historical levels, performance is typically viewed in a negative light (Greve 2002). Therefore, as long as the firm's profitability remains at or above a threshold level, the risks of the negative consequences associated with high failure rates are somewhat mitigated by this positive feedback. Indeed, positive performance feedback (despite a high failure rate) has been found to encourage more entrepreneurial endeavors, such as investments in R&D (see also Scherer 2001; Wolfe and Shepherd 2015k).

It is likely that the narratives organizations construct will be modified to include information from performance feedback and to portray firms' overall position. To investigate this issue, we (Wolfe and Shepherd, 2015k) analyzed annual reports from public firms that had submitted at least one drug-approval application to the EMA from 2002 to 2010. Because the performance events (e.g., project failure and profitability) occurred before narrative development (i.e., the construction of the annual report), there is a theoretical basis behind the causal relationship between these variables. Analyzing annual reports also proved advantageous because they represent narratives that are closely examined by important stakeholders and can therefore have important consequences for organizations (Stanton, Stanton, and Pires 2004). As a result, it is vital to top management that the narratives created within these reports appropriately portray the organization at hand as well as justify its past, present, and future activities. Our sample included 68 firms and a total of 356 observations (i.e., total number of annual reports).

In our study of how performance events – both negative (in the form of project failure) and positive (in the form of increases in profitability) – related to levels of positive and negative emotional content within organizational narratives, we found that both positive and negative performance events influenced the negative content of organizational narratives. Additionally, we discovered that not only did positive emotional content influence narratives' negative emotional content but that this relationship was moderated by gains or losses in profitability.

In this study, we found that even for large organizations, which usually construct relatively sanitized and standardized (e.g., mentions of failures restricted, negative emotional content minimized, etc.) narratives, such as annual reports, increased levels of project failure resulted in higher levels of negative emotional content. Additionally, narratives with more positive emotional content in general contained less negative emotional content. Moreover, Wolfe and Shepherd (2015a) found evidence that the negative relationship between the positive emotional content and negative emotional content of failure narratives was greater when there was high positive performance feedback than when there was low positive performance feedback. These findings have implications for our understanding of narratives' emotional outcomes related to performance feedback.

Project failure and narratives' negative emotional content

The first important implication of our findings is that the greater the failure rate of entrepreneurial projects, the greater the narrative's negative emotional content (controlling for narrative length) (Wolfe and Shepherd, 2015a). Although the development of new products and the R&D process in general are the foundation for success in the pharmaceutical industry (Del Monte and Papagni 2003; DiMasi et al. 2003), these projects by their very nature are higher in uncertainty and therefore result in higher project failure rates (DiMasi 2001). This is important to note because it has been shown that employees can develop high levels of psychological ownership of projects under their control (Pierce et al. 2001), which can in turn generate positive emotions that facilitate individual and organizational performance, particularly in situations of organizational change (Avey et al. 2008). However, as established in Chapter 2, the more important these projects are to project team members, the more grief they are likely to experience when the projects fail (Shepherd et al. 2009a; Shepherd, Patzelt, and Wolfe 2011a).

This type of negative emotional reaction can be felt at both the individual and the collective levels (Cannon and Edmondson 2001). As mentioned earlier, collective emotion refers to "emotions that are shared by a large number of individuals in a certain society" (Wolfe and Shepherd 2015k). The development of collective emotions from individual emotions can occur both implicitly and explicitly via a number of emotional processes. Implicitly, collective emotions can develop through emotional contagion (Hatfield et al. 1992) and vicarious affect (Bandura 1986). In terms of explicit processes, both affective influence (Ashkanasy and Tse 2000) and affective emotional displays (Kelly and Barsade 2001) can contribute to the development of collective emotions. Regardless of the mechanisms by which individual emotions become collective emotions, collective emotions arising from project failure can alter a narrative (Dutton et al. 2006).

Not surprisingly, because project failures often generate negative emotions (Cannon and Edmondson 2001; Shepherd et al. 2011a), the narratives constructed about those failures will have high negative emotional content. However, increased negative emotional content might not be the only way project failure influences organizational narratives. Because a narrative plot is constructed by an author in an attempt to make sense of past events (Vaara 2002), it is possible that the organization might use a project failure narrative to explain the activities leading up to the failure (Vaara 2002), modifying the plot as needed to alter how project failure is portrayed. That is, rather than simply reflect the consequences of the failure, the narrative might construct and reflect the antecedents to the project failure. In this manner, narratives could be used to signal to stakeholders the importance of failed projects to the firm and/or the firm's continued interest in similar entrepreneurial projects as a means to enhance firm performance.

An example of a passage containing higher levels of negative emotions as a result of project failure can be seen in the following passage detailing one organization's disappointment in having to withdraw a product from the market as well as ceasing development of another late-stage compound:

> These efforts will strengthen our long-term sustainability and help us to withstand the impact of some of the setbacks that we experienced with our pipeline this year. In February 2006, we withdrew our anticoagulant, Exanta, from the market and halted its development on patient safety grounds. We also stopped late-stage development of Galida, our potential diabetes therapy, and NXY-059, a potential treatment for stroke, because they were not demonstrating sufficient patient benefit. Whilst such decisions are disappointing to make, they are an indication of the challenges associated with delivering a new medicine and reflect our commitment to patient safety and to maintaining a portfolio of only the highest quality, highest potential candidates (AstraZeneca 2006).

Positive and negative emotional narrative content

A second important implication of our findings is that the greater the positive emotional content of the narrative, the lower the negative emotional content (again controlling for narrative length) (Wolfe and Shepherd, 2015a). Such a finding is consistent with the notion that positive emotions can "undo" the effects of negative emotions (Fredrickson et al. 2000) as well as broaden the set of thought–action resources, which may help regulate negative emotions generated by an unexpected failure (Tugade and Fredrickson 2004). In addition to the effects that positive emotions can have at the individual level, evidence suggests that they can prove to be similarly beneficial at the organizational level (Fredrickson et al. 2003). Emotions develop in social contexts and can thus influence social functions (Fischer and Manstead 2008). In this sense, positive emotions have been proposed to operate as a type of "social glue" that binds group members together on a social level (Fischer and Manstead 2008) and thereby increases the overall level of cooperation exhibited within the organization (Sekerka and Fredrickson 2008). This increased cooperation has been shown to be particularly useful in situations involving organizational change (Avey et al. 2008).

Examples of passages containing positive emotional elements include the following, wherein an organization is discussing positive results related to its drug-development activities:

> We made very significant progress in 2003 as illustrated by the FDA's decision to consider the company's injectable and dry product plants in Indianapolis to be in a state of compliance with current Good Manufacturing Practices. This subsequently led to a successful preapproval inspection for Zyprexa® IntraMuscular at Indianapolis. Based on this outcome, the FDA has indicated that it does not currently believe a preapproval inspection for Cymbalta will be necessary, although such an inspection remains at the discretion of the FDA. In addition, we've had two successful preapproval inspections for Cialis and Alimta. We are pleased with the progress we've made thus far and are committed not only to sustain it but to make Lilly the benchmark for quality within the industry (Eli Lilly, 2003).

Additionally, excerpts demonstrating the use of positive and negative emotional content within the same context can be seen in the following passage detailing disappointment at results of a drug trial in the United States but continued optimism for the drug's applications in East Asian markets:

> The disappointing results from a preliminary analysis of the ISEL study into Iressa patients' survival had little impact outside the US on sales in 2004. In 2005 in the US, we anticipate a rapid reduction in new prescriptions and sales will be recognized on confirmed patient usage. While commercial prospects have certainly been reduced in Western markets, the positive results in patients of East Asian origin offer the prospect of a continuing successful business in these important markets (AstraZeneca 2004).

Moderating role of profitability

Finally, the arrangement of narratives' positive and negative emotional content can be complex. Indeed, when positive performance events, such as increases in profitability, do occur, the relationship between positive and negative narrative content is amplified (Wolfe and Shepherd, 2015a). Positive outcomes in areas other than NPD might serve to mitigate the likelihood that individuals and organizations will over-identify with and ruminate over project failures within the organizational narrative. Such positive events can shift attentional focus away from the negative consequences of failure and onto other areas of importance to the organization (Ocasio 1997, 2011). This broadening of attention might reduce or even eliminate the possibility that project failures will become the driving focus of attention, thereby decreasing the potential for organizations to include high levels of negative emotional content in the narratives they construct. From an entrepreneurial point of view, this arrangement of emotional content – focusing more on the positive rather than the negative – provides support for the notion that "entrepreneurial action is characterized by the dominance of pride and the relative absence of shame" (Goss, 2005: 212). To better visualize the moderating role that profitability has on the relationship between a narrative's

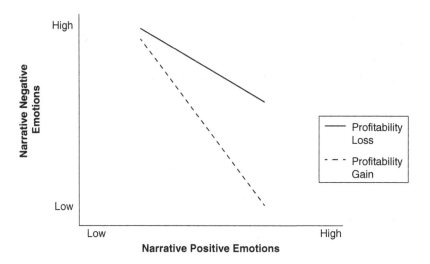

FIGURE 8.2: Positive emotional content, profitability, and negative emotional content

positive and negative emotional content, Figure 8.2 contains a graphical representation of this effect. As is evident in Figure 8.2, the negative influence that positive emotional content has on negative emotional content is more pronounced when organizations have experienced gains in profitability rather than losses in profitability.

NARRATIVE ELEMENTS AND BOUNCING BACK FROM FAILURE

While in the earlier sections, we established that performance events can influence the emotional content of organizational narratives, in the remainder of this chapter, we explore how narratives' emotional content can also influence subsequent action and performance. Although we again explore the emotional content of failure narratives, we believe it is important to include an important predictor of entrepreneurial action at the organizational level – an entrepreneurial orientation (EO) (see Lumpkin and Dess 1996; Rauch et al. 2009; Short, Broberg, Cogliser, and Brigham 2010). To explore the relationship between narratives' content and teams' ability to "bounce back" from failure, in the subsections that follow, we offer examples from a rich context – post-match press conference transcripts from head coaches of Division I college football programs directly after their first loss of the season (for a detailed description of the research method, see Wolfe and Shepherd 2015k). Indeed, sports teams have been shown to represent good examples of entrepreneurial organizations (Ratten 2010, 2011).

Entrepreneurial orientation content and bouncing back

Although the majority of previous evidence has supported the idea that EO has a positive effect on organizational performance (Rauch et al. 2009), recent research has suggested that this relationship is perhaps not linear (Zahra and Garvis 2000). In fact, a recent project examining the relationship between EO and performance in small- to medium-sized firms indicated that this relationship is U-shaped in nature (Kreiser, Marino, Kuratko, and Weaver 2013). Adopting a sensemaking perspective, narratives can be used to communicate the necessary amount of EO needed to effectively bounce back after failure. Because narratives give meaning to events (Orbuch 1997), they can be utilized not only to relate details about past events but also to influence future behaviors (Orr 1995). In this manner, they are particularly salient influences driving organizational change (Dunford and Jones 2000). Thus, the level of EO content contained within a narrative signifies an attempt to communicate how failure is interpreted and can thus have an important influence on subsequent performance.

An important point to make note of is that undertaking EO activities does not universally produce positive results (Hart 1992). Because entrepreneurial initiatives usually require considerable commitment of initial resources (Hornsby, Kuratko, Shepherd, and Bott 2009), it is possible that organizations might forego investing in activities critical for organizational survival in order to engage in entrepreneurial activities (Rosenbusch, Brinckmann, and Bausch 2011). Therefore, in terms of attempting to survive, organizations that have a relatively low EO may be better able to allocate resources to other more beneficial areas and may consequently experience increased performance. This low EO would be reflected in narratives containing fewer examples of language relating to the need to act entrepreneurially (e.g., proactive, innovative, risk taking, etc.). Examples of such language indicating a low need to act entrepreneurially include this from Coach Lynch after Indiana University's first loss of the season to Southern Illinois University:

> We didn't bounce back really at any one phase once they started gaining momentum, and that's on us. I do think that Southern Illinois is a very good football team, and they deserve a lot of credit for the way they played today. . . . We're going to find positives, and there is so much football left to play in the season; that's the thing about it. We'll watch tape, and we are going to move on. I really do believe we will get better. . . . I don't think there is a make-or-break, must-win game with nine games left, but you want to win every game. In that sense, they are all really important. In the big picture, it's important we get better and play a great game Saturday. . . . We aren't going to dramatically change what we do in practice. We believe in what we do and believe in the consistency we have developed. We need a new focus. To play against this kind of an opponent, we need to have mindset that we need to be at the top of our game. (Lynch 2006)

Similarly, Coach Roof of Duke University noted the following after his team's first loss of the 2006 football season:

> (We) are going to have opportunities and when opportunities come, whenever they come and however they come, we have to take advantage of it. I think that's true for our football team if you look at the game. Whatever mistakes we made, we still had opportunities to score and put ourselves in position to win and we weren't opportunistic. This football team is going to have to be opportunistic and take advantage of breaks whether we create them ourselves or whether they are given to us. (Roof 2006)

252 NARRATIVES OF ENTREPRENEURIAL FAILURE

Teams that act proactively (Lumpkin and Dess 2001) or engage in riskier behaviors in an attempt to increase performance (Covin and Slevin 1989) often find that such actions come with considerable costs (Li and Atuahene-Gima 2001; Rosenbusch et al. 2011). Because EO-related initiatives usually necessitate large initial expenditures of key resources (Hornsby et al. 2009) and are frequently linked with higher levels of uncertainty (Alvarez 2007), these types of entrepreneurial activities have a lower chance of producing rewards that outweigh the costs for the organization (Freel 2005). Indeed, moderate levels of EO narrative content could signal a lack of commitment to innovate and change, which could in turn translate into a lack of success in subsequent performances. By only moderately varying their activities, teams might suffer from a reduced ability to execute these activities because they have not had sufficient time or motivation to develop a deep understanding of the requisite changes. As a result, it is possible that the variations introduced through EO initiatives might not be different enough to confuse competitors, which could hinder performance.

While moderate levels of EO might lead to the costs outweighing the benefits, it is possible that teams willing to make substantial commitments to EO activities will experience benefits that outshine the associated costs (Kreiser et al. 2013). For teams that are highly committed to entrepreneurial initiatives, the costs are still substantially high. However, because of such teams' likely high level of commitment to and focus on their intended goals, the benefits of these actions could ultimately be greater than the initial costs. Examples of high EO content found within our sample include excerpts like the following from Coach Alvarez of Wisconsin following his team's loss to Northwestern in 2005:

> You have to correct mistakes and just show where we had breakdowns. And a lot of it was communication. That's something that we'll have to correct. And you go back to fundamentals. You've got a totally different game plan this week and a different type of team that you're defending. But you always correct mistakes and then move

forward. . . . I think for five games the communication and how they manage themselves and change during a game has been pretty good. That wasn't the case, and why, I don't know. (Alvarez, 2005)

Another example of higher EO content can be seen in the following passage from Coach Spurrier of South Carolina:

> Our defensive coaches have put in a little extra time trying to figure out all the assignments to stop the option run game. . . .There could be some scheme changes. We have to do something to try and create more offense, create getting the ball towards Sidney (Rice) and the other receivers and some big gains. We don't want to divulge all our new plans but we will be a different looking offense, I'll just say that to our fans. Hopefully, they hang with us a little while. Again, I'm embarrassed about the way we played the last game. Obviously, we did move the ball here and there. We got to the one-yard line, two-yard line but good teams can score second and goal from the two with three cracks and we couldn't do it. Next time we got down to the two-yard line we tried to throw it in and we couldn't do that either. We are re-evaluating everything and trying to do some things differently around here. (Spurrier 2006)

In summary, while the extant literature has stressed that EO is beneficial in general, recent investigations suggesting that this relationship is not linear in nature have lead us to further examine how EO influences a team's ability to bounce back from previous failure, to which we now turn. Our results indicate that in fact the relationship between narrative EO content and subsequent performance is U-shaped, with relatively low or high levels of EO content proving to be more beneficial than moderate levels of EO content. For a clearer representation of this relationship, see Figure 8.3.

Negative emotions and bouncing back

Throughout previous chapters, we have established that entrepreneurial activities are inherently risky endeavors (Covin and Slevin

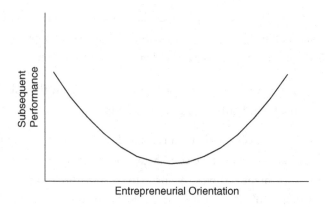

FIGURE 8.3: Entrepreneurial orientation and subsequent performance

1991; Lumpkin and Dess 1996) and are thus susceptible to failure (Wiklund and Shepherd 2011). We have also shown that failures of this nature can generate substantial negative emotional reactions among those involved (Shepherd et al. 2011b). These negative emotional reactions to project failure can have a positive impact on subsequent performance. That is, negative emotions are not always detrimental. Evidence has shown that negative emotions can help maintain attentional focus (Bless, Bohner, Schwarz, and Strack 1990), enhance information processing (Schwarz 1990), improve spatial performance (Gray 2004), increase perceived acceptable performance standards (Cervone, Kopp, Schaumann, and Scott 1994), and amplify the likelihood of eventual goal attainment (Brown and Eisenhardt 1997). Based on this evidence, it is likely that a complete absence of (or very low levels of) negative emotional content in narratives relating to failure might not be beneficial and could actually hamper subsequent performance.

While expressing little to no negative emotions regarding failure can prove detrimental to subsequent performance, excessive levels of negative emotions can also lead to negative consequences at both the individual (Pierce et al. 2001) and group levels (Cannon and Edmondson 2001). Evidence has indicated that over-identification with or rumination over failure can interfere with problem solving

(Lyubomirsky and Nolen-Hoeksema 1995) and impede attempts to understand and make sense of the failure event (Borders, Earleywine, and Jajodia 2010; Kross, Ayduk, and Mischel 2005). For these reasons, while a move from experiencing and expressing low levels of negative emotions to more moderate levels might prove beneficial, moving from moderate to high levels of negative emotional content in a failure narrative will likely result in decreased performance. Therefore, a moderate amount of negative emotional content within a failure narrative serves to adequately communicate information regarding future actions without focusing too much attention on the failure (i.e., considerable attention allocated to failure can lead to rumination and reduced performance) (Lyubomirsky and Nolen-Hoeksema 1995).

Interestingly, contrary to these expectations, the results of our recent study (Wolfe and Shepherd 2015k) do not substantiate the idea that moderate levels of negative emotional narrative content are the most beneficial for subsequent performance. In fact, the results of our recent study indicate that either high or low levels of negative emotional content produce better performance outcomes than moderate levels. It appears that low negative emotions can help maintain affective commitment to the organization (Belschak and Hartog 2009) – affective commitment to the team in this case – and affective commitment has been associated with enhanced performance outcomes (Sinclair, Tucker, Cullen, and Wright 2005). Examples of low-level negative emotional statements include passages like "You know, we didn't get the result that we hoped for today . . . but I want our players not to hang their heads"; "We are not satisfied obviously with losing the game"; and "We've got to work a little bit harder and come together a little bit more. . . . It's only devastating if you let it be devastating." While negative emotions have been associated with reduced affective commitment (Belschak and Hartog 2009; Shepherd et al. 2011b) and inhibited problem-solving ability (Lyubomirsky and Nolen-Hoeksema 1995), both of which are believed to diminish performance (Belschak and Hartog 2009; Rude, Maestas, and Neff 2007), it appears that – at least in the short run – an obsession with failure (reflected in ruminations Rude et al. 2007) may serve as a strong motivator to bounce back and perform well in the next project – namely, next week's game.

Excerpts from our study that exhibit higher levels of negative emotions include the following quote from Coach Smith of Michigan State University following their first loss of the 2005 season:

> We need to make more plays and get more big plays on the offensive side of the ball. If we can't get that done, that's our fault. Our kids played hard, but they need to be better prepared. You have to make more plays to win. Now we have to pick up the pieces and move on. We need to get through this week, work hard in the off week, and get ready for Ohio State. We didn't play well on the defensive side of the ball. We gave up way too many big plays in the first half. In the second half, we gave up a lot of opportunities on the offensive side, and our kicking stunk. We all played a part in it. It hurts, it hurts real bad, and it should hurt. I hope the players feel it and I hope they don't forget the feeling. It's tough, but we'll bounce back. (Smith, 2005)

This excerpt from Coach Mullen of Mississippi State University following their first loss in 2009 also illustrates this point:

> Last week I was disappointed in our coaching staff as far as not putting our players in better positions to make plays. There was a couple times we did do a good job and we made some plays and missed some plays, but we still have to be in better position to make plays when it comes to game time. We have a lot of things to still improve on. Not winning is not acceptable, I don't like using the "L-word." That is not acceptable for us and when you don't come out on top that is extremely disappointing. (Mullen, 2009)

Our findings indicate that indeed relatively low or high levels of negative emotional content contained within the failure narrative were more beneficial to subsequent performance than were moderate

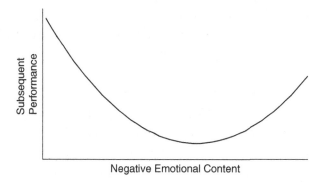

FIGURE 8.4: Negative emotional content and subsequent performance

levels of negative emotional content. A graph of this U-shaped relationship between the failure narrative's negative emotional content and subsequent performance can be seen in Figure 8.4.

Positive emotions and bouncing back

Just as it is important to understand the role negative emotions play in the relationship between failure narratives and subsequent performance, positive emotions' influence must also be taken into consideration. As touched upon earlier in this chapter, positive emotions can result in a "broaden-and-build" phenomenon (Fredrickson 1998, 2001). They have been shown to enhance individuals' performance in work-related tasks (Lyubomirsky, King, and Diener 2005) as well as in entrepreneurial tasks (Cardon, Zietsma, Saparito, Matherne, and Davis 2005; Cardon, Wincent, Singh, and Drnovsek 2009). By facilitating information integration through the broaden-and-build principle, positive emotions have been shown to improve individual reasoning and decision-making processes (Lyubomirsky et al. 2005). Furthermore, similar effects have been demonstrated to occur at the group level (Fredrickson 2003). Therefore, with regard to the positive emotional content of failure narratives, it is possible that including moderate levels of positive emotional content results in improvements to subsequent performance.

While positive emotions appear to enhance performance, their influence might not always be beneficial. The reasoning behind this lies in the relationship between positive emotions and optimism. Evidence suggests that positive emotions can increase the level of optimism after negative events (Fredrickson et al. 2003), which can prove useful because positive emotions, such as optimism, have been shown to enhance performance following negative events at both the individual (Isen 2002) and organizational (Avey et al. 2008) levels. However, high levels of optimism (i.e., over-optimism) can lead to poor decision making (Hmieleski and Baron 2008). Indeed, over-optimism is perhaps the most commonly noted bias among entrepreneurs (Baron 2004), and its negative influence on entrepreneurial performance is well documented (Lowe and Ziedonis 2006). The danger in developing over-optimism is that it can result in reduced ability and motivation to seek out and recognize the need for change and improvement. This blindness to the necessity of change and/or lack of motivation to do anything about it are the antithesis of the learning and change necessary to avoid project failure. Over-optimism can make project failure more likely by obstructing or delaying project adaptations. Therefore, although expressing some positive emotions regarding a failure event can produce benefits to subsequent performance, expressing extreme levels of positive emotions in a failure narrative could actually hinder future actions.

Examples of such passages from our study include the following from Coach Callahan of Nebraska following his team's first loss of the 2005 season:

> We had some opportunities today, but we just didn't get it done. I'm really proud of our kids. There's a lot of positive to draw from in this game. There are no moral victories of course, but I'm really proud of the way our guys fought today. It's important that we let this one go immediately and our players have a tremendous focus where they can adapt and change quickly and I think that's apparent in how

they displayed their efforts today when they were down. This is a resilient football team, it's a resourceful football team and I have a lot of confidence that they'll come back next week. (Callahan 2005)

This passage from Coach Stoops of Oklahoma University following his team's first loss of the 2008 season also demonstrates extreme positive emotions:

> As always, going back over last week's game with Texas, I really thought it was a hard fought game. I am very proud of our players for the effort. It was two really good football teams playing, and as I have said before, hats off to Texas for making the plays there in the fourth quarter to win the game. I thought for a good part of the game, we were able to play well on both sides of the ball. Texas is an excellent team. They kept coming back, and we kept hanging in there. (Stoops, 2008)

Our findings support the proposed inverted U-shaped relationship between the failure narrative's positive emotional content and subsequent performance, where moderate levels of positive emotional content are more beneficial than relatively high or low levels with regard to their influence on subsequent performance. A graph of this relationship can be seen in Figure 8.5.

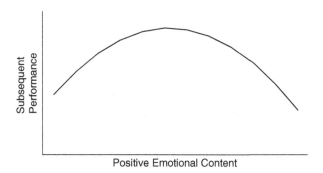

FIGURE 8.5: Positive emotional content and subsequent performance

DISCUSSION

Implications for entrepreneurship, failure, and organizational narratives

The findings of our first study represent important contributions to the study of corporate entrepreneurship, particularly as it relates to science-based organizations. It is imperative for science-based organizations to continue to maintain a high level of activity in R&D areas, for which technological feasibility is questionable at best and innovative activities (e.g., R&D) face inordinately high failure rates. In finding that organizations alter their narratives' content as a result of certain performance events, we presented evidence of how organizations attempt to understand these events and presumably apply that understanding to help maintain entrepreneurial and innovative activities. Additionally, our findings that failure rates alone are not the only important factor to consider with regard to narratives' levels of negative emotional content, we present evidence that not all failures are created equal and that failure events should not be viewed as homogeneous, universally identical experiences.

In addition, the results of our first study also indicate that if positive performance feedback occurs concurrently with failure, it is possible that organizations might choose to focus on communicating the positive aspects of their prior performance, essentially shifting focus away from project failures. This suggests that the interplay between positive and negative emotional content within organizational narratives is indeed complex in nature. Organizations must weigh a number of important factors when determining the configuration of these elements within the narratives they construct. This is particularly salient as the messages communicated within those organizational narratives will be influential in determining exactly how organizations understand and make sense of past events as well as how they enact and influence future actions.

Implications for failure, sensemaking, and subsequent performance

Our second study extended the findings of the first, examining the role that failure narratives play in sensemaking and how specific elements contained within these narratives influence bouncing back with regard to subsequent performance. With regard to evidence supporting our proposed U-shaped relationship between a failure narrative's EO content and subsequent performance, we believe this represents an important enrichment of our understanding of the EO–performance relationship. Unlike most previous research, which has focused on EO as a relatively stable and enduring characteristic, our study examined how EO relates to subsequent performance over a much shorter time frame. From this perspective, our results suggest that in order to effectively bounce back quickly, it is perhaps more beneficial to have a relatively high or low EO perspective rather than a more moderate EO outlook, essentially allowing for the opportunity to "stay the course" or "right the ship" depending on the situation at hand.

A second important implication with regard to this study can be seen in the finding of a similar U-shaped relationship between negative emotional content and subsequent performance. Whereas most conventional wisdom would point to the opposite relationship holding true, with moderate levels of negative emotions proving more beneficial than extremely high or low levels, our results suggest the exact opposite. Again, this could be related to the relatively short window of time over which these influences are measured. While high levels of negative emotions can lead to obsessive ruminations regarding a failure event, which can prove very detrimental over longer periods of time, such obsession might actually be beneficial in motivating individuals and organizations to bounce back quickly with regard to short-term performance. Therefore, rather than contradicting the existing prevailing thought that high levels of negative emotions adversely influence performance, our results provide a complementary perspective with regard to the potentially differential influence that negative emotions can have on failure over short versus long periods of time.

Finally, our results complement and extend existing literature regarding the influence of positive emotions. While we did find that positive emotions do enhance subsequent performance, this influence only holds true to a certain level, and in fact, further increases past this "optimal level" can actually result in diminished performance. This inverted U-shaped relationship between positive emotions and subsequent performance aligns with the idea that while low levels of positive emotions might restrict the cognitive processes underlying the narrative, essentially lowering the potential to change as a result of failure, high levels of positive emotions can produce heuristic biases (e.g., over-optimism) that can impede performance as well. As a result, this study provides evidence of a potential boundary condition to the broaden-and-build influence of positive emotions, indicating that higher levels of positive emotions might not always prove to be more beneficial – at least when it pertains to failure narratives' emotional content and their ability to influence bouncing back quickly with regard to subsequent performance.

CONCLUSION

In this chapter and its underlying studies (Wolfe and Shepherd, 2015a, 2015k), we examined the relationship between both performance events and narrative content as well as between narrative content and subsequent performance. While previous work has firmly established the role narratives play in the sensemaking process, these studies have primarily concerned themselves with the theoretical relationship between these two concepts. In order to complement the rich extant theoretical work regarding narratives and sensemaking, we developed a deeper understanding of the mechanisms underlying this relationship and provided some important novel insights into this area of study.

It appears that the circumstances surrounding a failure influence how that failure is experienced and understood. When failure is experienced in the context of larger overarching success, it is potentially not interpreted as being detrimental and, as a result, will lead to lower levels of negative emotional content conveyed in the organizational narrative. Furthermore, the narratives constructed about failures play an important role in the sensemaking process and can have implications for future success. Notably, both positive and negative emotional content as well as EO content have been shown to have significant but nonlinear influences on subsequent performance and success.

REFERENCES

Alvarez, B. 2005. *Northwestern University post-game press conference*: University of Wisconsin-Madison, 8th of October, 2005.

Alvarez, S. A. 2007. Entrepreneurial rents and the theory of the firm. *Journal of Business Venturing*, 22(3): 427–442.

Anderson, E. W., Fornell, C., and Lehmann, D. R. 1994. Customer satisfaction, market share, and profitability: Findings from Sweden. *The Journal of Marketing*, 58(3): 53–66.

Ashkanasy, N. M. and Tse, B. 2000. Transformational leadership as management of emotion: A conceptual review. In N. M. Ashkanasy, C. E. J. Hartel, and W. J. Zerbe (eds.), *Emotions in the Workplace: Research, Theory, and Practice*: 221–235. Westport, CT: Quorum Books.

AstraZeneca. 2004. *2004 Annual Report of AstraZeneca*. London.

AstraZeneca. 2006. *2006 Annual Report of AstraZeneca*. London.

AstraZeneca. 2007. *2007 Annual Report of AstraZeneca*. London.

Avey, J. B., Wernsing, T. S., and Luthans, F. 2008. Can positive employees help positive organizational change? Impact of psychological capital and emotions on relevant attitudes and behaviors. *The Journal of Applied Behavioral Science*, 44(1): 48–70.

Avey, J. B., Avolio, B. J., Crossley, C. D., and Luthans, F. 2009. Psychological ownership: Theoretical extensions, measurement and relation to work outcomes. *Journal of Organizational Behavior*, 30(2): 173–191.

Balogun, J. and Johnson, G. 2004. Organizational restructuring and middle manager sensemaking. *Academy of Management Journal*, 47(4): 523–549.

Bandura, A. 1986. *Social Foundations of Thought and Action: A Social Cognitive Theory.* Englewood Cliffs, NJ: Prentice-Hall.

Bar-Tal, D. 2001. Why does fear override hope in societies engulfed by intractable conflict, as it does in the Israeli society? *Political Psychology,* 22(3): 601–627.

Bar-Tal, D., Halperin, E., and De Rivera, J. 2007. Collective emotions in conflict situations: Societal implications. *Journal of Social Issues,* 63(2): 441–460.

Baron, R. A. 2004. The cognitive perspective: A valuable tool for answering entrepreneurship's basic "why" questions. *Journal of Business Venturing,* 19(2): 221–239.

Barry, D. and Elmes, M. 1997. Strategy retold: Toward a narrative view of strategic discourse. *Academy of Management Review,* 22(2): 429–452.

Barsade, S. G. 2002. The ripple effect: Emotional contagion and its influence on group behavior. *Administrative Science Quarterly,* 47(4): 644–675.

Bartel, C. A. and Garud, R. 2009. The role of narratives in sustaining organizational innovation. *Organization Science,* 20: 107–117.

Belschak, F. D. and Hartog, D. N. D. 2009. Consequences of positive and negative feedback: The impact on emotions and extra-role behaviors. *Applied Psychology,* 58(2): 274–303.

Bless, H., Bohner, G., Schwarz, N., and Strack, F. 1990. Mood and persuasion: A cognitive response analysis. *Personality and Social Psychology Bulletin,* 16(2): 331–345.

Boje, D. M. 1994. Organizational storytelling. *Management Learning,* 25(3): 433–461.

Bolton, M. K. 1993. Organizational innovation and substandard performance: When is necessity the mother of innovation? *Organization Science,* 4(1): 57–75.

Borders, A., Earleywine, M., and Jajodia, A. 2010. Could mindfulness decrease anger, hostility, and aggression by decreasing rumination? *Aggressive Behavior,* 36: 28–44.

Bristol-Meyrs Squibb. 2005. *2005 Annual Report of Bristol-Meyrs Squibb.* New York.

Brown, A. D., Stacey, P., and Nandhakumar, J. 2008. Making sense of sensemaking narratives. *Human Relations,* 61(8): 1035–1062.

Brown, S. L. and Eisenhardt, K. M. 1997. The art of continuous change: Linking complexity theory and time-paced evolution in relentlessly shifting organizations. *Administrative Science Quarterly,* 42(1): 1–34.

Callahan, B. 2005. *Texas Tech University post-game press conference:* University of Nebraska, 8th of October, 2005.

Cannon, D. R. 1999. Cause or control? The temporal dimension in failure sensemaking. *The Journal of Applied Behavioral Science,* 35(4): 416–438.

Cannon, M. D. and Edmondson, A. C. 2001. Confronting failure: Antecedents and consequences of shared beliefs about failure in organizational work groups. *Journal of Organizational Behavior*, 22(2): 161–177.

Cardon, M. S., Zietsma, C., Saparito, P., Matherne, B. P., and Davis, C. 2005. A tale of passion: New insights into entrepreneurship from a parenthood metaphor. *Journal of Business Venturing*, 20(1): 23–45.

Cardon, M. S., Wincent, J., Singh, J., and Drnovsek, M. 2009. The nature and experience of entrepreneurial passion. *Academy of Management Review*, 34: 511–532.

Cervone, D., Kopp, D. A., Schaumann, L., and Scott, W. D. 1994. Mood, self-efficacy, and performance standards: Lower moods induce higher standards for performance. *Journal of Personality and Social Psychology*, 67(3): 499–512.

Chuang, Y.-T. and Baum, J. A. C. 2003. It's all in the name: Failure-induced learning by multiunit chains. *Administrative Science Quarterly*, 48(1): 33–59.

Corbett, A. C., Neck, H. M., and DeTienne, D. R. 2007. How corporate entrepreneurs learn from fledgling innovation initiatives: Cognition and the development of a termination script. *Entrepreneurship Theory and Practice*, 31(6): 829–852.

Covin, J. G. and Slevin, D. 1989. Strategic management of small firms in hostile and benign environments. *Strategic Management Journal*, 10: 75–87.

Covin, J. G. and Slevin, D. 1991. A conceptual model of entrepreneurship as firm behavior. *Entrepreneurship Theory and Practice*, 16: 7–25.

Covin, J. G. and Miles, M. P. 1999. Corporate entrepreneurship and the pursuit of competitive advantage. *Entrepreneurship Theory and Practice*, 23(3): 47–63.

Covin, J. G., Green, K. M., and Slevin, D. P. 2006. Strategic process effects on the entrepreneurial orientation-sales growth rate relationship. *Entrepreneurship Theory and Practice*, 30: 57–81.

Czarniawska, B. 1998. *A Narrative Approach to Organizational Studies*. Thousand Oaks, CA: Sage.

Dasborough, M. T., Ashkanasy, N. M., Tee, E. Y. J., and Tse, H. H. M. 2009. What goes around comes around: How meso-level negative emotional contagion can ultimately determine organizational attitudes toward leaders. *The Leadership Quarterly*, 20(4): 571–585.

Deeds, D. L., DeCarolis, D., and Coombs, J. 2000. Dynamic capabilities and new product development in high technology ventures: An empirical analysis of new biotechnology firms. *Journal of Business Venturing*, 15(3): 211–229.

Del Monte, A. and Papagni, E. 2003. R&D and the growth of firms: Empirical analysis of a panel of Italian firms. *Research Policy*, 32(6): 1003–1014.

Diener, E. and Emmons, R. A. 1984. The independence of positive and negative affect. *Journal of Personality and Social Psychology*, 47(5): 1105–1117.

Diener, E., Larsen, R. J., Levine, S., and Emmons, R. A. 1985. Intensity and frequency: Dimensions underlying positive and negative affect. *Journal of Personality and Social Psychology*, 48(5): 1253–1265.

DiMasi, J. A. 2001. Risks in new drug development: Approval success rates for investigational drugs. *Clinical Pharmacology & Therapeutics*, 69: 297–307.

DiMasi, J. A., Hansen, R. W., and Grabowski, H. G. 2003. The price of innovation: New estimates of drug development costs. *Journal of Health Economics*, 22(2): 151–185.

Druskat, V. U. and Wolff, S. B. 2001. Group emotional intelligence and its influence on group effectiveness. In C. Cherniss and D. Goleman (eds.), *The Emotionally Intelligent Workplace*: 132–155. San Francisco, CA: Jossey-Bass.

Dunford, R. and Jones, D. 2000. Narrative in strategic change. *Human Relations*, 53(9): 1207–1226.

Dutton, J. E., Worline, M. C., Frost, P. J., and Lilius, J. 2006. Explaining compassion organizing. *Administrative Science Quarterly*, 51(1): 59–96.

Eli Lilly. 2003. *2003 Annual Report of Eli Lilly*. Indianapolis, IN.

Fiol, C. M. 1989. A semiotic analysis of corporate language: Organizational boundaries and joint venturing. *Administrative Science Quarterly*, 34(2): 277–303.

Fischer, A. H. and Manstead, A. S. R. 2008. The social functions of emotions. In M. Lewis, J. Haviland-Jones and L. F. Barrett (eds.), *Handbook of Emotions*, (3rd ed.): 456–468. New York: Guilford Press.

Fredrickson, B. L. 1998. What good are positive emotions? *Review of General Psychology*, 2(3): 300–319.

Fredrickson, B. L., Mancuso, R. A., Branigan, C., and Tugade, M. M. 2000. The undoing effect of positive emotions. *Motivation and Emotion*, 24(4): 237–258.

Fredrickson, B. L. 2001. The role of positive emotions in positive psychology: The broaden-and-build theory of positive emotions. *American Psychologist*, 56(3): 218–226.

Fredrickson, B. L. 2003. Positive emotions and upward spirals in organizations. In K. S. Cameron, J. E. Dutton, and R. E. Quinn (eds.), *Positive Organizational Scholarship: Foundations of a New Scholarship*: 163–175. San Francisco: Berrett-Kohler.

Fredrickson, B. L., Tugade, M. M., Waugh, C. E., and Larkin, G. R. 2003. What good are positive emotions in crisis? A prospective study of resilience and emotions following the terrorist attacks on the United States on September 11th, 2001. *Journal of Personality and Social Psychology*, 84(2): 365–376.

Freel, M. S. 2005. Perceived environmental uncertainty and innovation in small firms. *Small Business Economics*, 25(1): 49–64.

Gabriel, Y. 2000. *Storytelling in Organizations: Facts, Fictions, and Fantasies.* Oxford: Oxford University Press.

Garud, R., Dunbar, R. L. M., and Bartel, C. A. 2011. Dealing with unusual experiences: A narrative perspective on organizational learning. *Organization Science*, 22(3): 587–601.

Genzyme. 2008. *2008 Annual Report of Genzyme.* Cambridge, MA.

George, J. M. and Brief, A. P. 1992. Feeling good-doing good: A conceptual analysis of the mood at work-organizational spontaneity relationship. *Psychological Bulletin*, 112(2): 310–329.

George, J. M. 1995. Leader positive mood and group performance: The case of customer service. *Journal of Applied Social Psychology*, 25(9): 778–794.

Gioia, D. A., Thomas, J. B., Clark, S. M., and Chittipeddi, K. 1994. Symbolism and strategic change in academia: The dynamics of sensemaking and influence. *Organization Science*, 5(3): 363–383.

GlaxoSmithKline. 2007. *2007 Annual Report of GlaxoSmithKline.* London.

Goss, D. 2005. Schumpeter's legacy? Interaction and emotions in the sociology of entrepreneurship. *Entrepreneurship Theory and Practice*, 29: 205–218.

Gray, J. R. 2004. Integration of emotion and cognitive control. *Current Directions in Psychological Science*, 13(2): 46–48.

Greve, H. R. 2002. Sticky aspirations: Organizational time perspective and competitiveness. *Organization Science*, 13(1): 1–17.

Grinyer, P. and McKiernan, P. 1990. Generating major strategic change in stagnating companies. *Strategic Management Journal*, 11: 131–146.

Hart, S. L. 1992. An integrative framework for strategy-making processes. *Academy of Management Review*, 17(2): 327–351.

Hatfield, D. E., Cacioppo, J. T., and Rapson, R. L. 1994. *Emotional Contagion.* Cambridge, UK: Cambridge University Press.

Hatfield, E., Cacioppo, J. T., and Rapson, R. L. 1992. Primitive emotional contagion. In M. S. Clark (ed.), *Review of Personality and Social Psychology: Vol. 14. Emotions and Social Behavior*: 151–177. Newbury Park, CA: Sage.

Hayward, M. L. A., Forster, W. R., Sarasvathy, S. D., and Fredrickson, B. L. 2009. Beyond hubris: How highly confident entrepreneurs rebound to venture again. *Journal of Business Venturing*, 25(6): 569–578.

Hmieleski, K. M. and Baron, R. A. 2008. When does entrepreneurial self-efficacy enhance versus reduce firm performance? *Strategic Entrepreneurship Journal*, 2(1): 57–72.

Hornsby, J. S., Kuratko, D. F., Shepherd, D. A., and Bott, J. P. 2009. Managers' corporate entrepreneurial actions: Examining perception and position. *Journal of Business Venturing*, 24(3): 236–247.

Huy, Q. N. 1999. Emotional capability, emotional intelligence, and radical change. *Academy of Management Review*, 24(2): 325–345.

Iacovoc, C. L. and Dexter, A. S. 2005. Surviving IT project cancellations. *Communications of the ACM*, 48(4): 83–86.

Isen, A. M. 2002. Missing in action in the AIM: Positive affect's facilitation of cognitive flexibility, innovation, and problem solving. *Psychological Inquiry*, 13(1): 57–65.

Kelly, J. R. and Barsade, S. G. 2001. Mood and emotions in small groups and work teams. *Organizational Behavior and Human Decision Processes*, 86(1): 99–130.

Khandawalla, P. N. 1977. *The Design of Organizations*. New York: Harcourt Brace Jovanovich.

Kreiser, P. M., Marino, L. D., Kuratko, D. F., and Weaver, M. K. 2013. Disaggregating entrepreneurial orientation: The non-linear impact of innovativeness, proactiveness and risk-taking on SME performance. *Small Business Economics*, 40(2): 273–291.

Kross, E., Ayduk, O., and Mischel, W. 2005. When asking "why" does not hurt distinguishing rumination from reflective processing of negative emotions. *Psychological Science*, 16(9): 709–715.

Lant, T. K., Milliken, F. J., and Batra, B. 1992. The role of managerial learning and interpretation in strategic persistence and reorientation: An empirical exploration. *Strategic Management Journal*, 13(8): 585–608.

Li, H. and Atuahene-Gima, K. 2001. Product innovation strategy and the performance of new technology ventures in China. *Academy of Management Journal*, 44(6): 1123–1134.

Lindsley, D. H., Brass, D. J., and Thomas, J. B. 1995. Efficacy-performance spirals: A multilevel perspective. *Academy of Management Review*, 20(3): 645–678.

Lowe, R. A. and Ziedonis, A. A. 2006. Overoptimism and the performance of entrepreneurial firms. *Management Science*, 52(2): 173–186.

Lumpkin, G. T. and Dess, G. G. 1996. Clarifying the entrepreneurial orientation construct and linking it to performance. *Academy of Management Review*, 21(1): 135–172.

Lumpkin, G. T. and Dess, G. G. 2001. Linking two dimensions of entrepreneurial orientation to firm performance: The moderating role of environment and industry life cycle. *Journal of Business Venturing*, 16(5): 429–451.

Luscher, L. S. and Lewis, M. W. 2008. Organizational change and managerial sensemaking: Working through paradox. *Academy of Management Journal*, 51(2): 221–240.

Lynch, B. 2006. *Southern Illinois post-game press conference*: Indiana University, 19th of October, 2006.

Lyubomirsky, S. and Nolen-Hoeksema, S. 1995. Effects of self-focused rumination on negative thinking and interpersonal problem solving. *Journal of Personality and Social Psychology*, 69(1): 176–190.

Lyubomirsky, S., King, L., and Diener, E. 2005. The benefits of frequent positive affect: Does happiness lead to success? *Psychological Bulletin*, 131(6): 803–855.

March, J. G. 1991. Exploration and exploitation in organizational learning. *Organization Science*, 2(1): 71–87.

McGrath, R. 1999. Falling forward: Real options reasoning and entrepreneurial failure. *Academy of Management Review*, 24: 13–30.

Mills, J. H. 2003. *Making Sense of Organizational Change*. London, UK: Routledge.

Minniti, M. and Bygrave, W. 2001. A dynamic model of entrepreneurial learning. *Entrepreneurship Theory and Practice*, 25(3): 5–17.

Morrison, E. W. and Milliken, F. J. 2000. Organizational silence: A barrier to change and development in a pluralistic world. *Academy of Management Review*, 25(4): 706–725.

Mullen, D. 2009. *Auburn University post-game press conference*: Mississippi State University, 12th of September, 2009.

Nadler, D. A. 1979. The effects of feedback on task group behavior: A review of the experimental research. *Organizational Behavior and Human Performance*, 23(3): 309–338.

Napier, N. K. and Nilsson, M. 2006. The development of creative capabilities in and out of creative organizations: Three case studies. *Creativity and Innovation Management*, 15(3): 268–278.

Ocasio, W. 1997. Towards an attention-based view of the firm. *Strategic Management Journal*, 18: 187–206.

Ocasio, W. 2011. Attention to attention. *Organization Science*, 22(5): 1286–1296.

Orbuch, T. L. 1997. People's accounts count: The sociology of accounts. *Annual Review of Sociology*, 23: 455.

Orr, J. 1995. *Talking about Machines: An Ethnography of a Modern Job*. Ithaca, NY: ILR Press.

Pierce, J. L., Kostova, T., and Dirks, K. T. 2001. Toward a theory of psychological ownership in organizations. *Academy of Management Review*, 26(2): 298–310.

Pisano, G. P. 2010. The evolution of science-based business: Innovating how we innovate. *Industrial and Corporate Change*, 19(2): 465–482.

Popper, M. and Lipshitz, R. 2000. Organizational learning. *Management Learning*, 31(2): 181–196.

Quinn, R. W. and Worline, M. C. 2008. Enabling courageous collective action: Conversations from United Airlines Flight 93. *Organization Science*, 19: 497–516.

Ratten, V. 2010. Developing a theory of sport-based entrepreneurship. *Journal of Management & Organization*, 16(4): 557–565.

Ratten, V. 2011. Sport-based entrepreneurship: Towards a new theory of entrepreneurship and sport management. *International Entrepreneurship and Management Journal*, 7(1): 57–69.

Rauch, A., Wiklund, J., Lumpkin, G. T., and Frese, M. 2009. Entrepreneurial orientation and business performance: An assessment of past research and suggestions for the future. *Entrepreneurship Theory and Practice*, 33(3): 761–787.

Roche. 2006. *2006 Annual Report of Roche*. New York.

Roof, T. 2006. *University of Richmond post-game press conference*, 2nd of September, 2006: Duke University.

Rosenbusch, N., Brinckmann, J., and Bausch, A. 2011. Is innovation always beneficial? A meta-analysis of the relationship between innovation and performance in SMEs. *Journal of Business Venturing*, 26(4): 441–457.

Rude, S. S., Maestas, K. L., and Neff, K. 2007. Paying attention to distress: What's wrong with rumination? *Cognition & Emotion*, 21(4): 843–864.

Salanova, M., Llorens, S., Cifre, E., Martínez, I. M., and Schaufeli, W. B. 2003. Perceived collective efficacy, subjective well-being and task performance among electronic work groups: An experimental study. *Small Group Research*, 34(1): 43–73.

Scherer, F. M. 2001. The link between gross profitability and pharmaceutical R&D spending. *Health Affairs*, 20(5): 216–220.

Schwarz, N. 1990. Feelings as information: Informational and affective functions of affective states. In E. T. Higgins and R. M. Sorrentino (eds.), *Handbook of Motivation and Cognition: Foundations of Social Behavior*, Vol. 2: 527–561. New York: Guilford.

Sekerka, L. E. and Fredrickson, B. L. 2008. Establishing positive emotional climates to advance organizational transformation. In N. M. Ashkanasy and C. L. Cooper (eds.), *Research Companion to Emotion in Organization*: 531–545. Cheltenham, UK: Edward Elgar Publishing.

Shepherd, D. A. 2009. Grief recovery from the loss of a family business: A multi- and meso-level theory. *Journal of Business Venturing*, 24(1): 81–97.

Shepherd, D. A., Covin, J. G., and Kuratko, D. F. 2009a. Project failure from corporate entrepreneurship: Managing the grief process. *Journal of Business Venturing*, 24(6): 588–600.

Shepherd, D. A., Wiklund, J., and Haynie, J. M. 2009b. Moving forward: Balancing the financial and emotional costs of business failure. *Journal of Business Venturing*, 24(2): 134–148.

Shepherd, D. A., Patzelt, H., and Wolfe, M. T. 2011. Moving forward from project failure: Negative emotions, affective commitment and learning from the experience. *Academy of Management Journal*, 54(6): 1229–1259.

Short, J. C., Broberg, J. C., Cogliser, C. C., and Brigham, K. H. 2010. Construct validation using Computer-Aided Text Analysis (CATA). *Organizational Research Methods*, 13(2): 320–347.

Sinclair, R. R., Tucker, J. S., Cullen, J. C., and Wright, C. 2005. Performance differences among four organizational commitment profiles. *Journal of Applied Psychology*, 90(6): 1280–1287.

Smith, J. 2006. *University Of Michigan post-game press conference*: Michigan State University.

Sperber, M. 2004. College sports, Inc. In D. G. Stein (ed.), *Buying In or Selling Out?: The Commercialization of the American Research University*: 17. Piscataway, NJ: Rutgers University Press.

Spurrier, S. 2006. *University of Georgia post-game press conference*: University of South Carolina, 9th of September, 2006.

Stanton, P., Stanton, J., and Pires, G. 2004. Impressions of an annual report: An experimental study. *Corporate Communications: An International Journal*, 9(1): 57–69.

Stephan, W. G. and Stephan, C. W. 2000. An integrated theory of prejudice. In S. Oskamp (ed.), *Reducing Prejudice and Discrimination*: 225–246. Hillsdale, NJ: Erlbaum.

Stoops, R. 2008. *University of Texas post-game press conference*: Oklahoma University. 11th of October, 2008.

Tugade, M. M. and Fredrickson, B. L. 2004. Resilient individuals use positive emotions to bounce back from negative emotional experiences. *Journal of Personality and Social Psychology*, 86(2): 320–333.

Vaara, E. 2002. On the discursive construction of success/failure in narratives of post-merger integration. *Organization Studies*, 23: 211–248.

Weick, K. E. 1995. *Sensemaking in Organizations*. London: Sage.

Weick, K. E., Sutcliffe, K. M., and Obstfeld, D. 1999. Organizing for high reliability: Processes of collective mindfulness. *Research in Organizational Behavior*, 21: 81–123.

Weick, K. E., Sutcliffe, K. M., and Obstfeld, D. 2005. Organizing and the process of sensemaking. *Organization Science*, 16(4): 409–421.

Wiklund, J. and Shepherd, D. A. 2011. Where to from here? EO-as-experimentation, failure, and distribution of outcomes. *Entrepreneurship Theory and Practice*, 35(5): 925–946.

Wolfe, M. T. and Shepherd, D. A. 2015a. What do you have to say about that? Performance events and narratives' positive and negative emotional content. *Entrepreneurship Theory and Practice*, 39(4): 895–925.

Wolfe, M. T. and Shepherd, D. A. 2015k. "Bouncing back" from a loss: Entrepreneurial orientation, emotions, and failure narratives. *Entrepreneurship Theory and Practice*, 39: 675–700.

Zahra, S. A. and Garvis, D. M. 2000. International corporate entrepreneurship and firm performance: The moderating effect of international environmental hostility. *Journal of Business Venturing*, 15(5–6): 469–492.

9   What can we do to learn more from our failure experiences?

Entrepreneurial action occurs in both *de novo* (i.e., the creation of a new organization) and *de alio* (i.e., the creation of a new venture within an established organization) contexts. What is common about entrepreneurial action in these two contexts is that both represent modes for exploiting what is believed to be an opportunity. We refer to opportunity belief (or a potential opportunity) because signals of an opportunity's features and attractiveness are surrounded by high levels of uncertainty. It is impossible to tell with certainty whether an opportunity belief is accurate; we can only know this after attempts to exploit the potential opportunity. Given this high uncertainty, entrepreneurial actors are sometimes (and perhaps frequently) going to "get it wrong" and find that their entrepreneurial ventures fail. Because opportunity belief, uncertainty, and failure are intimately intertwined, this book sets out to investigate these interrelationships. We use this final chapter to reflect on what we have learned from the social science research underpinning each chapter and to offer some practical implications.

Given the uncertainty of an entrepreneurial opportunity's attractiveness, entrepreneurial action results in outcomes that vary extensively in terms of success. For example, an entrepreneurial organization will have new ventures with greater variance in the outcomes (i.e., larger upside and larger downside) than less entrepreneurial firms. This is important because if actors (i.e., individuals or firms) can benefit from the upside of their entrepreneurial ventures and somehow minimize the costs of the downside, this will have a positive impact on their overall performance. While there are many books indicating how we should generate and capitalize on the upside, the neglected half of the story is how to minimize the downside costs of entrepreneurial action. This is why we conduct research on failure and wrote the current book – we can offer practical advice on how to manage failure to reduce the costs of entrepreneurial action (that goes wrong) and thus help enhance overall performance for entrepreneurial actors.

In the sections that follow, we offer practical implications derived from the findings discussed in each chapter. Specifically, we discuss variance in responses to failure at multiple levels: individuals who create independent organizations, entrepreneurial project team members within established organizations, and entrepreneurial organizations themselves. Many of the practical implications of this book apply in a similar way to all these entrepreneurial actors; however, there can be differences and even competing interests between actor groups, which we highlight when applicable. We now turn to these implications.

YOU FEEL GRIEF AFTER FAILURE BECAUSE YOU HAVE LOST SOMETHING IMPORTANT (CHAPTER 2)

A basic and fundamental premise of the book (based on our social science research) is that failure can generate a negative emotional reaction and that this negative emotional reaction can exacerbate the costs of failure. Although we explore how these costs can be more rapidly reduced, it is important to investigate the implications of our understanding of what generates this negative emotional reaction. The negative emotional reaction – grief – from the failure of an entrepreneurial endeavor is generated by the loss of something important. An implication of this finding is that while entrepreneurial actors may feel grief over the failure of a new venture, they may not understand why they feel this way. This lack of understanding of their emotions can create additional anxiety (and other negative emotions), making it difficult to find a solution.

Projects are important to the extent they satisfy psychological needs

A new venture may help satisfy an actor's psychological needs for competence, belongingness, and autonomy. As a result of the importance of new ventures to actors' psychological well-being, individuals engaged in entrepreneurial endeavors often make substantial personal investments into their new ventures. These investments (mostly non-financial investments, such as time, energy, and emotional commitment) are critical for overcoming obstacles in an attempt to achieve new venture success. Understanding the role new ventures can play in satisfying the psychological needs of those involved has implications for thinking about which ventures they should pursue or be assigned. Ideally, people should focus their entrepreneurial activities on ventures that best satisfy their basic psychological needs. When a venture meets an individual's needs, that person is more likely to persist in overcoming challenges and ultimately succeed, making necessary investments where required.

In the established entrepreneurial firm context (i.e., corporate setting), managers can design or choose projects for organizational members that help satisfy their specific psychological needs for competence, belongingness, and autonomy. That is, while all people have these basic psychological needs, the strength of each need varies across people. For example, some individuals' need for competence is stronger than their needs for belongingness or autonomy, and others have different combinations. Therefore, in new venture and corporate settings, understanding the needs ventures fulfill for individuals is relevant for both motivating venture success and overcoming psychological need related grief associated with failure. In this section, we discuss grief-management implications for the three different psychological needs discussed in Chapter 2 (i.e., competence, belongingness, and autonomy).

Reduce grief by managing the psychological need for competence: Individuals value projects, work assignments, or entrepreneurial pursuits that match their competences. As such, managers can assign people to projects that allow them to use their current skills, knowledge, and experience and also provide them opportunities to further develop existing skills and build new ones. This involves developing a systematic approach to identifying individuals' competences and then aligning work assignments and activities to those particular skill sets.

In doing so, managers are able to build competences and motivate organizational members to make the sorts of investments that enhance the chance that individuals will be fully engaged and that as a result, the project will succeed. Similarly, an entrepreneur looking to create an independent new organization may be well served to pursue an opportunity that requires the sorts of skills, knowledge, and experience possessed by him or her or the founding team. Although this might seem rather obvious, the implication is clearer when an entrepreneur faces two potential opportunities and decides to pursue the one that "fits" his or her competences despite a lower anticipated upside relative to the alternative that is less related to his or her competences. Furthermore, the implication is important for those who potentially misidentify their competence levels and therefore invest resources in a venture that demands skills or experience they do not possess.

While it is useful to identify work to satisfy the psychological need for competence, this need extends to work that enhances or builds new skills, knowledge, and experiences. That is, work that pushes individuals to develop and build upon existing competences provides even greater psychological benefit for some individuals than work that simply meets existing competence levels. Some organizational members appreciate being assigned to new ventures that allow them to grow their professional and personal selves. Knowing which members want to capitalize on their existing competences and those wishing to build new competences can be important knowledge for managers when designing new ventures and/or assigning people to various entrepreneurial projects. Similarly, although entrepreneurs are encouraged to pursue opportunities whose exploitation relies on their current skills, knowledge, and experience, some entrepreneurs may become bored with such ventures because they feel they are not growing – they are not being pushed and are therefore not building new competences. Therefore, it is important for people to know how best to satisfy their psychological need for competence.

While managing individual projects with competences is important in general, it becomes more relevant in the context of failure when
managers hope to reduce grief and encourage learning. Failure events
could challenge how one perceives his or her competence levels, which
provides an opportunity to enable growth within that competence.
Project failure itself may help satisfy project team members' need for
competence. That is, although the failure of a project may (or may not)
reflect team members' competences to perform project tasks, satisfying
the psychological need goes beyond simply exploiting individuals'
competences; it can also involve the development of competences.
Therefore, if the team members feel that they were able to learn a great
deal from the project failure, then initial feelings of inadequacy may be
somewhat offset by the new competences gained from learning from
the experience. Therefore, to the extent that managers can help team
members learn from their failure experiences and reinforce how this
learning helps build their competence in a way that makes them even
more useful to the organization, they can reduce negative emotional
reactions and better prepare team members for the next project.

Reduce grief by managing the psychological need for belongingness:
Both team members and managers are interested in creating a sense
of fit between organizations, project teams, and individuals. When
individuals fit in an organizational structure, there is a sense of belongingness that positively influences performance outcomes. To satisfy the
psychological need for belongingness, managers can select people for a
project and/or provide an environment in which individuals feel part of
the team – they identify with the project and the group of individuals
working on the project. To the extent that project team members satisfy
their psychological need for belongingness, the project takes on greater
importance. These team members are more likely to make the sorts of
commitment that enhances the likelihood of venture success, which in
turn may further increase these individuals' identification with the team.

The need for belongingness is similarly applicable for individual
entrepreneurs. Although the individual who creates a new organization

278 WHAT CAN WE DO TO LEARN FROM OUR FAILURE?

can be a lone wolf, the new venture can still help him or her satisfy the psychological need for belongingness. This need for belongingness may be satisfied through interactions with other members of the management team, employees, and perhaps even through business-group affiliations. Many new organizations are created by teams of entrepreneurs, and the founding team may help the individual satisfy his or her psychological need for belongingness. Similar to managers of established organizations, entrepreneurs must also consider fit when creating a sense of belongingness both for themselves and their employees. Specifically, the entrepreneur could use fit, over and above individual qualifications, as a selection criterion for hiring managers and/or other organizational members.

In the context of failure events, managers and individual entrepreneurs should consider the impact of a team member's sense of belongingness and how this might influence grief. To the extent that managers see each team member as a resource to be redeployed after project failure, they underestimate the importance of the team to individual team members. A focus on the individual and the breaking up of a team often does not reflect the power of the team. When a team is broken up, the psychological need to belong can be disrupted. That is, when a project fails and people are reassigned, they often have negative emotional reactions to the loss of relationships with other people on the team. This grief can negatively affect cognitive processing, learning, and the motivation to make personal investments in subsequent projects.

To the extent managers recognize the importance of team members' psychological need to belong and the negative consequences of thwarting that need, managers might attempt to keep teams or perhaps a subset of the team together. This will lead to less thwarting of the psychological need for belongingness from project failure. Furthermore, there could be additional benefits from maintaining team structures that profit subsequent work, including tapping into the team's tacit knowledge of tasks, each other, and the team as a whole. This could preserve the valuable information gleaned from the failure event, which could then be applied to subsequent projects.

Reduce grief by managing the psychological need for autonomy: While many factors are likely to motivate venture creation, the desire for independence – that is, the autonomy to make decisions that impact one's life – is one of the strongest motivators. Despite the strength of this motivator, other desires (e.g., job security, reduced uncertainty) can attenuate an individual's desire for autonomy. Therefore, the individual or corporate entrepreneur needs to have a clear understanding of the strength of his or her need for autonomy.

Within established organizations, individuals and teams can be given more or less autonomy. Indeed, some new ventures might require greater autonomy than others to be successful. The manager who has a good understanding of the strength of organizational members' psychological needs for autonomy is in a better position to allocate people to projects that help satisfy this need, which in turn creates a greater fit between the needs of the individual and the attributes of the entrepreneurial venture. Similarly, managers can communicate to employees the tradeoffs between autonomy and alternatives, such as a job with more structure (i.e., less uncertainty) and fewer risks. The primary implication is that managers should proactively match individuals who have a high need for autonomy with jobs for which this is possible.

For individual entrepreneurs, there are similar autonomy trade-offs depending on the lifecycle stage of the venture. For example, in the founder's dilemma (Wasserman, 2012), entrepreneurs who are successful are likely to grow their businesses quickly and, as a result, increase the need to raise funds from external sources. Although this growth can make the entrepreneur rich, it also means potentially relinquishing decision-making authority to others (i.e., financial investors to fund the growth), who subsequently have a greater say in how the business is run. This greater say could include decisions regarding the management of day-to-day operations, products offered, geographic location, and even the possibility of replacing the entrepreneur with a professional manager. To address this founder's dilemma, entrepreneurs need to weigh the importance of independence

versus growth or whether they prefer to be rich (and give away autonomy) or be what Wasserman (2012) labels a "king" (i.e., maintain
autonomy but sacrifice personal wealth). Understanding what satisfies
one's psychological need for autonomy can facilitate decision making
at multiple stages of a venture's lifespan.

In the context of failure, managers should consider employees'
need for autonomy when determining subsequent project or role
assignments as this is likely to influence grief and recovery. Specifically, if managers remove employees' autonomy as a result of a failure,
then over and above the negative signals they send about engaging in
entrepreneurial action, the managers are likely magnifying the feelings of grief team members feel over project failure. Importantly, team
member perceptions of changes in autonomy (e.g., loss of autonomy)
on subsequent projects (whether or not intended by managers) will
create more severe negative reactions to project failure and therefore
likely diminish performance on these subsequent projects. Managers
need to realize that team members can learn from project failure
and are thus likely more deserving of greater autonomy rather than
less autonomy.

Beyond recognizing how employees might react to new assignments, managers should proactively communicate to project team
members the degree of autonomy they will have with a new project
(e.g., whether it will be similar to what they experienced with the
previous project). To the extent that team members believe these
reassurances, there is less thwarting of the psychological need for
autonomy and therefore less grief interfering with their cognitive
processing on the next project as well as less grief diminishing their
motivation to invest in the subsequent project.

For individual entrepreneurs, a failure event is likely to disrupt
autonomy, forcing individuals to either find a job as an employee or
pursue another venture. To the extent individual entrepreneurs can
manage the grief associated with venture failure, learn from the failure, and apply that knowledge to new ideas, the desire for continued
autonomy could fuel new venturing. Furthermore, a failure event may

lead the individual to re-evaluate his or her preference for autonomy, balancing that desire with other objectives, such as job security. These individuals might pursue different opportunities in "safer" settings, such as working on corporate-level initiatives, with some autonomy being sacrificed for security. Failure events provide strong signals that something went wrong, including perceptions of how much one needs autonomy. As a result of this disruption, entrepreneurs can apply learning to a new venture, maintaining previous levels of autonomy, or they can apply learning about themselves that leads to a new career.

Reduce grief by managing the extent of loss through constructing alternative opportunities: Up to this point, we have primarily discussed how entrepreneurial ventures at the individual or corporate level can satisfy individual needs. However, there is a potential downside to new ventures satisfying entrepreneurial actors' basic psychological needs: the more a new venture satisfies an individual's psychological needs, the more important the venture is to the actor and the more grief he or she will experience if it fails. Therefore, managers and entrepreneurs face a potential dilemma in considering how closely to connect themselves (and/or employees) with activities that meet psychological needs. On the one hand, ventures that satisfy the psychological needs of the actor are more likely to be successful. On the other hand, however, if they do fail, they will likely create more negative emotional reactions because the satisfaction of those needs has been thwarted by venture failure.

In considering this dilemma, it is important to highlight another factor that influences grief responses to failure. Specifically, the extent to which venture failure thwarts actors' psychological needs depends on the extent to which *the next best alternative* satisfies these psychological needs. For the entrepreneurs whose businesses fail, the next best alternative may not be particularly good at satisfying their psychological needs. Perhaps if they were able to start another new organization immediately, this might help lessen the generation of grief. However, the immediate creation of a new

282 WHAT CAN WE DO TO LEARN FROM OUR FAILURE?

organization after a business failure is often not a viable option. Entrepreneurs of failed businesses may face unemployment (which is unlikely to be effective at satisfying their psychological needs). Alternatively, they may seek employment. Employment varies in terms of the extent to which it offers (ex-)entrepreneurs the opportunity to satisfy their psychological needs for competence, belongingness, and autonomy. For example, perhaps the entrepreneur of a failed business has an employment alternative in the research and development (R&D) department of a highly entrepreneurial organization where project teams are assigned highly challenging tasks, team spirit is fostered, and the team is given considerable latitude in making decisions and taking actions. In such a case, the extent to which the satisfaction of his or her psychological needs is thwarted may be minimal.

The implication of the next-best-alternative understanding of the generation of grief over venture failure likely has greater applicability to team members who experience project failure within established organizations. By realizing that team members will feel grief when project failure thwarts their needs for competence, belongingness, and autonomy, managers have the opportunity to think about and construct transitions to new projects. That is, by understanding what is thwarted (or even most thwarted) by project failure for a team member, the manager can provide a subsequent project that also satisfies that psychological need or at least minimizes the gap between the previous (failed project) and the new project.

If managers are unable to provide replacement projects to satisfy team members' psychological needs, they will likely face a greater negative emotional reaction to project failure, and these negative emotions can spill over to subsequent project performance. Specifically, these negative emotions from a gap in the satisfaction of team members' psychological needs can diminish cognitive processing for learning from project failure and for motivating emotional investment in and commitment to subsequent post-failure project assignments. This means that unless managers can somehow overcome the generation of negative emotional reactions from project failure (or dissipate those emotions quickly), they will likely have a negative impact on the next project's success. Namely, such emotions could create a domino (or negative spiral) effect.

Although many of the implications mentioned here have to do with minimizing the level of grief by selecting or generating next best alternatives that help satisfy basic psychological needs, we must acknowledge that over and above these attempts, actors are likely to experience some level of grief over entrepreneurial venture failure. These entrepreneurial actors need to understand that such reactions are a normal part of the entrepreneurial process and that failure represents an opportunity to learn important lessons and provides a direction for moving forward. Therefore, experiencing these negative emotions should not be considered a personal defect. In the entrepreneurial firm context, to the extent that managers can communicate the normality of feelings of grief and failure as an opportunity to learn, they can help reduce the secondary costs of grief over project failure. For example, by communicating these messages, managers may prevent team members from isolating themselves from everyone else when they feel grief because they believe that they are the only one suffering. Rather, when they come to realize that grief is a somewhat normal outcome, they are more likely to stay connected with others, which will also likely help them more quickly recover from grief, make sense of the failure, and be motivated to move on to the next project.

Organizations and entrepreneurs often struggle to manage grief associated with projects, particularly in making failure feel like one of several natural outcomes of a project. Similarly, if failure becomes normalized in an organization, individuals might become blunted to possible lessons that failure events can provide. In building on this concept of managing grief and avoiding the normalization of failure, we now turn to the managerial implications from Chapter 3, focusing on the notion of self-compassion and how this perspective facilitates positive outcomes from a failure experience, including learning.

ENGAGE SELF-COMPASSION TO LEARN FROM
FAILURE EXPERIENCES (CHAPTER 3)

As has been a prominent theme in this book, entrepreneurial failure is an event that can generate negative emotions for the individuals involved. In Chapter 3, we discussed two different perspectives in responding to failure. A view of failure from a hedonic perspective explains that individuals are motivated to seek pleasure and avoid situations that can generate pain, including the emotional pain of failure experiences. Thus, a response to a failure event would be to remove the object, inducing pain, as quickly as possible. In contrast, from a personal growth (i.e., eudaimonic) perspective, individuals may need to put themselves in vulnerable positions and face adversity in order to grow and improve. These challenging and perhaps adverse situations should not necessarily be avoided but could be seen as situations for individuals to endure and learn from because as the saying goes, "whatever doesn't kill us makes us stronger." Indeed, it is the hedonic perspective of avoiding negative feedback that can be destructive because in seeking pleasure, people tend to blame others for adverse conditions and avoid learning opportunities, which ironically may be driving them to suffer a larger, more negative outcome in the long run.

By understanding why people react to failures in the ways they do, entrepreneurial actors can develop and use capabilities that overcome some of the important barriers to learning from failure. For example, by recognizing that people are motivated to maintain high self-esteem and that they often see failure as a challenge to that esteem, managers will gain a deeper understanding of the type of ego-defensive mechanisms team members may use to protect their self-esteem (but which obstruct learning from their failure experiences), including why they use those mechanisms following a failure event.

In this section, we discuss how self-compassion helps prevent defensive mechanisms that obstruct learning. We highlight three components of self-compassion at the individual level, explore the indirect effect self-compassion has on positive emotions, and then highlight how organizations can use self-compassion to provide a more optimal environment for learning from failure.

Use self-compassion to avoid ego-defensive mechanisms that obstruct learning

Self-compassion offers a way to protect feelings of self-worth without the sort of maladaptive mechanisms that obstruct learning from failure experiences that might occur in attempts to protect self-worth. Therefore, if entrepreneurial actors can develop self-compassion, this represents an important resource that reduces the level of grief generated from venture failure, inhibits the implementation of ego-protective mechanisms that obstruct learning from failure, and provides a stronger motivational basis for subsequent entrepreneurial action. In the context of a failure event, an individual shows him- or herself self-compassion when his or her emotional response to the failure involves feeling care and kindness toward oneself, recognizing that one's experience is part of the common human experience, and understanding one's inadequacies and flaws in a non-judgmental way (adapted from Neff 2003). The key implication here is that self-compassion can be a critical catalyst to both returning individuals back to productivity following a failure event and, perhaps even more importantly, enabling those individuals to learn and grow from the experience.

Self-compassion and cognition: Not only are team members who have self-compassion likely to be happier, more optimistic, and more mindful than those who show less self-compassion, these individuals are also less likely to engage in the mental or cognitive tactics used to try and buffer their self-esteem from the perceived threat of a failure. As managers encourage and coach team members to be more self-compassionate, team members' self-worth becomes less contingent on the outcomes of entrepreneurial tasks (the outcomes of which we know are uncertain), so that they are less self-critical and defensive in the face of a failure.

Importantly, showing self-compassion does not mean that these individuals give themselves a pass by perhaps blaming others for the failure. Blame, denial, or other maladaptive reactions to failure are symptomatic of a cognitive strategy to protect one's self-worth and come at the expense of the opportunity to learn from the failure experience. For individuals seeking to protect their self-worth, there is little to learn from failure when they are unable to perceive their role in it. In contrast, entrepreneurial actors with greater self-compassion are able to process information about what went wrong, including their role in the failure, without the need to attempt to protect their self-worth.

Self-compassion and emotion: The use of self-compassion in the aftermath of venture failure not only has implications for cognition but also for emotions. Showing self-compassion does not mean that actors will not make emotional investments in their ventures and does not mean that they will not experience negative emotional reactions if they fail. Following a negative event, such as project failure, self-compassionate individuals will likely experience a negative emotional reaction because they have lost something important to them. However, in contrast to those seeking to protect self-worth, those with self-compassion acknowledge their negative emotions and do so without being overwhelmed by them.

Negative events can be unique opportunities to initiate change, learn from mistakes, and move an organization forward inasmuch as the organization understands how to manage the potentially adverse consequences of these events. Recognizing the importance of self-compassion for reactions to failure as well as the ability to learn from the experience and maintain the motivation to try again highlights the importance of "tapping into" and/or building self-compassion. In Chapter 3, we explored three specific ways managers and individuals can develop self-compassion – namely, by building self-kindness, common humanity, and mindfulness. We now discuss each of these components of building self-compassion and the implications for individuals and managers.

Use self-kindness to learn from failure: Managers can encourage team members – and entrepreneurs can encourage themselves – to extend kindness to themselves when experiencing a failure rather than harsh self-criticism. That is, while we often think that people blame others for a failure (which some do), another but opposite response is to come down too hard on oneself for a failure. Coming down hard on oneself – namely, harsh self-criticism – is not showing self-kindness, and this kind of self-bullying can exacerbate negative emotional reactions to the failure event and generate ruminations and other forms of anxiety. Managers can encourage self-kindness by asking team members to recognize that they are going through a tough time and that in such situations, they should be tolerant of their flaws. Being tolerant of one's flaws does not mean giving oneself a free pass. On the contrary, with self-kindness, the entrepreneurial actor can take a more "considered" and "balanced" perspective of his or her flaws and how they were connected to the failure event as a basis for learning. In the same way, entrepreneurs whose businesses have failed can show themselves self-kindness by recognizing but tolerating their flaws as a cause of business failure.

In other words, entrepreneurial actors need to be encouraged to show themselves the same kindness that they would show a friend who is suffering in the aftermath of a failure. This self-kindness is not about forgetting or ignoring the situation but encouraging action toward dealing with the current situation through gentleness and patience. This is a difficult balance for entrepreneurial actors because failure events may create urgent situations requiring that things be done quickly. However, consistent with the saying "less speed, more haste," through the gentleness and patience of self-kindness, these actors can more quickly move in a productive direction.

Use common humanity to learn from failure: The second way to develop self-compassion is through common humanity – "perceiving one's experiences as part of the larger human experience rather than seeing them as separating and isolating" (Neff 2003: 85). Those entrepreneurial actors who are feeling bad about a failure event can stimulate a common-humanity perspective by asking themselves whether other people also experience failure events; whether it is a common occurrence; and when others do experience failure, whether they also have negative emotional reactions to the failure event. That is, self-talk (or talk with others) helps the entrepreneurial actor realize that the way he or she is feeling in response to a failure is very similar to many other people who also experience failure.

To stimulate these discussions, managers might organize discussions among employees to talk about the shared experience of failure, involving team members from the failed project as well as others who failed previously and overcame the failure to go on to succeed. Similarly, individual entrepreneurs might seek out mentor entrepreneurs who likely have failed many times in the process of finding success. These relationships as well as other "entrepreneurial community" resources are likely to provide the perspective that failing in a project is not unique but quite common in the process of moving toward success. The types and methods of forming communities to discuss overcoming failure is limited only by an individual's or manager's creativity and could include in-person discussions, group interactions, online communities, and many other forms.

The benefits of engaging this common-humanity perspective is that entrepreneurial actors become less likely to isolate themselves from others under the false belief that they are unique in their feelings. This enables the individual to instead focus on moving forward, learning, and building off the information gained through the failure experience. Isolation can exacerbate negative emotions – for example, loneliness and related anxieties – and can also separate the individual both from sources of information critical for learning from failure and from important others necessary for moving on.

Use mindfulness to learn from failure: Entrepreneurial actors can build self-compassion through the process of mindfulness – "holding painful thoughts and feelings in balanced awareness rather than over-identifying with them" (Neff 2003: 85). Although entrepreneurial actors are often encouraged to approach novel situations in an open-minded way, there is less encouragement in terms of how to approach the emotions of an event. That is, when it comes to mindfully addressing a failure event, entrepreneurial actors should approach the failure situation not only in an open-minded way but also in an open-hearted way.

In an open-hearted mindful approach, negative emotions are not dismissed nor ignored but rather held and investigated with curiosity. Emotions are explored with curiosity when individuals are able to separate themselves (and their self-worth) from the situation for the purpose of analysis. In doing this, one can hold negative emotions in balance – that is, entrepreneurial actors can explore their negative emotions without these negative emotions "running wild" through, for example, ruminations. Mindfulness, on the one hand, provides the opportunity to use negative emotions to highlight situations as inputs to the learning process and, on the other hand, enables individuals to hold these negative emotions in check so as not to obstruct the cognitive process of learning from failure.

Managers of entrepreneurial projects and individual entrepreneurs can develop and practice mindfulness by how they construct post-project activities. While "post-mortem" discussions can be useful, they lose value when the discussion devolves into a mindless focus on everything that was negative and when problems and mistakes are exaggerated or blown out of proportion. In selecting mechanisms for project reflection, managers and entrepreneurs should ensure activities encourage an open-hearted perspective toward the failure event. This does not mean that negative emotions are denied but that events are put in their proper place and perspective, maximizing the opportunity for learning and progress.

Use self-compassion to generate positive emotions

Over and above the direct implications of self-compassion for learning from failure and maintaining the motivation to re-engage in entrepreneurial action, self-compassion has a number of indirect implications. Specifically, self-compassion can be fostered to generate positive emotions in entrepreneurial actors even in the face of venture failure. Generating and tapping into these positive emotions is important because positive emotions can help "undo" negative emotions and thereby remove obstacles to learning from the failure experience. Similarly, positive emotions can enhance the cognitive processing necessary for novel tasks, such as both learning from failure and engaging in subsequent entrepreneurial tasks. Moreover, positive emotions facilitate the motivation to move on to the next venture. Therefore, as entrepreneurial actors are able to use self-compassion to generate positive emotions, they enhance their ability and motivation to learn from the experience and move on.

Organizations using self-compassion to learn from failure

The role of self-compassion to help entrepreneurial actors learn from their failure experiences also has implications for organizations. Organizations can be more self-compassionate, which will enhance their ability to learn from their project failures. An organization that is more self-compassionate is one in which the collective emotional response of organizational members to organizational failures involves collectively feeling care and kindness toward the organization and its members; recognizing that these negative emotions are part of organizational experiences; and understanding, in a non-judgmental way, the inadequacies and missteps of the organization and its members. Therefore, managers can build norms, routines, and systems for developing self-compassion at a collective level. As organizations incorporate these practices into existing structures and routines, they will likely develop organizational mindfulness, providing the context needed for individuals, teams, and the organization to experience self-compassion following failure events.

BE AWARE OF PERSISTING WITH A LOSING COURSE OF ACTION (CHAPTER 4)

Up to this point, we have primarily discussed how individuals respond to failure events and how differences across responses influence learning, subsequent actions, and the effectiveness of these actions. Implicit in this discussion was the fact that the failure event had occurred, individuals had noticed it, and they were then subject to its consequences. In the next two sections of this chapter, we discuss implications from Chapters 4 and 5, where the focus was on failing projects, the decision to persist in a failing course of action, and these decisions' influence on responses to the eventual failure and learning from the overall experience. These chapters offer several important practical implications for managers and entrepreneurs who are managing projects or ventures that are failing but have not yet failed.

Conventional wisdom is that when it comes to entrepreneurial action, persistence is a virtue. This is understandable given the many unforeseen obstacles that must be overcome to achieve entrepreneurial success. Persistence in an entrepreneurial venture, corporate project, or business requires additional investments of time, energy, and money. Although persistence is more likely to lead to a successful outcome, the additional investments associated with persistence can also lead to increased costs of failure – greater costs of failure than if the project had been terminated earlier. In this book, we explored this darker side of persistence, which occurs when entrepreneurial actors persist with a venture despite poor performance.

Persistence in a failing venture occurs for both entrepreneurs of under-performing firms and managers of poorly performing projects within established organizations. An important implication of this behavior is that when entrepreneurial actors persist in failing projects, they not only increase the cost of a potential failure but also use resources in inefficient and counterproductive ways. Specifically, resources are inefficiently or inadequately deployed when invested in a dead-end project; they could have been used for other more productive uses that would benefit the entrepreneur or organization more. The implication is that the timing of the decision to terminate a poorly performing venture is important, not only for the efficient use of resources tied up in the failing venture or project but also for the entrepreneurial actor's recovery in terms of learning from the experience and his or her ability and motivation to try again. In this section of the chapter, we highlight three primary takeaways for entrepreneurial actors to avoid over-persisting in failing projects (and the consequences): avoiding procrastination to enhance recovery time, setting performance thresholds to avoid the high costs of persistence, and creating awareness of the double-edged sword of collective efficacy.

Avoid procrastination to enhance recovery from failure

Entrepreneurial actors often delay the termination of failing ventures. By understanding why entrepreneurial actors persist despite poor performance, we are in a better position to avoid escalation of commitment to a losing course of action. One of the reasons for persisting with a poorly performing course of action is procrastination. In the entrepreneurial context, procrastination involves deferring the termination of a poorly performing project because the act of termination is anticipated as being emotionally unpleasant (in the short run). As such, the anticipated negative emotions in the short term override the fact that a more rapid termination would benefit the entrepreneurial actor in the long run. Given this dilemma, entrepreneurial actors should deploy structures or systems to help overcome their aversion to short-term negative emotions.

A first step toward reducing the procrastination associated with a failing project is recognizing when one is doing it. By recognizing procrastination, the entrepreneurial actor can more explicitly consider the short-term benefits of delaying the termination of the failing entrepreneurial endeavor in relation to the long-run benefits of terminating immediately. That is, by highlighting the presence and nature of a bias, the individual is more likely not to succumb to that bias. However, the push away from taking actions that will hurt in the short run is powerful. Individuals and organizations alike could develop systematic reminders to help direct attention to procrastination. Project decision makers might have a team member assigned to bring up concerns about procrastination should a project begin to fail, or they could hold recurring monthly meetings to assess the project and consider whether or not a termination decision is being procrastinated (as a specific agenda item). At the very least, these or similar approaches would provide a mechanism to direct decision makers' attention toward the possibility of procrastination, allowing for more proactive project management.

After entrepreneurial actors recognize the tendency to procrastinate by delaying the termination of poorly performing projects, the next step is to determine how to overcome the emotions and other factors driving procrastination. In the established-organization context, the likelihood of procrastination may be lowered by managers who reduce the anticipated negative consequences of failure among project team members, thereby reducing the benefits of delaying action to terminate. This could be done through many of the mechanisms mentioned throughout this book. For example, to the extent self-compassion can reduce the threat of failure on feelings of self-worth, the negative consequences to be avoided in the short term are reduced, so procrastination becomes less alluring. Similarly, if the individual is more confident in his or her ability to more quickly reduce the negative emotions associated with failure (e.g., an oscillation orientation), the negativity of the failure in the short run does not loom as large.

As a final step, decision makers can focus on the long-term benefits of project termination (as opposed to only or primarily focusing on the negative consequences of project termination). If managers can emphasize more on the long-run costs associated with delaying the termination decision, this may also change the equation such that the benefits of acting to terminate are greater than the benefits of prolonging the project (by avoiding negative consequences of failure), thus making immediate termination more attractive. However, given the influence of the more immediate benefit gained through delay, a more effective way to reduce procrastination is to reduce members' anticipation of failure's negative consequences.

Setting performance thresholds to avoid costly persistence

While it is important to attend to the possibility of procrastinating project-termination decisions, it may still fail to persuade actors that a change of course is needed. Specifically, persistence in a failing project may not be just that some procrastinate and others do not but instead could be that some people (or the same person under different circumstances) have different performance thresholds. Beyond procrastination, it is this difference in performance thresholds that explains why some persist despite poor performance and others terminate ventures. If we can understand the role of performance thresholds and how these thresholds are set, then we may have some control over setting performance thresholds to avoid costly delays in venture termination. Setting performance thresholds involves a number of psychological processes, including perceptions of uncertainty surrounding outcomes, individual-level decision-making biases, and the availability of alternative career options.

Uncertainty of future performance: Although it might be clear that the firm is performing poorly, it is often difficult to determine with certainty its future performance, and this is even more difficult in some environments than in others. Decision makers can lower their threshold for current performance when they are more uncertain about the nature of future firm performance. Namely, in such circumstances, they are likely to maintain a belief that firm performance will turn around. With little solid information to go on, they believe there is a chance of a turnaround. However, such a belief is more likely based on wishful thinking than actual facts. In contrast, if an entrepreneurial actor has a high degree of certainty about the future status of a project (e.g., the project is very likely to fail), he or she will be more willing to terminate the project as opposed to holding out for a turnaround. The major implication here is for entrepreneurs, managers, and organizational members to recognize that they are more likely to lower their performance thresholds in more uncertain environments.

Individual decision-making biases: Entrepreneurial actors and other individuals have certain biases that may encourage lowering performance thresholds and thus persisting with a poorly performing venture. One such bias is the desire to justify previous decisions. It is important to note that the decision to terminate a venture is often not one decision made in isolation; in the mind of the decision maker, it is a decision that can potentially build upon or go against prior decisions. Venture founders or organizational members who start new entrepreneurial projects may thus be inclined to justify their decision to start the venture or project. One way to justify that decision is to avoid terminating the venture or project (as that would seem to be inconsistent with the decision to start the venture or project) by maintaining a low performance threshold. Thus, rather than establishing criteria to facilitate the termination decision, these entrepreneurial actors use criteria designed primarily to justify prior decisions. Entrepreneurial actors can overcome this bias by recognizing that there are sunk costs associated with the venture (e.g., start-up costs, time investments, etc.), but that these sunk costs should not be considered when deciding whether to make further investments in keeping the venture going. However, this is not easy. Indeed, we know that across many different contexts, people know they should not use sunk costs in their decision making, but do so anyway. It is a powerful bias that is difficult to overcome.

Another biasing factor that influences the decision to terminate a project is that people want to see themselves as being consistent. This desire can lead to a confirmation bias such that entrepreneurial actors look for information that confirms their initial beliefs. As influenced by this bias, entrepreneurial actors might only look for information that supports their belief that an opportunity is attractive, leading them to ignore, discredit, or fail to recognize and consider information that runs contrary to their beliefs. To address this decision-making bias, entrepreneurial actors (including project team managers) need to look for disconfirming evidence because this is generally more informative about the veracity of an opportunity conjecture. This might include selecting a team member to consistently provide a contrarian viewpoint or identifying an outside consultant or advisor to provide an alternative point of view. Similarly, in entrepreneurial teams, managers should create an environment in which many alternative viewpoints are encouraged and welcomed so as to avoid a confirming bias that might result in wasted resources due to delayed termination. When decision makers are encouraged to look for more disconfirming evidence and to suspend criticisms of that source or content, they are more open to information suggesting that the poorly performing venture should be terminated.

Entrepreneurial actors should also be aware of projecting too much on to the current situation from previous organizational successes. Rather than assuming that the current entrepreneurial endeavor and environment are the same as the past when they had achieved success, they could ask themselves in what ways the situation and conditions are different and what the impact of those differences is. Recognizing differences might help break the need for consistency with previous decisions and action because those previous decisions and actions may not directly apply to the current situation and conditions.

Availability of alternative career options: Decision makers' performance thresholds will likely be lower when they have few other attractive career alternatives. They will persist with their best option despite that option being unattractive in an absolute sense and despite delayed failure being costly. An implication of this is to create more career alternatives such that one does not create a low threshold for the focal entrepreneurial venture. That is, the decision maker is more willing to terminate the current entrepreneurial venture (and reduce the costs of escalating commitment) when he or she has other attractive career opportunities that he or she can pursue. To the extent that the switching costs from the entrepreneurial endeavor can be lowered, the person feels less stuck with the under-performing firm and will terminate and move on to the next best career alternative. Indeed, earlier, we offered some practical ways that managers can create alternatives to the current venture, alternatives that are made more attractive by acknowledging and targeting the satisfaction of team members' psychological needs.

Be aware of the double-edged sword of collective efficacy

While we have primarily focused on individual-level factors influencing decision making, there is also a group dynamic that has implications for persistence despite poor performance. Specifically, although collective efficacy provides an advantage in overcoming obstacles to achieving success, it can also encourage persistence despite poor performance such that when failure occurs, the financial costs of the failure are much larger than they need to be. The implication is not necessarily to reduce collective self-efficacy but to design teams in such a way that it ensures that collective efficacy does not drown out dissenting opinion and information, such as evidence that disconfirms the underlying opportunity belief. Consistent with the suggestions mentioned earlier, team leaders might specifically assign individuals to provide a dissenting opinion at each meeting to challenge the core assumptions of the group. Consistent with this, team members should assign members as core team members rather than simply accepting volunteers (who may all share common beliefs regarding the project). Similarly, outsiders could be utilized to provide dissenting opinions as long as they are in a position to provide objective, unbiased feedback. Finally, a team might also consider identifying an "exit champion" – an experienced person who points to the facts to make the case that the poorly performing venture needs to be terminated.

In sum, there are many factors that influence the costly decision to delay terminating an entrepreneurial venture. Yet, entrepreneurial actors have many tools at hand to manage these situations. By proactively acknowledging and addressing potential issues with terminating projects before engaging in a venture, actors can reduce the risks of succumbing to individual biases and in-group influences when weighing termination decisions.

SOME DELAY IN TERMINATING A POORLY PERFORMING VENTURE IS BENEFICIAL (CHAPTER 5)

As suggested in the previous section of this chapter, the decision to terminate a venture involves nuances, including uncertainty about the future of the venture as well as biases and perceptions that influence thresholds for poor performance. Although there are a number of factors that drive entrepreneurial actors to persist with their ventures, this persistence makes the financial costs of failure greater. These increased financial costs have a negative impact on the entrepreneurs of independent firms: they are in deeper financial holes that will be more difficult and time consuming to climb out of.

However, overall recovery involves more than just financial return, and there are additional nuances that managers and entrepreneurial actors should consider in the decision to terminate a project or entrepreneurial venture. Throughout this book, we have acknowledged that the negative emotional reactions to venture failure can obstruct learning from the failure experience and the motivation to move on. It is important to acknowledge that in certain circumstances, when entrepreneurial actors realize failure will occur, some delay in termination can help them emotionally prepare for the failure such that when it does occur, they are in a better position to emotionally recover *and learn* from the failure event.

Therefore, the common wisdom that any delay in terminating an entrepreneurial endeavor that will eventually fail will diminish recovery needs to be tempered by the recognition that overall recovery involves *both* financial and emotional recovery. While financial recovery is facilitated by rapid termination, emotional recovery (and therefore overall recovery, including learning from the failure event) can be enhanced by some delay in termination whereby the individual engages in anticipatory grieving. The key here is that when entrepreneurial actors realize that their ventures will fail, they can use a delay in venture termination to engage in anticipatory grieving but not so

long as to create emotional exhaustion. During the period of anticipatory grieving, entrepreneurial actors can engage in activities to reflect
on, articulate, and document lessons learned from the project, enhancing both learning and recovery.

In the sub-sections that follow, we provide suggestions for
balancing the goals associated with venture-termination timing by
discussing termination delay and its usefulness for learning, the
importance of redeploying individuals to attractive projects following
termination, and the need for negative emotions as a signal to motivate change.

Delay termination to learn from experiences with the failing venture

Building on the recognition of the importance of timing the decision
to terminate an entrepreneurial venture, there are some specific
implications for terminating projects, particularly regarding the speed
of termination. The speed at which projects are terminated is an
important mechanism by which organizations manage uncertainty.
These projects represent probes into an uncertain future, and as they
reveal information, resources are withdrawn from those that do not
show promise (i.e., they are terminated) and redeployed to those that
do. The implication for management is that to manage uncertainty,
firms need to be entrepreneurial in creating multiple small new ventures to explore potential future products or businesses. Similarly,
management must be prepared to rapidly terminate and redeploy the
resources of those that do not show promise. The value of this
approach is that even those ventures that "fail" provide information
from which project team members and the organization as a whole
can learn. However, as we have discussed throughout the book, not all
individuals and organizations learn from their projects, and not
all rapidly terminate those ventures that do not show promise.

It is important to realize that this logic for managing uncertainty
is from the perspective of top management members of the organization
who are interested in utilizing the portfolio approach to managing

uncertainty. In this way, each new venture is consistent with the notion of a real option. However, the perspective of top management members who have multiple new ventures is different from team members who are working on one of the projects. That is, the perspective of those "who own the option" is likely different from those "who are the option" (McGrath 1999). To the extent that top management members understand the perspective of those team members working on a specific venture and understand how they feel and think about the termination process, these managers may be able to better use the portfolio approach to manage the uncertainty surrounding the organization.

We have consistently emphasized that failure is a frequently occurring event within the entrepreneurial context (independent new venture and new ventures within existing organizations), and the challenge is to make sure that members (and the organization) learn from their failure experiences and are motivated to try again. Indeed, managers need to try and capitalize on members' attention captured by the failure event to learn from their experiences but, at the same time, try and minimize the negative emotional obstacles to learning and to the motivation to try again. Based on our research of entrepreneurial projects in a multibillion dollar organization, we offer a number of managerial implications.

Reduce negative emotions by redeploying individuals to a more attractive project: Although we might suspect that rapid project termination would create higher levels of post-failure grief because the individuals had less time to emotionally prepare for the loss, negative emotional reactions to project failure are somewhat eliminated when people are redeployed to a project they believe is superior to the one that was terminated. At first glance, this implication seems inconsistent with Chapter 2, where we made the case for why entrepreneurial actors feel grief when their ventures fail (i.e., how venture failure can generate grief because the next best alternative is inferior in satisfying the basic psychological needs for competence, belongingness, and autonomy). However, it need not be the case that the "next" project is anticipated to be inferior to the current failing project. Indeed, the fact that the venture is failing can be seen as an indication that it was no longer fulfilling an important need for team members (i.e., the need to be challenged), and redeployment to another new venture may be seen as a superior option. Therefore, the implication is that it may not be necessary to prepare to help team members deal with the negative emotions of project failure when they are redeployed to what they believe is a superior venture alternative (relative to the satisfaction of their basic psychological needs). There is little benefit in giving attention to regulating negative emotions when there is little, if any, negative emotional reaction to project failure.

Without some grief, there is little motivation to learn from the failure experience: This book establishes that venture termination typically generates grief for the entrepreneurial actors, and this grief obstructs learning and the motivation to try again; hence, many of the implications of this book are focused on reducing the level of grief. However, in the situation of rapid redeployment to what is believed to be a superior career alternative, there is little to no grief generated and little to no learning taking place. This suggests a number of implications. If the failure event does not generate a negative emotional reaction, the event may not be considered sufficiently important to capture team members' attention for sensemaking purposes. That is, some negative emotional reaction may be an important input to the learning process. Another important implication is that rapid redeployment, especially to what is considered to be a superior career alternative, does not provide sufficient time for team members to learn. Therefore, in the context of rapid redeployment after project failure, delay in the decision to terminate the venture is likely to create a negative emotional reaction (i.e., creeping death) that motivates and provides the time for learning from the failure experience – that is, the motivation and time for team members to formulate, articulate, and codify lessons learned from their experiences with the failing venture. Therefore, in this situation, mangers can facilitate learning from the failing project by delaying the termination decision.

Create the opportunity to reflect on and learn from the experience with a failing (or failed) venture: Learning is facilitated (even with the rapid termination of a poorly performing project) when team members dedicate time to reflecting on, articulating, and codifying their project failure experiences before being reassigned to a new project. For example, implementing debriefing sessions may provide similar benefits to those gained by delayed termination and perhaps with reduced costs in terms of the continued funding of a poorly performing project and the negative emotions associated with creeping death. That is, managers can encourage team members (whether during the period of creeping death or after failure in a debriefing session) to articulate what the project issues were and offer potential solutions to others in the team. By articulating the issues surrounding the project failure, the individual is better able to understand and question his or her assumptions about the failure, and articulating them to others encourages feedback so that a more plausible explanation for the project failure is developed. After articulation, more time provides the opportunity to codify lessons learned and thereby begin to convert individual learning to organizational learning. That is, during creeping death (or a debriefing session), team members should begin to document the problems, solutions, and lessons learned from the project failure.

EMOTIONAL INTELLIGENCE, CAPABILITY, AND BOTH GRIEF RECOVERY AND SENSEMAKING (CHAPTER 6)

Entrepreneurial failure can result in a variety of adverse outcomes for individuals and organizations. As indicated earlier, this could include grief over the loss of something that is valued and could include the project itself or, in some instances, the loss of interesting and challenging work. However, a fundamental view in this book is that entrepreneurial individuals are first and foremost *action minded*. In other words, entrepreneurial actors are accustomed to solving problems, identifying opportunities, and enduring hardship to bring about business ideas in what are often harsh and uncertain external environments. Consistent with this perspective, we now focus on the actions individuals and organizations take to regulate grief associated with entrepreneurial failure. We consider these actions in the context of key outcomes discussed throughout the book: overcoming grief and learning from failure.

Regulating grief rather than eliminating grief

As highlighted earlier in Chapter 6, individuals orient themselves through different grief-recovery modes. These modes include a loss orientation (where individuals attend to causes of the failure), a restoration orientation (where cognitive capacity is freed up to focus on actions to move forward), and an oscillation orientation (where individuals and organizations transition between a loss and restoration orientation). The primary implication here for managers of entrepreneurial organizations and individual entrepreneurial actors is that the oscillation orientation is an ideal grief-recovery mode and should therefore be developed and encouraged.

By oscillating between grief modes, entrepreneurial actors make sense of a failure situation by scanning for relevant information (e.g., why did the project fail, what are the various factors to consider, etc.) and then interpreting that information (e.g., how does this information fit together and what will we do differently in the future?). However, if the negative emotions associated with grief are too high, individuals will be less able to make sense of what went wrong, which could greatly reduce learning. Similarly, if individuals or organizations become desensitized to failure or failure becomes an organizational norm, grief will be eliminated but so too will the opportunities to learn from the failure event.

From a practical standpoint, entrepreneurial actors face a dilemma in responding to negative events. On the one hand, if they eliminate grief associated with failure, learning is likely to be reduced, enhancing the risk of subsequent failures. On the other hand, if grief is not appropriately regulated, the organization could suffer both from a lack of learning as well as in ongoing performance. In response to this dilemma, we offer several suggestions for entrepreneurial actors at both the individual (i.e., building emotional intelligence) and organizational (i.e., developing an emotional capability) levels to facilitate the healthy regulation of grief that can result in better learning, decreased risk of future failures, and enhanced performance.

Individuals regulating grief: Building emotional intelligence: Emotional intelligence at the individual level offers one explanation for the selection and effectiveness of grief-recovery modes. Emotionally intelligent individuals are aware of and understand their emotions. This basic awareness is critical for regulating and managing those emotions moving forward. Individuals can enhance awareness by identifying specific triggers that drive emotional responses, including social settings, events, and other factors. Following a failure event, team members could be guided through these processes to provide clarity surrounding the emotional experience associated with failure.

Similarly, emotionally intelligent individuals can regulate their emotions, recognizing when their emotions are beginning to escalate. As such, these individuals recognize emotional signals that suggest transitioning from one grief orientation to another (e.g., a loss orientation to a restoration orientation). These individuals also recognize how to respond to others' emotional reactions and sensitivities, understanding the influence of emotions on social interaction. They recognize that individuals respond differently to similar events and therefore make adjustments to accommodate a variety of emotional reactions to negative events. Entrepreneurial actors who develop the ability to regulate emotions are likely to be more open to a variety of responses to grief. This openness is essential for the oscillation mode and likely exposes the individual to a more diverse set of information that he or she can process in making sense of failure.

An implication from this discussion is that entrepreneurial actors should proactively consider individuals' emotional intelligence when considering them for teams where project failure (at least at some point) is highly likely. Managers could build emotional-intelligence tools into hiring procedures and employee-development programs, which could in turn enhance efforts to regulate grief.

Organizations regulating grief: Developing an emotional capability: While developing individual-level emotional intelligence is helpful, there are factors at the organizational level – namely, developing an emotional capability – that can also contribute to improved grief regulation. An organization's emotional capability is manifest in its routines and structures that recognize, monitor, and attend to organizational members' emotional states. That is, the organization does not actively seek to *remove* emotion from a failure event but rather attempts to facilitate the healthy regulation of emotion. Entrepreneurial actors who develop the emotional capability of their organizations are likely to be better equipped to regulate grief associated with failure, converting a project loss into learning and other gains.

Managers can develop a systematic failure response or routine to help recognize and acknowledge the emotional state of organizational members. For example, a specific protocol could be established to allow team members to voice emotions following project loss, such as one-on-one meetings, team meetings, or post-mortem reports that include sections on emotional responses. Alternatively, managers could utilize online tools through which team members can voice their concerns about a project and interact with others who might be feeling the same way. As these routines are supported (by management and through reward structures), organizations can regularly access critical information on how team members are responding emotionally to a failure, enabling subsequent action customized to the situation.

Similarly, routines might be put in place to highlight and reward emotion sharing throughout a project (i.e., before it has failed). This can help gauge team members' emotional investment throughout a project and, if a project is enduring creeping death as discussed in Chapter 5, can help focus team leaders on initiating learning activities before the project is terminated. As the organization identifies creative approaches to help team members express and resolve emotional concerns, it can develop customized follow-up solutions that help team members oscillate between loss and restoration orientations, search for information on the project failure, and analyze that information in hopes of creating future improvements. These routines and structures, combined with rewards that support desired behaviors, will likely enhance learning as well as performance in subsequent projects.

Threat of normalizing failure through habituation or desensitization: While structures and routines can provide the contextual structure necessary for grief recovery and regulation, entrepreneurial actors considering routines to address failure in their organizations should avoid habituating their members to failure and desensitizing them to its consequences.

Habituation is developed through social processes, including classifying events (e.g., failure) and associating value with those events (e.g., failure is bad, good, normal, etc.). Entrepreneurial organizations should attend to these social processes as they will influence behavior and in turn learning and future project performance. Specifically, if failure is stigmatized, organizational members will be less likely to take risks or associate themselves with innovative but uncertain projects. In contrast, if failure is celebrated extensively, organizational members might blindly pursue projects with little thought of the possible consequences of a failure outcome. At the very least, entrepreneurial actors should actively construct the values they desire and then aggressively associate those values with organizational events.

The second mechanism that contributes to the normalization of failure is desensitization. When desensitization occurs, events that one would typically view as extraordinary (e.g., the loss of millions of dollars on a project, the failure of a team to achieve projected results, etc.) become viewed as ordinary, justifiable, and even commonplace. This dilution of a critical signal (i.e., a failure event) masks the key problems that caused the failure, essentially shielding the entrepreneurial actor from information that may be critical to subsequent activities and performance. Organizations may attempt to reduce or eliminate negative emotions by desensitizing their members to failure. However, there is a cost associated with removing the emotional element, which is greater than appropriately managing and regulating negative emotions.

In Chapter 6, and as summarized here, we explored a simple question: why are some individuals and organizations more effective at responding to failure in a healthy way such that they learn from failure and apply lessons learned to future activities? In response, we found that individuals can develop their emotional intelligence and organizations can provide structures and routines that foster emotional capability. Therefore, the key takeaway from this discussion is that organizations should develop routines and structures that incorporate emotional intelligence and regulation activities. In doing so, they can avoid normalizing failure, providing a culture that acknowledges and then rapidly responds to negative emotions and the drivers of those emotions to help members learn from failure experiences.

MANAGE STIGMA TO ENHANCE PSYCHOLOGICAL WELL-BEING (CHAPTER 7)

As indicated in the previous section, organizational routines can be used to normalize failure, leading entrepreneurial actors to ignore or fail to recognize opportunities to improve. While habituation and desensitization normalize failure, other actions by individuals, organizations, or even regional communities go to the opposite extreme by identifying and stigmatizing those who fail. As with normalization, stigmatization disrupts the psychological well-being of entrepreneurial actors and damages future performance. In this section, we discuss how individuals can avoid and manage stigmatization. Specifically, we discuss the factors influencing stigma and opportunities for how entrepreneurial actors can minimize the threats stigmatization poses on their well-being.

Stigma and failure

Up to this point, we have primarily focused on how entrepreneurial actors manage the narrative surrounding failure events. However, there are other important actors who contribute to the overall narrative of failure, including other organizational members, investors, community members, and society at large. Sometimes, the stories told of a failure by these others are heroic; other times, the stories are unflattering. However, in some situations, stories cut much deeper and go so far as to stigmatize the individuals associated with the failure. Stigma is a deeply discrediting social devaluation of an individual who behaves in a way that deviates from social norms. This could include the norms of a variety of social units, including a department, organization, or broader community. Whether from the failure of a business or the failure of a project within an established organization, stigma can be sufficiently powerful to result in feelings of anxiety and social exclusion for the individual who experienced the failure. Indeed, social exclusion in a person's professional life can substantially delay financial recovery due to difficulties in finding a job, and re-entering self-employment can exacerbate feelings of loneliness and negative emotions, further diminishing psychological well-being.

Minimizing stigma poses a unique challenge for entrepreneurial actors as it comes from an outside force. Despite these challenges, there are a number of options actors can pursue to avoid or minimize stigmatization and the resulting adverse outcomes of that stigmatization. Specifically, our recommendations involve (1) reflection on stigma, including determining one's role in avoiding stigma, and (2) actions individuals can take to influence others' impressions and opinions to reduce stigma and/or enhance psychological well-being.

Self-reflection and avoiding stigma

Recognize one's vulnerabilities to stigmatization from failure: Not all individuals associated with a failure are stigmatized to the same extent. Not surprisingly, it is often the leader of the business or the team who are singled out for blame and harsh criticism. The stigma is particularly strong for those who were previously celebrities, were deceitful or unethical in their conduct, and/or were perceived as greedy. In one of our own studies, we found that the extent of stigmatization from failure depends on attributes of the entrepreneurial actor that are largely independent of the attributes of the failure. Specifically, we found that people who are homosexual are stigmatized more than those who are heterosexual for the very same failures. It seems that there is still some stigma with being homosexual and that this stigma magnifies the stigma of failure. We hesitated to make too many recommendations on this because it touches on social issues we are not experts in, but many of the same impression-management strategies are likely to apply and likely to become more important. Fortunately, it appears that the stigma with being homosexual is reducing over time (although faster in some regions than in others).

In contrast to this negative bias against those who are homosexual, there appears to be a positive bias for those who form ventures that try to do good (in this case, ventures that offer technologies that help protect the environment). That is, the stigma associated with business failure is reduced when that failure is associated with an attempt (albeit a failed one) to help others or preserve the natural environment. Therefore, to reduce the level of stigma for a particular failure, the individual can communicate one's good intentions to help others underlying the venture, which is likely to help reduce the level of grief (if the audience believe the good intentions). In sum, entrepreneurial actors might consider reflecting on their vulnerability to stigma from failure prior to engaging in a venture, potentially factoring these considerations into their broader decision structure. By doing this, entrepreneurs can better understand the personal risks associated with starting a new venture, including enduring a social devaluation if their venture fails.

Conceal failure to reduce stigma: As mentioned earlier, stigma is a social judgment that can be difficult to manage. However, one way to reduce the effect of stigma is to reduce the number of stigmatizers.

This can be done for certain types of events that can largely remain hidden. That is, failure can be considered an invisible stigma such that it can be hidden, and the more it is hidden, the less stigma and damage it can cause to the individual. However, we note that the very act of hiding something about oneself that others might find important can be challenging and carry some negative consequences. Specifically, the negative emotions and stress associated with hiding a stigma can be substantial.

The key takeaway from this discussion is that individuals should proactively choose their approach to managing stigma. By doing as much, they can proactively choose which negative outcome (i.e., concealing versus revealing a stigmatized behavior) they are best equipped to manage, thereby increasing their likelihood of enhanced well-being after project failure.

Enhance psychological well-being by engaging self-verification strategies: While the first two suggestions could actually reduce the negative impact of stigma, this suggestion (i.e., engaging self-verification strategies) serves more to temporarily attenuate the intensity of negative emotions associated with stigma. An underlying assumption of impression-management strategies is to avoid stigma and maintain a positive image in one's own eyes and the eyes of others. However, the goal of impression management is not always to establish a positive image; sometimes, individuals' goal could be to have people see them as they see themselves. This means that the extent to which failure creates a negative self-view, these individuals may engage in impression-management strategies to ensure that those with whom they interact have a similar impression of them – that is, to ensure that the people surrounding them also hold this negative self-view, which, somewhat counter-intuitively, enhances the individual's psychological well-being despite the potential for greater stigmatization.

Individuals who have a negative self-view after experiencing failure may enhance their psychological well-being (at least temporarily) by seeking out and choosing to interact with those who also hold a negative view of them regarding their failure. Interestingly, when they come into contact with others who hold a positive view of them, individuals with a negative self-view after failure may engage in impression-management strategies to change the others' view from positive to negative. If these impression-management strategies do not work to bring the others' view in line with their own, the individuals who experienced failure may flee from those who hold a positive view of them. While this seems highly counter-intuitive, there are psychological benefits to interacting with people who "see you as you really are" (at least in terms of how one perceives oneself). As explained earlier, self-verification is an impression-management strategy that involves both reflection on oneself and the pursuit of others who reaffirm that self-view. While providing temporary relief, this strategy does not address the core issues associated with stigma. In the following section, we discuss additional impression-management strategies that directly target the stigmatized perceptions of outside observers with the intention of reducing stigma and its consequences in the long term.

Reducing stigma by influencing others' impressions and opinions

Understand the region in which you are situated: Not all cultures or social groups perceive social norms in the same way. As a result, there is variance in perceptions of what constitutes deviation from social norms. Therefore, entrepreneurial actors should consider the perceptions of failure within their region when attempting to influence impressions and opinions because the "rules" of stigma do not apply uniformly across regions.

First, regions differ on what constitutes normative expectations and therefore what violates those normative expectations and the extent to which they do. Indeed, bankruptcy laws vary by country and are indicative of – and perhaps reinforce – variance across regions in the stigmatization of failure. Specifically, bankruptcy laws differ in the extent to which they punish entrepreneurs for bankruptcy.

Although this reflects the institutional norms of the country specific to the failure of a business, it could also reflect cultural norms of failure more generally, including project failure within established organizations. To the extent that individuals can anticipate the stigma from failure, regions with punitive bankruptcy laws provide a disincentive for people to engage in entrepreneurial pursuits. The key takeaway here is that risk assessments for entrepreneurial projects should include the possibility of negative stigmatization as well as challenges associated with "punishment" should the venture fail. The punishment could be formal (e.g., prosecution in a court of law) or informal (e.g., negative perceptions among members of one's social communities) depending on regional norms.

Second, there are also regional differences in the visibility of business failure. Indeed, in regions that highly stigmatize failure and provide the public substantial information about those who fail, the negative impact of stigma is magnified. That is, by making failure more visible, it becomes less of an invisible stigma and therefore harder to hide or conceal. In other areas, business failure might be harder to detect given privacy rules or norms, which would influence stigma outcomes.

Finally, although bankruptcy laws and the visibility of failure help explain variation in stigmatization across nations, there are cultural variations within countries as well. For example, how the media report on failure can reduce or increase the stigma associated with failure. Although the media may reflect the norms of the region it "speaks to," it can also represent a sensegiving function such that the stories it tells of failure influence its readers' opinions of failure and ultimately the level of stigmatization for those who experience failure.

Furthermore, differences in perceptions occur not only across countries but also across regions within a country, and these differences likely impact the level of stigmatization from failure. We mentioned earlier how in one of our studies we found that individuals who are homosexual are stigmatized more for their failures than their heterosexual counterparts, but we also found evidence of regional differences. We found that the increased stigmatization of failure based on sexual orientation existed in a region with strong religious values but less so in a region that had weaker religious values. The implications of recognizing that there are regional differences in the level of stigmatization for failure are complex. For some individuals, it might be necessary to relocate to a different region although such a move might take them away from their social networks, which might make failure more likely. Regional differences in stigmatization and ultimately in the attractiveness (or unattractiveness) of entrepreneurial action given the high likelihood of failure has important implications for policymakers, but this requires substantially more research before we can offer prescriptions to governments.

Seek those who are less likely to stigmatize: As indicated here, entrepreneurial actors can minimize the threat of stigma by considering the broader context of their business venture, including the country, region, and community in which they choose to operate. Beyond the broader business context, individuals can also pursue social relationships that reduce the risk of stigma (and its associated negative consequences).

Even when others know of the stigmatizing event – failure – not everyone in the social network is likely to attach a stigma to the person (or attach one with less severe consequences). For example, when those in the social network can voluntarily associate (but also disconnect) with the individual who experienced failure, they are less likely to feel that the stigma will "rub off" on them and therefore not feel it necessary to socially exclude the potentially stigmatized individual. Therefore, by signaling the voluntary notions of social relationships, the individual who has experienced failure "shields" the other person from the contagion of stigma and is able to maintain important social relationships – relationships that stave off loneliness, regulate grief, and facilitate recovery. Given the various responses individuals have to others' failures, entrepreneurial actors should seek out those who are supportive even when an entrepreneurial failure occurs.

Even strangers vary in the extent they stigmatize someone for failure. We know that people who take others' perspective are better able to put themselves in the shoes of the individual experiencing failure and are therefore less likely to stigmatize them for the event. Perhaps those who experience failure are well advised to approach for help (or for any form of assistance) those individuals who are good at perspective taking. The challenge with this approach is recognizing those who are good at perspective taking. This is not easy, but it is likely revealed in the job they have, the extent to which they have helped people in the past, and their own experiences with adversity. Rather than select people with perspective-taking skills, individuals can prime this form of thinking in others. This might be as simple as asking them to put themselves in your shoes and/or asking them to think about when they had a major failure or faced adversity and reflect on how they felt, how others treated them, and what they needed to recover.

Therefore, even if an individual's broader social environment is such that failure is stigmatized, entrepreneurial actors can still seek out social support from understanding individuals. This social support could be critical in recovering and learning from the failure event. Furthermore, this support could be instrumental in motivating future entrepreneurial action in which the lessons of the initial failure can be applied.

Engage impression management to minimize stigma over failure: Over and above attempts to avoid or minimize stigma, those who experience failure can engage in other strategies to reduce stigma and/ or reduce its negative consequences. While the previously mentioned obstacles to overcoming stigma are formidable, our research suggests that individuals are not helpless in confronting stigma. Specifically, we suggest four impression-management tactics entrepreneurial actors could deploy to address stigma.

First, individuals can engage in sensegiving by defining their failure to others in a positive light. That is, rather than accepting that others will perceive the failure event as a negative occurrence, individuals who experience failure can communicate the positive benefits generated from the failure. For example, such individuals may emphasize how much they learned from failure, how others learned from their failure to develop a project that generates value for the economy and society, and how the failure has revealed other opportunities. In emphasizing the benefits of failure, others' harsh evaluations of those who experience failure may be softened such that there is less stigma.

Second, individuals can deny responsibility for failure. If the individual is not responsible for the failure, then it is more difficult for others to blame him or her for the failure event, thereby eliminating or minimizing stigmatization. The challenge is whether the audience believes the story that the leader (of the failed business or project) was not responsible. People know that people often attribute successes to themselves and failures to external causes. External audiences are likely to be aware of this attribution bias and will take some convincing that the leader was not responsible for the failure. The individual who experienced the failure is going to need to tell a plausible story for the responsibility lying elsewhere for this impression-management strategy to work.

Third, an opposite impression-management strategy to the one mentioned earlier is to take responsibility for the failure. While consistent with the notion in the previous paragraph that taking responsibility might lead to harsher evaluations that strengthen stigmatization, it is possible that by taking responsibility for the failure, the individual can claim with more authority that there are benefits from the failure event (a combination with the first impression-management strategy, such as learning from the failure event). Also, along with realizing that one's audience probably recognizes that most people engage in the attribution bias of blaming others for negative events, taking responsibility for failure indicates a more mature approach and one that is more worthy of forgiveness.

Finally, to avoid the stigma from a failure, individuals can try and withdraw from the situation. The extreme instance of this approach is when managers of a failing firm or members of a team whose project is failing "jump ship" to avoid being characterized in the same way as those who remain and experience the failure. However, the effectiveness of this jumping-ship strategy depends on when the person jumps: if the person waits too long, then even though he or she may have left before the failure event occurred, others may still associate the person with the ship's sinking, so he or she may still be stigmatized by the failure.

In conclusion, entrepreneurial failure evokes a response from those outside the venture. This response can vary depending on various factors at the country, region, and group levels but can include stigma, which inhibits learning and threatens future performance. While the scope of this research is limited in making recommendations that influence the causes of stigma at all levels, entrepreneurial actors have a number of options to both avoid and minimize the stigma of failure. As mentioned in this section, sensegiving is one of the key impression-management tools entrepreneurial actors can use in attempting to shape the stigmatization of failure. We now explore in greater detail how sensegiving (and sensemaking) influences positive outcomes from failure events, including learning.

BUILD NARRATIVES TO MAKE SENSE OF AND GIVE SENSE TO FAILURE EVENTS (CHAPTER 8)

Throughout this book, we have repeatedly made the case that entrepreneurial actors need to process, interpret, and understand the causes of failure to inform and motivate future entrepreneurial action. In making this case, we discussed obstacles to this process (i.e., grief, stigma, etc.) and how individuals can overcome those obstacles to learn and venture (successfully) again. However, above and beyond overcoming obstacles to learning, it is also important to recognize that the process of understanding a failure event is often an emerging story – one that can be offered as a narrative. That is, the lessons from a failure event frequently are not immediately self-evident but require a process of emergence and internalization.

Narratives of failure events

As detailed throughout the book, the experience of failure and the negative emotional reactions to it can have a demotivating impact on engaging in subsequent entrepreneurial action. A repercussion of this demotivation is that entrepreneurial actors become more conservative and tend to focus on exploiting existing technologies and/or markets, thereby avoiding the exploration for more radical opportunities. A substantial managerial implication stemming from this tendency is the idea that how project failure is *communicated* within entrepreneurial groups, teams, and organizations as well as to (potential) stakeholders is important for making sense of the failure experience. That is, narratives of failure are important in understanding, explaining, and communicating the impact that project failure can have on the performance of subsequent entrepreneurial projects to the entrepreneurial actor, stakeholders, and other audiences.

Narratives, not a collection of facts: By recognizing that narratives are more than a collection of facts, managers can begin to link the causes and outcomes of previous actions to develop a plausible story of failure. Articulating the narratives of failure events identifies thematic components of the failure that go above any one action, helping both to disassociate the failure event from a single person while simultaneously enhancing the value of the full range of information and facts generated in a post-failure inquiry. A plausible failure story not only conveys messages regarding past events but also informs future actions that reveal additional information critical to learning from failure.

Narratives and the broader story: Importantly, narratives can put a single project failure into perspective. Specifically, although project failure is considered a negative event, the overall performance of the entrepreneurial firm can be enhanced by engaging in multiple new ventures. With enhanced overall performance, organizational members are likely to experience positive emotions, and these positive emotions can begin to undo the negative emotions generated from a specific project failure. Therefore, for entrepreneurial organizations where project failure is likely to be a common occurrence, directing members' (and other important stakeholders') attention to positive overall firm performance (or at least the potential for positive performance by engaging in entrepreneurial probes) helps instill the belief that the organization can actually benefit from project failures. The benefits of this focus on positive overall performance can be exhibited in areas like increased group pride, involvement, and cooperation.

Sharing a narrative that incorporates the "long view" or the broader context of a failure event reduces grief associated with failure while simultaneously encouraging actors to identify themes of behavior, practice, or action to avoid/continue in subsequent ventures. However, these broader themes will be more effective when cast in a positive light. Therefore, to the degree that narratives can focus stakeholders' attention on positive feedback, such as firm performance, this focus will serve to somewhat negate negative emotional reactions to individual project failures.

Expression of emotion and entrepreneurial orientation in failure narratives

Beyond the general recommendations discussed earlier, our research also identified specific expressions within narratives that facilitate or discourage learning from failure events. These include the expression of negative and positive emotions as well as entrepreneurial orientation (EO).

Expressing high or low negative emotions in failure narratives: Our research has implications for the role of negative emotions in both failure narratives and entrepreneurial actors' ability to bounce back from failure events. For failure narratives, including low negative emotional content within narratives appears to be effective in that this level of negative emotions helps maintain stakeholder commitment to the organization, which is important for organizational success. Including high negative emotional content within narratives appears to be effective because it creates a sense of urgency for subsequent – and perhaps crucial – corrective actions and thereby enhances performance. The implication of the either/or approach to negative emotional content in narratives is that a moderate level of negative emotional content appears to tap into the worst of both worlds: it reduces affective commitment to the organization and inhibits problem solving but without creating the sense of urgency that facilitates and motivates corrective actions. Therefore, entrepreneurial actors should carefully consider the actions they hope to motivate with their narratives and then utilize negative emotions accordingly within those narratives.

Expressing positive emotions in failure narratives: Some but not too much

Understanding the negative emotional content of narratives is important but so too is understanding positive emotional content, especially because positive emotions are not simply at the opposite end of a continuum from negative emotions. Narratives that include positive emotional content can enhance performance in that they can counteract – and even undo – negative emotions that constrict attention and cognitive processes. That is, the positive emotional content in narratives can reflect thinking that is broader in scope in capturing information about the reason for venture failure as well as more cognitively flexible in interpreting and understanding this information. However, including positive emotional content within narratives is not without risk. Based on our findings, it appears that too much positive emotional content in the narrative may diminish individuals' ability to "bounce back" after a project failure because it can lead to over-optimism, which reduces people's ability and motivation to learn and act on that learning to alter and hopefully improve performance in the next project.

Expressing high or low entrepreneurial orientation in failure narratives: While it is important to understand the importance of the emotional content of narratives regarding project failure, it is also imperative to recognize the influence that EO content can have on firms' ability to bounce back from failure. When constructing failure narratives, much like having relatively high or low (but not moderate) levels of negative emotional content is most beneficial for bouncing back from failure, so too is having high or low levels of EO content. That is, high levels of EO content suggest a "need-to-right-the-ship" approach such that individuals begin engaging in higher levels of entrepreneurial activities to proactively innovate and alter routines and actions in order to realize dramatically different outcomes. Therefore, if managers of entrepreneurial teams believe that "righting the ship" is an important outcome after project failure, they should express high levels of EO in failure narratives.

In contrast, low levels of EO content relate to more of a "stay-the-course" approach such that failure is realized to be somewhat of an anomalous event and is not indicative of the need for systemic wide-scale change. Therefore, maintaining existing activities and routines will produce desired results. In these situations, entrepreneurial managers might perceive that the organization is on track, but they just "missed" on a particular opportunity and have little need to deviate substantially from the current course. Conversely, moderate levels of EO suggest a "middle-of-the-road" approach to entrepreneurial initiatives, the consequences of which are reduced subsequent performance and an increased likelihood of future failure.

To summarize, narratives' EO content can be beneficial in assisting individuals in bouncing back from failure but only if such content is present in high or low levels. Similarly, emotional expressions are beneficial when they are consistent with the organization's objectives (i.e., staying the course or motivating a fundamental change in modus operandi).

CONCLUSION

Failure is a common outcome of entrepreneurial venturing and can produce a number of positive and negative outcomes. Throughout this book, we have focused on why failure elicits certain responses for both individuals and outside observers as well as how and why that response is attenuated. Furthermore, we discussed the various consequences of the methods used to attenuate negative responses to failure, with some responses enhancing learning and other positive outcomes, and others effectively shielding entrepreneurial actors from these same benefits (but providing some relief from the negative emotions associated with failure).

By compiling our research in this format, our hope is to provide entrepreneurial decision makers with a set of tools that can enhance their understanding of failure, particularly managing it effectively. First, entrepreneurial actors should proactively identify the source of grief following a failure event. Is it the loss of the project, the loss of the ability to work on a technical challenge, the loss of personal identity? To address grief associated with failure, entrepreneurial actors must first understand the drivers of the negative emotional response. Second, we discussed how some efforts to bolster self-esteem following a failure obstruct learning from the experience. In contrast, engaging in self-compassion creates a path for honest reflection on the project's failing, avoiding common pitfalls (e.g., assigning blame elsewhere, self-loathing) that obstruct learning and future performance.

Third, we discussed the dangers of persisting with a failing course of action and explained how entrepreneurial actors should consider a number of factors when deciding to "pull the plug" on a failing project. These factors include resources assigned to the project (as real options) as well as learning that occurs while the project is failing. If actors do not sufficiently consider both of these factors, they will likely miss opportunities to enhance performance on future projects. Finally, we discussed a number of strategies for individuals and organizations to develop capabilities for regulating emotions and managing outside perceptions associated with entrepreneurial failure. No matter what an individual might think about his or her current ability to manage failure, there are opportunities to develop emotional intelligence, impression-management skills to manage stigma, and failure narrative construction tools such that those individuals can achieve more positive outcomes from failure events. Furthermore, organizations can develop capabilities, routines, and structures to similarly create positive environments for learning and growing from failure.

While there remains much to learn about how entrepreneurial failure impacts individuals and organizations, how they respond to it, and how society in general can better support positive outcomes from failure events, this book represents one (important) step in what we hope is a long journey in coming to a better understanding of this important (yet largely neglected) aspect of entrepreneurship.

REFERENCES

McGrath, R. 1999. Falling forward: Real options reasoning and entrepreneurial failure. *Academy of Management Review*, 24: 13–30.

Neff, K. 2003. Self-compassion: An alternative conceptualization of a healthy attitude toward oneself. *Self and Identity*, 2(2): 85–101.

Wasserman, N. 2012. *The Founder's Dilemmas: Anticipating and Avoiding the Pitfalls that can Sink a Startup.* Princeton, NJ: Princeton University Press.

Index

innovation influenced by, 231–232
interpreting information about, 166–167
as loss, 146–147
loss orientation and, 168–169
managers and, 30–31
motivational consequences of, 16–20
narratives for, 244–246
need for autonomy and, 12–14
need for competence and, 8–12
need for relatedness and, 14–16
negative emotional reactions to, 7–8, 231–232, 244–246
normalization of, 160
NPD and, 231
performance spirals as result of, 231–232
physical consequences of, 20
R&D and, 138–139
restoration orientation and, 168–169
scanning and, 164–165
self-determination theory and, 7–8
social impacts of, 15–16
social stigma from, 199–200
well-being influenced by, 11–12
project termination, delaying of
articulation opportunities as result of, 134–135
benefits from, 298–302
codification of information as result of, 135–136
as creeping death, 125–131, 142–143
by entrepreneurship organizations, 116
financial incentives for, 121
grief while, 301–302
as learning experience, 299–302
negative emotions from, 125–131
performance-monitoring systems for, 122
portfolio management implications from, 143–147
positive outcomes from, 132–133
redeployment of individuals during, 300–301
reflection during, 302
reflection opportunities as result of, 134
psychological needs, 274–283. See also specific needs

R&D. See research & development
reflection, 134
social stigma and, 308–311
while delaying project termination, 302

relatedness. See need for belongingness
research & development (R&D)
learning from failure and, 119, 139–141
need for autonomy and, 13
project failures and, 138–139
resources. See learning resources
restoration orientation
in grief recovery, 162–163, 168–169
negative emotions and, 166
project failures and, 168–169
rituals, coping through, 178
ruminations, 165

scanning
grief recovery and, 164–165
in sensemaking activities, 163–164
Schramm, Stephan, 198
self-blame, 217–218
self-compassion
through broad perception, 45–51
from Buddhist philosophy, 39–41
as buffer against negative events, 39–40
cognition and, 285–286
common humanity as component of, 42–43
connectedness and, 39
constructs of, 37–38
curiosity and, 39
ego-defensive mechanisms and, 285–289
emotion and, 286
eudaimonic approach to, 37
failure and, 39
happiness and, 39
learning from failure and, 37–55, 284–290
as learning model, 37–55
managers and, 63
mindfulness and, 43–45
optimism and, 39
organization theory and, 38–41
organizational use of, 290
personal growth from, 39
positive emotions and, 55–58, 289–290
research implications for, 59–61
resources for, 51–54
self-kindness as component of, 41–42
self-concept, 37
self-criticism
as buffer against negative events, 39–40
self-kindness and, 41

Printed in the United States
By Bookmasters